Moonstruck,
Joe versus the Volcano,
and Five Corners

Moonstruck, Joe versus the Volcano, and Five Corners

Screenplays by

John Patrick Shanley

Grove Press
New York

First edition

Published simultaneously in Canada
Printed in the United States of America

Library of Congress Cataloging-in-Publication Data

Shanley, John Patrick.
    [Moonstruck]
    Moonstruck; Joe versus the volcano; and, Five corners:
screenplays / by John Patrick Shanley. — 1st ed.
        p.   cm.
    ISBN 0-8021-3471-8
    1. Motion picture plays.   I. Shanley, John Patrick. Joe versus
the volcano.   II. Shanley, John Patrick. Five corners.   III. Title.
IV. Title: Moonstruck; Joe versus the volcano; and, Five corners
V. Title: Joe versus the volcano.   VI. Title: Five corners.
PS3569.H3337M66   1996
791.43'75—dc20   96-4216

Design by Laura Hammond Hough

Grove Press
841 Broadway
New York, NY 10003

10 9 8 7 6 5 4 3 2 1

I would like to dedicate this book to Tony Bill, Norman Jewison, and Steven Spielberg. These men were my first champions in film and my first mentors. Tony Bill saw that a door was opening in my life and expansively, patiently guided me into a new world. Norman Jewison showed me the muscular side of the film business; he challenged me to stand up and be strong; and he respected the text, I think, even more than I did. Steven Spielberg was bold, generous, courageous, and brilliant. He showed me the excitement and the possibility of moviemaking. All three of them knew more about the movies than I did, and they still do. They all tested me to see what I was made of. They all supported me when the crunch came. I've been angry at each of them at one time or another, but they are my heroes.

Contents

Introduction

I decided to try my hand at screenwriting because I was broke. I watched many movies on cassette. I thought about action as opposed to dialogue. I read the screenplays of other writers. I read a screenplay by Oliver Stone called *Scarface*, and something clicked in my head. Stone was in love with his main character and made no secret of it. He described the appearance of Tony, the guy Al Pacino would play, the way a lover would. This really struck me. No ironic distance. The writer is not on Olympus regarding his creations struggling far below. The writer of a certain kind of screenplay is struggling *with* the characters, hoping for them, afraid of them even, but most of all *loving* them. Something about the heat of that involvement that I noticed in Stone's writing made me know how to write a screenplay.

I thought to write a screenplay about my childhood, most especially about my childhood outside my home. I grew up in a neighborhood in the Bronx. I had many memories of this place, of things that happened there, of people who made an impression on me, and of stories that were told to me. I remembered hearing that a man had been murdered on his way to the train station. Someone had shot him with an arrow. The murderer was never caught. I remembered hearing many times about another neighborhood in the Bronx with the peculiar name Five Corners. The name of my neighborhood was Archer Street (the arrow thing again). So many images, names, stories, feelings were swirling around this idea of writing about this place. I began to imagine a story that could contain these elements. I outlined the first several scenes of the story, and then I began to write.

I'd been writing plays for about ten years. I was writing my first movie. I wrote the first five pages over and over, creating and deepening the style, making friends with the new format. I wrote the first several scenes, stopped, and outlined several more. Then I moved forward again. I noticed I wasn't very interested in the dialogue. What began to take hold of me was the fascination, the passion, really, of structure. This scene leads to that scene. This character drives away in a car. Where does he go? I was juggling multiple story lines. I had introduced all these characters, set them in motion. They were like parallel lines that must eventually intersect.

Somewhere in the middle of writing this thing, the phone rang. The phone rang in the apartment where I was working. I looked up, honestly confused. Why was the phone ringing? *I hadn't told it to ring.* That's when I knew I'd lost my mind. And that's when I understood for the first time the narrative pull and power of storytelling in this form. Screenwriting is another world. You go there, and everything is yours, everything is alive, even inanimate objects do what you want. Phones ring because you tell them to ring.

When I finished writing *Five Corners*, I burst into tears because all the stories came together; and I couldn't believe it. I had gone into each story line, pushed it along to the next development, and then gone on to the next set of characters. At the end, all the characters suddenly stood up on their own and resolved their stories. My experience of that moment of writing was kind of magical.

That was *Five Corners*. The writing of it. The movie was made, and that was another whole story, much more complicated, because it involved all these people who were not under my control. They were like the phone. They rang when they felt like it, not when I told them to. So of course the whole thing was very stressful. In fact, two weeks before the shooting finished, I collapsed with the flu and poisoning from a bad tooth and God knows what else, and had to go home.

When I saw the movie, I liked it. It made me feel like I felt when I thought about my childhood and that Bronx neighborhood. I cannot describe that feeling to you. The best I can say is that that feeling inhabits that movie. How that happens I do not know.

Then I wrote *Moonstruck*. Actually, the original title was *The Bride and the Wolf*. Norman Jewison, who directed the picture, said, "John, it sounds like a horror picture." I knew immediately that he was right, and gave him a list of alternate titles. One of those was *Moonstruck*. For a while, Cher insisted that the film be called *Moonglow*, a title that made me sick. They even had the scripts distributed with this title on the front page. But MGM/UA's marketing department sided with me in the end. And the film's title reverted to *Moonstruck*.

I wrote the film for several reasons. First, I'd had lunch with Sally Field. I told her I'd write a movie for her, on speculation, and that if she liked it, she could option it. She was more than agreeable. And, I thought, if not her, somebody else. I had noticed that female stars who "read" in their late thirties were always looking for something to do. There never seemed to be enough material that was right for them. So there was a market for this kind of script in terms of casting.

And then there was my experience since my divorce. I had been dating a lot. And what I began to realize was I kept meeting women who were in a certain predicament. They were not married. They wanted to get married. They wanted to have children, and time was running out. *But where was Mr. Right?* Often these women knew someone they *could* marry. But he was a compromise guy. He was not *the* guy. So the question for these women became, Should I wait, even though my years of childbearing are nearing their end? Or should I marry and settle for this guy and get on with my life?

So I came up with the premise of a woman who makes the choice of marrying a man she likes but does not love, because she has lost faith. And once she agrees to marry him, *then* have Mr. Right show up and claim her.

Now, these were and are important issues to me. And I am a very particular person. So this premise was and is very lively for me. I am full of feelings about it. And thoughts. And myths. And images. And language. I've read and written a lot of poetry. I've had a tempestuous love life, filled with confusions and happiness and just plain slapstick. So I brought all this to the table when I began to write. I brought my heart to the table and my craft. And as not too often but sometimes happens, everything came together, and I wrote a very nice script. What it turned out to be about was not so much my premise, which makes sense since a premise is where you start from. It turned out to be about the incredible potential beneficial power of family to help its members. To live. To love. To incorporate change.

It's a movie about a family that works. Even now that concept is like a glittering distant star to me. How wonderful and strange it would be if people in a family actually loved and helped each other.

It was not hard for me to write that film. The shooting went very smoothly. The movie came out, everybody loved it, and it was a big hit. I won the Writers Guild Award and the Academy Award for best screenplay. Sometimes, not often, things go that way. All you can do is shake your head, enjoy it, and say, Go figure. You don't learn much from an experience like that. Except that success is easy and fun. At least at first.

Which brings me to *Joe versus the Volcano*. Actually, there was another film before that called *The January Man*. A thriller without guns, car chases, or any particular interest in who done it. Unfortunately, due to a Writers Guild strike, I was not allowed to work on that film once it began shooting. Almost an hour of screen time was cut from the final product, leaving something perhaps not worthy of prolonged perusal. Hence its absence from this volume.

In a way, *Joe versus the Volcano* is the story of my life to that point. I had grown up in this violent neighborhood. I remember, for instance, when I was about seven years old, I threw a snowball at an older guy. He and his friend chased me into a building, up five flights of stairs, and caught me on the roof. They then proceeded to hang me off the roof by my feet and threatened to drop me. Things like that stay with you. When I was a teenager, I had a string of horrible jobs. One of the jobs was for a truly surreal medical supply company located in a desolate region of the Bronx. Like a sleepwalker, I worked there for the better part of a year. Dreaming about sex, having none. Dreaming about life itself, which I was somehow apart from. I was paralyzed, dreaming. The drawer of my desk was full of these oval plastic things. I asked what they were. They were artificial testicles.

At the point when I wrote *Joe*, I had just managed to complete the saving of my own life. I had gotten out of the Bronx. I had gotten out of a marriage that was no good for me. I had broken through in my career and established myself as a writer. I was supporting myself. I'd married again, more happily. Now, for the first time, I could afford to admit how frightened I had been.

I made it that Joe had been a fireman, in terrific danger many times, but that he'd always come through. Finally, the fear gets to him, and he becomes constantly afraid. A hypochondriac. The life force deserts him because of his misdirected after-the-fact terror. He drifts out of his job and ends up working in this medical supply company. A place that pictorializes the inside of his own head.

He goes to a doctor, the last of many he has wearied with his meaningless symptoms. But this meeting turns out differently. This doctor tells Joe the thing he most needs to hear. He tells Joe that he is going to die. This message, the news that he is mortal, frees Joe from the bondage of his fear. He can feel again. His symptoms disappear. He grabs a girl, quits his job, and goes out to celebrate.

But that's when things get more difficult. When the girl finds out that Joe is condemned, she recoils. She can't handle it. Joe finds out that in his knowledge of death is not only freedom but also isolation.

At this point, the powerful, mysterious Mr. Graynamore appears and makes Joe a proposition. A proposition involving a volcano. If Joe will promise to jump into a volcano, Mr. Graynamore will make the remaining days of Joe's life a great adventure. Joe accepts the proposition.

When I finished writing *Joe versus the Volcano*, I sent it off to various movie people to see if anyone wanted to make it. And then I kind of forgot about it. Then one day, my phone rang. It was Steven

Spielberg. He said he had read *Joe* and loved it, and he thought that I should direct it. What did I think? I said, "Yes, I'd like to direct it." Spielberg was my Mr. Graynamore. When I hung up the phone, I knew my life had taken an unexpected turn and that I was embarking on a great adventure. I cannot begin to share that adventure without going on far longer than this introduction can endure, but let me just say this.

Writing these screenplays led me to places I never dreamed I would go. It has been a great adventure, a fabulous school, a tempestuous marriage. I can't wait to see where I'm taken next. But I'm scared, too.

Moonstruck

The cast of *Moonstruck* includes:

Loretta Castorini	Cher
Ronny Cammareri	Nicolas Cage
Cosmo Castorini	Vincent Gardenia
Rose Castorini	Olympia Dukakis
Mr. Johnny Cammareri	Danny Aiello
Rita Cappomaggi	Julie Bovasso
Perry	John Mahoney
Raymond Cappomaggi	Louis Guss

Music	Dick Hyman
Costume Designer	Theoni V. Aldredge
Production Designer	Philip Rosenberg
Editor	Lou Lombardo
Director of Photography	David Watkin
Producers	Patrick Palmer and Norman Jewison
Writer	John Patrick Shanley
Director	Norman Jewison

FADE IN:

INTERIOR: ZITO'S BREAD STORE. DAY.

Several dozen loaves of golden Italian bread are standing on end in a shaft of morning sunlight. They stand in bins in Zito's front window. In the window, ZITO'S can be read in reverse. We leave the loaves and drift down to a Progresso Products calendar, which hangs from the wall by a nail. The month is November. Various phone numbers and delivery dates have been penned in a rough scrawl. Now we go to a white Formica counter, scuffed and pocked from long use. On the counter, in a rinsed-out olive jar filled with water, are three fat red roses. The title appears in black script against the white background: MOONSTRUCK.

Now the faint voice of ZITO *himself and a low tapping sound are heard. Some credits roll.*

ZITO'S VOICE (barely discernible): Three times they cancel the order with me, and three times they come back. Who they kidding? They cheap, cheap, cheap. The other bread they get is no good. They save pennies. Everybody complain, and they come back. "Zito, your bread is the best." They're like children stupid in school who cannot learn. The water. It's the water. You buy bread in Hoboken, you get Hoboken water. Hoboken water is dry. Ask anybody who knows. Ask your father. He knows.

(*During Zito's plaintive words, we leave the roses and move down the counter to a calculator being tapped very efficiently with the eraser end of a pencil. When the results appear, the pencil notes the figure in a threadbare old ledger.*)

Now we see ZITO. *He's a middle-aged Italian man with a kind face. But it's early in the day, and he has already been working for hours, so he's a little tired and disgruntled.)*

ZITO: You want me to make you some coffee?

(*Now we see* LORETTA *for the first time. She's entering a few final figures in the ledger.* LORETTA *is Italian, thirty-seven. Her black hair, done in a dated style, is flecked with gray. She's dressed in sensible but unfashionable clothes of a dark color.*)

LORETTA: What d'you know about coffee? Gimme a loaf of bread.

EXTERIOR: ZITO'S BREAD STORE. DAY.

LORETTA *emerges with her little weathered leather bookkeeping satchel and a loaf of Zito's bread in a white paper bag. She moves off briskly.*

EXTERIOR: A. J. CONTI FUNERAL CHAPEL. DAY.

This is a little Italian funeral parlor.

INTERIOR: THE "WAKE ROOM." DAY.

A generic little room filled with many flowers and wreaths, many folding chairs, a few old people sitting, and up front, the star of the show, the corpse on display in his gold and Formica casket. Before the casket kneels a small figure, an OLD WOMAN, *who crosses herself and rises. She goes and sits by* RUBY, *another old woman.*

OLD WOMAN (leaning over): He looks great.

RUBY: That Al Conti is a genius.

INTERIOR: THE OFFICE OF THE FUNERAL PARLOR. DAY.

First we see a nameplate on a desk. The plate reads ALFONSO CONTI.

CONTI'S VOICE: I am a genius.

(*The shot widens to include the loaf of bread, which is half cut up and being buttered. Next to the bread are two steaming mugs of coffee. We hear the subdued tapping of Loretta's tabulations.*)

LORETTA'S VOICE: If you're such a genius, why can't you keep track of your receipts? How am I going to do your income tax?

CONTI'S VOICE: I am an artistic genius.

(*The shot widens, and now we can see* AL CONTI *and* LORETTA *sitting at the desk having Zito's buttered bread and mugs of coffee.* LORETTA *has got her calculator going and is entering figures in Al's black, gold-lettered ledger.*)

LORETTA: If you're an artistic genius, how come you got butter on your tie?

(CONTI *looks down and sees the stain. He's at a loss.*)

LORETTA (continuing): Give it here. I'll give you this, Al, you make good coffee.

(LORETTA *downs her coffee, accepts the stained tie, which* AL *has taken off, and slams the ledger shut.*)

INTERIOR: ROBERT'S DRY CLEANERS. DAY. MORE CREDITS ROLL.

A wall of dry-cleaned clothes in plastic bags. They are hanging from an automated grid. The wall starts to move off to the left. A gap appears where no clothes are hung. The gap creates a visual frame. In the frame is ROBERT. *He is operating the grid with a little stick shift. He stops it and takes down a garment. He leaves the frame, heading off to the counter. When he moves away, we see that* LORETTA *is behind him, working her calculator, entering figures in a ledger. She slams the led-*

*ger shut, waves good-bye, and goes. After a beat, she reappears, pro-
duces Conti's tie, says something to* ROBERT, *who is out of view, leaves
the tie, and reexits.*

INTERIOR: A BUTCHER SHOP. DAY.

A cleaver is whacking an oxtail into sections.
    Now we see LORETTA, *a few feet away, tabulating on a chopping
block that is partially obscured by a row of hanging rabbits, unskinned.*

INTERIOR: A FLORIST SHOP. DAY.

A long white box is being filled with red roses.

FLORIST'S VOICE: Red roses. Very romantic. The man who sends these
knows what he's doing.

(*Now we see* LORETTA *tabulating and the* FLORIST *working on the box of
roses.*)

LORETTA: The man who sends those spends a lot of money on something that ends up in the garbage can.

(*The* FLORIST *gives her a look and then smiles.*)

FLORIST: I'm glad everybody ain't like you, Loretta. I'd be outta business.

LORETTA: Without me, you'd be out of business. I like flowers.

(LORETTA *gives him a sudden, brief, blinding smile. It's the first time we've
seen her smile. She has gold work around one of her two front teeth.
The* FLORIST *grunts and hands her a red rose. The camera moves close
to* LORETTA *and the rose.*
    End of credits.
    Dissolve into:)

EXTERIOR: THE GRAND TICINO, AN ITALIAN RESTAURANT. NIGHT.

A red neon sign hangs in the window.
   It's a quaint downstairs restaurant in Greenwich Village. A young couple stop, look at the menu, become more interested in each other, kiss, and decide to go in.

INTERIOR: THE GRAND TICINO. NIGHT.

White tablecloths and dark green walls, a tiny bar up by the door. The waiters all look a little alike. That's because they're all related. The place is about half full and bustles along pleasantly.
   Music: a violin plays a melancholy Neapolitan air.
   MR. JOHNNY *and* LORETTA *sit at a table for two talking quietly. They have their menus and glasses of red wine.* MR. JOHNNY *is Italian, around forty-two. His wavy salt-and-pepper hair is impeccably combed back, but there is so much that it threatens to fall forward someday and engulf his face. He is wearing a pinky ring, a dark suit, a gold watch, a mustache, and a look of incredible seriousness.* MR. JOHNNY *is really timid of life, an overgrown boy who hides these qualities behind a veil of dignity.* LORETTA *is tough and efficient, loyal and watchful; she watches out for* MR. JOHNNY *and defends him against life.* BOBO, *an old-world Italian waiter, comes over to take their order.*

BOBO: Are you ready?

MR. JOHNNY: Hello, Bobo. How are you tonight?

BOBO: Very good, Mr. Johnny.

MR. JOHNNY: We will both have the salad Ticino.

BOBO: Uh-huh.

MR. JOHNNY: And I'll have the special fish.

LORETTA: You don't want the fish.

MR. JOHNNY: No?

LORETTA: It's the oily fish tonight. Not before the plane ride.

MR. JOHNNY: Maybe you're right.

LORETTA: Give him the manicotti, Bobo. Me, too.

BOBO: Yes, Miss Loretta.

LORETTA (to MR. JOHNNY): That will give you a base. For your stomach. You eat that oily fish, you go up in the air, halfway to Sicily you'll be green and your hands will be sweating.

MR. JOHNNY (smiles): You look after me.

(*A distinguished man's voice rises out of the babble. They turn and look. The man's name is* PERRY.
        Loretta's point of view: PERRY *and* PATRICIA. PERRY *is a university professor.* PATRICIA *is his girlfriend and student. He's in his fifties. She's about twenty-five years younger. She's getting her coat on in a huff.*)

PERRY: Patricia, please don't go!

PATRICIA: What do you think I am, a talking dog?

PERRY: I was just making a point about the way you said . . . the way you stated your aspirations.

PATRICIA: You can kiss my aspirations! Professor!

(PATRICIA *storms out, leaving* PERRY *muttering to himself.*)

PERRY: Kiss my aspirations. Oh, very clever. The height of cleverness. Waiter!

(*An abnormally* SHY WAITER *stops.*)

SHY WAITER: Yes?

PERRY: Could you do away with her dinner and any evidence of her, and bring me a big glass of vodka?

SHY WAITER: But absolutely!

(*The* SHY WAITER *begins to clear efficiently.*
MR. JOHNNY *and* LORETTA *exchange a glance.* MR. JOHNNY *is amused.*
BOBO *serves them their salad.*)

MR. JOHNNY: A man who can't control his woman is funny.

LORETTA: She was too young for him.

(MR. JOHNNY *considers this a point well taken.*
   BOBO *and his nephew* EDDIE *stand near the kitchen, which can be seen through a serving window. They can look out over the restaurant tables.* BOBO *is melancholy and philosophical.* EDDIE *is a young waiter.*)

EDDIE: Whatsamatter, Uncle Bobo?

BOBO: Tonight Mr. Johnny's gonna propose marriage.

EDDIE: How you know that?

BOBO: He arranged it with me. When he asks her, then he'll wave to me and I'll bring champagne. Good bachelor customer for twenty years. But who knows? Maybe he'll lose courage.

(PERRY, *feeling no pain, collars the* SHY WAITER. PERRY *holds out his empty glass.*)

PERRY: Can I get another one of these?

SHY WAITER: Definitely!

PERRY (taking the Shy Waiter's arm): May I presume to ask you a question?

SHY WAITER: Sure!

PERRY: Do you have a girlfriend?

SHY WAITER: I am alone in the world.

(PERRY *lets go of his arm. He and the* SHY WAITER *commiserate a moment. Then, wordlessly, the* SHY WAITER *goes.*)

PERRY: That's very sad.

(BOBO *is clearing the remains of Mr. Johnny's dinner. He has already cleared Loretta's.*)

BOBO: How's things?

LORETTA: Fine, Bobo. We'll take the check.

MR. JOHNNY: No. I want to see the dessert cart.

BOBO: Very good.

(BOBO *goes.*)

LORETTA (surprised): You never have dessert.

MR. JOHNNY: Never is a long time.

(MR. JOHNNY *is uneasy. He massages his head.*)

LORETTA: What's the matter?

MR. JOHNNY: My scalp is not getting enough blood sometimes.

(LORETTA *looks at him strangely.* BOBO *rolls up the dessert cart. We see* LORETTA *and* MR. JOHNNY *through the frame of the dessert cart. They turn and look at the desserts.*)

MR. JOHNNY: Have something.

LORETTA: I shouldn't.

MR. JOHNNY: Will you marry me?

LORETTA: What?

MR. JOHNNY: Will you marry me?

LORETTA: Bobo, take the cart away.

(BOBO *takes the cart away.*)

LORETTA: Are you proposing marriage to me?

MR. JOHNNY: Yes?

LORETTA: You know I was married and that my husband died. But what you don't know is, I think he and I had *bad luck*.

MR. JOHNNY: What do you mean?

LORETTA: We got married at the city hall, and I think it gave *bad luck* to the whole marriage.

MR. JOHNNY: I don't understand.

LORETTA: Right from the start, we didn't do it right. Could you kneel down?

MR. JOHNNY: On the floor?

LORETTA: Yes, on the floor.

MR. JOHNNY: This is a good suit.

LORETTA: I helped you buy it. It came with two pairs of pants. It's for luck, Johnny. When you propose marriage to a woman, you should kneel down.

MR. JOHNNY: All right.

(MR. JOHNNY *slowly gets out of his chair. There's not enough room for him to kneel down. He has to ask two off-duty professional wrestlers,* BOB *and* MOOK, *who are eating dinner to move their chairs. They do so with bemused expressions.*
The SHY WAITER *brings* PERRY *a fresh glass of vodka.*)

PERRY (to the SHY WAITER): Is that man praying?

MR. JOHNNY (on his knees addressing LORETTA): So. Will you ma—

LORETTA (interrupting): Where's the ring?

MR. JOHNNY (at a loss): The ring?

(BOB *and* MOOK *are watching Mr. Johnny's performance. They are dead-pan mugs.*)

BOB (to MR. JOHNNY): A ring. That's right.

MOOK: I woulda sprung for a ring if it was me.

(BOBO *and* EDDIE *stand near the kitchen, watching.*)

BOBO: She's got him on his knees. He's ruining his suit.

(LORETTA *and* MR. JOHNNY *continue.*)

LORETTA: You could use your pinky ring.

MR. JOHNNY: I like this ring.

LORETTA: You propose to a woman, you should offer her a ring of engagement.

(MR. JOHNNY *takes off the ring and holds it out to her.*)

MR. JOHNNY: Loretta. Loretta Castorini Clark. On my knees. In front of all these people. Will you marry me?

(LORETTA *meekly accepts the ring from him and takes his hands.*)

LORETTA: Yes, Johnny. Yes, John Anthony Cammareri. I will marry you. I will be your wife.

(MR. JOHNNY *slowly stands up, brushes off his knees. The restaurant has fallen utterly silent.* LORETTA *smiles. They embrace.* LORETTA *kisses him quickly.*

Having heard the proposal, a middle-aged woman, SUSAN, *has become maudlin.* BOBO *stands very near her table.* SUSAN *is about to applaud the proposal. She brings her hands together. Bobo's hand flashes out and neatly captures her hands before they can part again. The single sound dies abruptly in the silent room.*

MR. JOHNNY *is in control now. He looks around once, regally.*)

MR. JOHNNY: Bobo! The check!

(PERRY *and the* SHY WAITER *look at* MR. JOHNNY *and* LORETTA.)

PERRY: I feel like I have just witnessed a car accident.

(*The* SHY WAITER *sits down at Perry's table.*)

SHY WAITER: When I was twenty-seven years old, in Jersey City, I asked a woman to marry me. She had red hair. She smelled a jasmine. She wore black shoes with pointy white tips.

PERRY: What happened?

SHY WAITER: She didn't hear me. She asked me to repeat, so she could understand what I said. But I wouldn't repeat it. Outta shyness. So I'm a bachelor.

(MR. JOHNNY *is helping* LORETTA *get on her coat.*)

LORETTA: What time is it?

MR. JOHNNY: Seven-thirty.

LORETTA: So we'll pick up the car; we'll make the plane in plenty of time.

(MR. JOHNNY *puts on his coat.*)

MR. JOHNNY: My mother will be happy I'm getting married.

(BOBO *approaches with the bucket of champagne. He's flustered.*)

BOBO: I forgot to bring the champagne, Mr. Johnny.

MR. JOHNNY: I forgot to wave. We'll have it at the wedding.

EXTERIOR: MIDTOWN TUNNEL. THE CREAM-COLORED LTD SPEEDING. NIGHT.

INTERIOR: THE CREAM-COLORED LTD. NIGHT.

LORETTA *is driving, and* MR. JOHNNY *is sitting beside her. In the backseat are two suitcases.*

LORETTA: What about the wedding?

MR. JOHNNY: My mother is dying. When she is dead, I'll come back and we'll be married.

LORETTA: How near is she to death?

MR. JOHNNY: A week. Two weeks. No more.

LORETTA: Then let's set the date. How about a month from today?

MR. JOHNNY: Must it be so definite? Can't we just say that we will be married when I get back?

LORETTA: Where? At the city hall? No! I want the whole wedding, or we will have *bad luck*. For a whole wedding to be planned, a date must be set.

MR. JOHNNY: All right. A month. In a month.

LORETTA: A month from today?

MR. JOHNNY: Yeah.

LORETTA: I'll take care of it, Johnny. I'll take care of the whole thing. All you have to do is show up.

INTERIOR: A TERMINAL AT KENNEDY INTERNATIONAL AIRPORT. NIGHT.

Many people, most of them Italian, are lined up to board the plane.

VOICE (over PA system): International Flight Number Six-oh-four boarding for Rome and Palermo at Gate Twenty-six.

(MR. JOHNNY *and* LORETTA *are saying good-bye.*)

LORETTA: Call me when you get in.

MR. JOHNNY: I'll call you when I get to Mama's house.

LORETTA: You've made me very happy, Johnny.

(MR. JOHNNY *takes a piece of paper from his wallet.*)

MR. JOHNNY: There's one thing about this wedding I want you to do. Call this number. It's a business number. Ask for Ronny. Invite him to the wedding.

LORETTA: Who is he?

MR. JOHNNY: He's my younger brother.

LORETTA: You have a brother?

MR. JOHNNY: We haven't spoken in five years. There was some bad blood. I want you to call him and invite him to the wedding. Will you do it?

LORETTA: Sure.

VOICE (voice-over): This is the last call for International Flight Number Six-oh-four boarding at Gate Twenty-six for Rome and Palermo.

MR. JOHNNY: I've got to go.

(*He clumsily kisses* LORETTA. *Then he quickly turns and leaves. She waves, but he doesn't look back.*)

EXTERIOR: AIRPORT RUNWAY. NIGHT.

Close shot on plane's wheels and underbelly as it slowly begins to move. Red lights are flashing.

An old Italian CRONE *is looking out the terminal window.*

In the background the accordionlike ramp that had led to the departing aircraft slowly folds up. LORETTA *walks up beside her and looks out the window, too. The* CRONE *is dressed in black and has a black scarf on her head. The* CRONE *notices* LORETTA.

CRONE: Do you have someone on that plane?

LORETTA: Yeah. (Smiles.) My fiancé.

CRONE: I have put a curse on that plane. My sister is on that plane. I have put a curse on that plane that it should explode. Burn on fire and fall in the sea. Fifty years ago she stole a man from me. Today she told me that she didn't even love him. She took him to feel strong with me. Now she goes back to Sicily. I have cursed her that the green Atlantic water should swallow her up.

LORETTA: I don't believe in curses.

CRONE (smiles): Neither do I.

(*The plane takes off.* LORETTA *looks after it anxiously. All her hopes are on that plane.*)

INTERIOR: A PARKING GARAGE IN LITTLE ITALY. NIGHT.

The LTD pulls into the entrance, and LORETTA *gets out. An* ATTENDANT *appears.*

ATTENDANT: Mr. Johnny's, right?

LORETTA: Right. The key's in it.

ATTENDANT: Good night.

LORETTA: Night.

(LORETTA *walks off into the night.*)

EXTERIOR: THE SWEETHEART LIQUOR STORE. NIGHT.

The camera frames the window with a heart in neon.

EXTERIOR: THE SWEETHEART LIQUOR STORE. NIGHT.

LORETTA *walks up the street and enters the store.*

INTERIOR: THE SWEETHEART LIQUOR STORE. NIGHT.

LORETTA *walks in.* IRV *and* LOTTE, *the middle-aged couple who own and run the place, are having an argument.*

LOTTE: I've seen how you look at her, and it isn't right.

IRV: How do I look at her? (To LORETTA:) Can I help you?

LORETTA: A split of Moët.

LOTTE (to IRV): Like a wolf.

IRV (getting the split): Like a wolf, huh? You never seen a wolf in your life. (To LORETTA:) That's seven-fifty-seven.

(LORETTA *pays and waits for her change.*)

LOTTE: I seen a wolf in everybody I ever met, and I see a wolf in you.

IRV (giving the change): That makes ten. Thanks. Have a nice night.

LORETTA: You, too.

(LORETTA *walks out.*)

IRV: You know what I see in you, Lotte?

LOTTE: What?

IRV: The girl I married.

(LOTTE, *caught off guard, blushes.*)

EXTERIOR: THE CASTORINI HOUSE. NIGHT.

It's a big, old, eccentric, three-story corner house. To one side, it has got a gated arch that leads to an inner courtyard where three cars could park. It has got two cast-iron balconies. About a third of the windows in the house are lit.
From within can be heard the faint strains of Vicki Carr singing and one dog barking. Loretta appears, carrying champagne, approaches the front door, unlocks it, and goes in.

INTERIOR: THE CASTORINI HOUSE. FRONT HALL. NIGHT.

Music: Vicki Carr is singing "It Must Be Him."
The front hall is typical of large, old brownstones. There's a big, old oak coatrack with a built-in mirror and an umbrella stand. There are several coats hanging from it. The floor is littered with boots. There's also a side table. On the table is a large cut-glass bowl filled with a couple of pounds of hard candy.
LORETTA *comes in and takes off her coat. A single mad howl is heard, followed by a pandemonium of barking. Five dogs charge into the hall to greet* LORETTA. *They are totally cockeyed, crackpot mutts. Their names are Judas, Lucy, Leo, Fatboy, and Jones.*

LORETTA: Hello, boys and girls. Guess what happened to me?

OLD MAN'S VOICE (calling out from upstairs): How long must I wait? *Quanto tempo devo aspettare?!*

(*The five dogs turn away from* LORETTA *and charge up the staircase toward the voice.* LORETTA *walks toward the living room.*)

INTERIOR: THE CASTORINI HOUSE. LIVING ROOM. NIGHT.

This is the source of the Vicki Carr song, which is just ending. COSMO CASTORINI, *Loretta's father, is just turning off the old stereo. He's a powerful man, about sixty-five, with a huge shock of white hair and gold wire glasses. He's wearing a big, old red silk robe over blue pajamas, and royal blue slippers. The room is filled with lumpy upholstered furniture, once grand, now threadbare; shawls and doilies cover holes in failing fabric. There's a fireplace containing a dying fire. Cosmo's wing chair, with his newspaper on it, is beside a lit fringed lamp.* COSMO *sees* LORETTA *as she comes in.*

COSMO: Hi.

(COSMO *sits in his chair and puts his feet up on an old needlepoint ottoman. He starts to read the paper.*)

LORETTA: Where's Ma?

COSMO: Bed.

LORETTA: You're not sleepy?

COSMO: I can't sleep anymore. It's too much like death.

LORETTA: Pop, I got news.

(COSMO *puts down the paper and takes his feet off the ottoman.*)

COSMO: All right. Let's go in the kitchen.

(COSMO *gets up and heads for the kitchen. He hums and continues as* LORETTA *opens champagne.*)

INTERIOR: THE CASTORINI HOUSE. KITCHEN. NIGHT.

LORETTA *and* COSMO *sit at the kitchen table. It's a big tin table with a black-and-white design.* LORETTA *has put two old-fashioned champagne glasses on the table, the split of champagne, a bag of sugar cubes, and a bottle of bitters. She pours the champagne, drops a little lump of sugar into each glass, and adds a dash of bitters. She hands one of the drinks to* COSMO.

LORETTA: Here. (Toasts.) *Ti amo.*

COSMO: *Ti amo.*

LORETTA: You look tired.

COSMO: What's your news?

LORETTA: I'm getting married.

COSMO: Again?

LORETTA: Yeah.

COSMO: You did this once; it didn't work out.

LORETTA: The guy died.

COSMO: What killed him?

LORETTA: He got hit by a bus.

COSMO: No! *Bad luck!* Your ma and I been married fifty-two years, an' nobody died. You were married, what, two years, and somebody is dead. Don't get married again, Loretta. It don't work out for you. Who's the man?

LORETTA: Johnny Cammareri.

COSMO: Him? He's a big baby. Why isn't he here with you telling me?

LORETTA: He's flying to Sicily. His mother's dying.

COSMO: More *bad luck!* I don't like his face, Loretta. I don't like his lips. When he smiles, I can't see his teeth. When will you do it?

LORETTA: In a month.

COSMO: I won't come.

LORETTA: You've got to come. You've got to give me away.

COSMO: I didn't give you away the first time.

LORETTA: And maybe that's why I had the *bad luck.* Maybe if you gave me away, and I got married in a church, in a wedding dress, instead of at the city hall with strangers standing outside the door, maybe then I wouldn't a had the *bad luck* I had.

COSMO: Maybe.

LORETTA: I didn't have no wedding cake, no reception or nothing. Johnny got down on his knees and proposed to me at The Grand Ticino.

COSMO: He did?

LORETTA: Yeah.

COSMO: That don't sound like Johnny. Where's the ring?

LORETTA (showing it): Here.

(COSMO *examines it.*)

COSMO: It looks stupid. It's a pinky ring. It's a man's ring.

LORETTA: It's temporary.

COSMO: Everything is temporary. That don't excuse nothing.

LORETTA: So you'll come to the wedding, right?

COSMO: Let's go tell your mother.

(LORETTA *smiles.* COSMO *doesn't. They rise from the table.*)

INTERIOR: THE CASTORINI HOUSE. DARKENED MASTER BEDROOM. NIGHT.

The door to the hall opens, and the light from without dimly illumi-
nates a massive four-poster bed. COSMO *enters, followed by* LORETTA. *He*
speaks a calm and measured summons into the dark.

COSMO: Rose. Rose. Rose. Rose.

(*A lamp by the bed is switched on by* ROSE. *She is in her sixties and is*
very, very beautiful. Her abundant white tresses frame a face of por-
celain delicacy. She's wearing an old and richly beautiful white night-
gown.)

ROSE: Who's dead?

COSMO: Nobody. Loretta is getting married.

ROSE: Again? Johnny Cammreri.

(COSMO *goes and sits on the bed.*)

COSMO: I don't like him.

ROSE: You're not gonna marry him, Cosmo. Do you love him, Loretta?

LORETTA: No.

ROSE: Good. When you love them, they drive you crazy 'cause they know they can. But you like him?

LORETTA: Oh, yeah. He's a sweet man. I wanna have a big church wedding, Ma. And a reception.

ROSE: And who's gonna pay for that?

LORETTA: Pop.

COSMO: What?!

(ROSE starts laughing.)

LORETTA: Father of the bride pays.

COSMO (walking out): I have no money!

ROSE: You're rich as Roosevelt. You're just cheap, Cosmo.

COSMO (shouting from the stairs): I won't pay for nothing.

LORETTA: It's his duty as a father to pay for my wedding, Ma.

ROSE: He didn't used to be cheap. He thinks if he holds on to his money, he will never die.

(*Music: Vicki Carr's "It Must Be Him" starts playing.*
     ROSE *looks weary.*)

ROSE: Now he's gonna play that damn Vicki Carr record. And then when he comes to bed, he won't touch me.

EXTERIOR: THE CASTORINI HOUSE. MORNING.

The first golden rays of sunlight touch the great old house. The front door opens. Close shot of dogs coming into camera as door opens. The OLD MAN *comes out. The* OLD MAN, *who is Cosmo's father, is eighty-three years old. He is taking the five dogs out for their morning walk. He has their five leashes bundled in one hand. In the other hand, even though it is a cloudless November morning, he carries an open black umbrella. He walks off down the block with the dogs.*

EXTERIOR: A SMALL CITY PARK SURROUNDED BY HURRICANE FENCING. DAY.

The OLD MAN *and the five dogs appear and enter the park. He approaches a park bench where* FELIX *and* LUCY *are already sitting.* FELIX *and* LUCY *are about the same age as the* OLD MAN. *They each have a well-behaved dog. When the* OLD MAN *sits down, he lets the five dogs go. The dogs run off, barking like mad.*

FELIX: It's wrong to just let them go.

OLD MAN (ignoring FELIX): Good morning, Lucy.

LUCY: Good morning.

FELIX: They run around, they mess up the whole park.

OLD MAN: What do you want me to do? Pick up after five dogs? I am eighty-three years old. God in his heaven understands that I cannot pick up after five dogs.

FELIX: You have too many dogs.

(*The dogs can be heard in the distance. It sounds like they're killing each other.*)

OLD MAN (goes back to ignoring FELIX): Lucy. There are big things going on in my house. My granddaughter, Loretta, the only daughter of my son Cosmo, has engaged herself to be married a second time.

LUCY: I have heard that Johnny Cammareri got down on his knees in The Grand Ticino and proposed to her.

OLD MAN: My son does not like this Johnny Cammareri. He says he is a big baby.

FELIX: You should have one dog. Like Lucy. Like me. I wish I hadda gun. If I hadda gun, I would shoot four of your dogs.

(*The* OLD MAN *makes a low, threatening noise.*)

LUCY: Don't fight.

OLD MAN: My granddaughter wants my son to pay for the wedding. But he does not want to pay.

LUCY: He should pay.

OLD MAN: I don't know.

LUCY: He owes her a wedding from the first time when there was none.

OLD MAN: Maybe. I don't know. He has not asked my advice. If he asks my advice, I don't know what I will say.

(*The sound of the dogs fighting becomes intense again.*)

FELIX: I won't have to shoot those dogs. They will kill each other.

OLD MAN: You think so, huh, stupid? Those dogs love each other.

EXTERIOR: THE CASTORINI HOUSE. DAY.

The gates in the big archway are opened from the inside. It's COSMO. *He's wearing a good but old-fashioned suit, an overcoat, and a homburg. He's pulled his car, a 1965 black Buick, up to the gate. Now that he has the gates open, he gets in the car and drives out to the curb. He gets out and goes back to lock the gates. As he does this, the* OLD MAN *approaches the house with the five dogs and the open umbrella. The* OLD MAN *and the dogs go to the front door of the house.* COSMO *goes to the door of his car. The two men, father and son, see each other at the moment they grab their respective door handles. They each raise a hand in greeting; it is the same gesture for both men, an eccentric chopping motion. Then they open their respective doors. The* OLD MAN *disappears within the house.* COSMO *drives slowly away in his car.*

INTERIOR: THE CASTORINI HOUSE. KITCHEN. DAY.

A red-hot, well-seasoned cast-iron frying pan receives a big lump of butter with a hissing gasp of satisfaction. A wooden spoon pushes the sinking lump around until the pan is coated. Two square slices of yellow bread with round holes punched in their middles land in the pan. Two circles of green pepper land next to the bread. A spatula flips over the bread, which has become glistening gold on the cooked side.

Two eggs are broken and dropped sunny-side up into the holes in the bread. The circles of green pepper are pushed around by the spatula, scooped up deftly, and each is made to frame one of the eggs. A woman's hand garnishes each bright yellow yolk with a slash of red pimento. The spatula reappears and lifts the results from the pan and slides them onto two small dark blue plates.

Now we see that LORETTA *is just finishing setting the tin table for two. In the background* ROSE *is turning away from the big, old-fashioned six-burner gas stove where an old speckled coffeepot is steaming up a sun-drenched window.* ROSE *comes toward the table with the laden blue plates. She's wearing a nice old apron over a blue housedress. She's thoughtful. As* ROSE *comes to the table,* LORETTA, *in a blue denim work shirt and pants, goes to the stove and gets the coffee. As* ROSE *puts breakfast on the table, she speaks to* LORETTA, *who's at the stove.*

ROSE: Will you live here?

LORETTA: No.

ROSE: Why not?

LORETTA: Pop don't like Johnny.

(LORETTA *returns with the coffeepot to the table, and pours. Then she takes the pot back to the stove.*)

ROSE: So we'll sell the house.

LORETTA: I got married before, you didn't sell.

(LORETTA *comes to the table. They sit down·to breakfast.*)

ROSE: Grandma was still alive. Chiro was still home going to school. Now he's married and gone to Florida. If you and Johnny moved in, hadda baby . . .

LORETTA: I'm thirty-seven years old.

ROSE: What's thirty-seven? I had Chiro after I was thirty-seven. It ain't over till it's over.

LORETTA: Johnny has a big apartment. We'll live there.

ROSE: And we'll sell the house.

LORETTA: I'd like to stay, Ma. I love the house. But Pop don't like Johnny.

ROSE: No. He don't.

(*The wall phone in the kitchen rings.* LORETTA *goes and answers it.*)

LORETTA: Hello? Yeah, this is Loretta Castorini—yeah—is that you, Johnny?

INTERIOR: A DARKENED BEDROOM IN PALERMO. DAY.

MR. JOHNNY *is calling on an old European-style phone. In the background is the sickbed. In the sickbed lies* VESTA, *Mr. Johnny's mother, her gray hair spread out on a golden pillow. By the bed are three mourners, old crones dressed in black. One clutches a missal; the other two clutch rosaries. All three are grieving in a steady, low, wordless whine.* MR. JOHNNY *speaks into the phone in a confidential manner. There is some long-distance crackle.*

MR. JOHNNY: Ssh, it's me. I'm calling from the deathbed of my mother.

(LORETTA *on the phone.*)

LORETTA: How was your plane ride?

(MR. JOHNNY *on the phone.*)

MR. JOHNNY: The waitresses were very nice. (*Glances over at his mother.*) My mother is slipping away.

VESTA (calling to the heavens): *Quanto tempo devo aspettare?* (*Aiming more at* JOHNNY:) How long must I wait?!

MR. JOHNNY: I can't talk long.

(LORETTA *on the phone.*)

LORETTA: Have you told her we're getting married?

(MR. JOHNNY *on the phone*)

MR. JOHNNY: Not yet. I'm waiting till a moment when she's peaceful.

LORETTA'S VOICE (over his receiver): Just don't wait until she's dead.

MR. JOHNNY: Have you called my brother?

LORETTA'S VOICE: Not yet.

MR. JOHNNY: Will you do it today? Call him, make him come to the wedding. Five years is too long for bad blood between brothers. Nothing can replace your family. I see that now.

(LORETTA *on the phone.*)

LORETTA: All right. I'll call him. Today. Listen, Johnny. Call me after you tell your mother. All right? All right. And don't stand directly under the sun. You've got your hat, use your hat. All right. Bye-bye.

(LORETTA *hangs up the phone. She thinks.* ROSE *speaks from the table, where she's still sitting.*)

ROSE: How's the mother?

LORETTA: She's dying. But I could still hear her big mouth.

ROSE: Did he tell her?

LORETTA: Not yet. That old lady makes him sweat. (*To herself:*) Where's that card?

(ROSE *gets up and takes the dishes to the sink.* LORETTA *fishes in her pocket and comes out with the business card* MR. JOHNNY *gave her. She dials the number.*)

ROSE: Who are you calling?

INTERIOR: CAMMARERI BAKE SHOP. DAY.

CHRISSY, *a woman with a Queens accent, answers.*

CHRISSY: Cammareri's Bake Shop.

(LORETTA *in Castorini kitchen*.)

LORETTA: Is Ronny there?

(CHRISSY *in Cammareri bake shop*.)

CHRISSY: Hold on. (*Yells into intercom:*) Ronny, the phone!

INTERIOR: CAMMARERI BAKE SHOP. OVEN ROOM. DAY.

RONNY: Yeah, this is Ronny.

(LORETTA *in Castorini kitchen*.)

LORETTA: I'm calling for your brother Johnny. He's getting married, and he wants you to come.

(*There's a long pause*.)

(RONNY *in oven room*.)

RONNY (hoarse with emotion): Why didn't he call himself?

(LORRETA *in Castorini kitchen*.)

LORETTA: He's in Palermo.

(RONNY *in oven room*.)

RONNY: What's wrong can never be made right.

(RONNY *hangs up phone*.)

(LORETTA *in Castorini kitchen.*)

(LORETTA *hangs up the phone. She looks at the card again, makes a decision and pockets the card.*)

EXTERIOR: A FOUR-STORY TOWNHOUSE OFF WASHINGTON SQUARE. DAY.

Cosmo's black Buick is parked out front.

INTERIOR: TOWNHOUSE. BATHROOM. DAY.

It's an old-fashioned bathroom not in good repair. Water pours weakly from the faucet in the tub. COSMO, *his homburg in his hand, regards the faucet soberly. A middle-aged married couple,* LOWELL *and* NANCY *stand next to* COSMO, *waiting for his verdict.* LOWELL *and* NANCY *are rarified, bookish people with Locust Valley lockjaw.*

LOWELL: Well, Mr. Castorini, what do you think?

COSMO: Ten thousand, eight hundred dollars.

NANCY: That seems like a lot.

COSMO: It's a lot of work.

LOWELL: Is there any way you could do it for less?

COSMO: There are three kinds of pipe. There is the kind of pipe you have, which is garbage, and you see where that's gotten you. There is bronze, which is very good unless something goes wrong. And something always goes wrong. And then there's copper, which is the only pipe I use. It costs money. But it costs money 'cause it saves money.

LOWELL (to NANCY): I think we should follow Mr. Castorini's advice, Heart.

(NANCY *makes a face.*)

EXTERIOR: THE TOWNHOUSE. DAY.

COSMO *comes out the front door and gets in his car.*

EXTERIOR: THE TOWNHOUSE/INTERIOR: THE BUICK. DAY.

As COSMO *drives away, he's in a very good mood. He's whistling. He laughs to himself.*

EXTERIOR: CAMMARERI'S BAKE SHOP AND THE STREET IN FRONT OF IT. DAY.

LORETTA *arrives. She's wearing a long, navy blue cloth coat and a knit hat. She looks up at the sign and at the business card in her hand, and enters the shop.*

INTERIOR: CAMMARERI'S BAKE SHOP. DAY.

*It's a nice Italian bake shop. Three Italian women—*CHRISSY, BARBARA, *and* MA—*wait on three women shoppers at the counter.* CHRISSY *and* BARBARA *are in their late twenties or early thirties;* MA *is old, old.* LORETTA *comes in.*

LORETTA (speaking to CHRISSY): Is Ronny Cammareri here?

CHRISSY: He's down at the ovens. What do you want?

LORETTA: I would like to speak to him.

EXTERIOR: CAMMARERI'S BAKE SHOP. DAY.

CHRISSY *comes out, and* LORETTA *follows. They walk around to an outdoor staircase that descends into the sidewalk.*

CHRISSY (shouting down): Hey, Ronny!

EXTERIOR: AN OLD DOOR AT THE FOOT OF THE STAIRCASE. DAY.

The door slides open, revealing ROCCO, *a baker missing a few teeth. He is surrounded by bread.*

ROCCO: What?!

CHRISSY'S VOICE: Somebody to see Ronny.

(ROCCO *slides back the door all the way.* CHRISSY *and* LORETTA *make their way past him. He slides the door three-quarters shut behind them.*)

INTERIOR: THE BASEMENT OVEN ROOM. DAY.

There are two coal-fired ovens, one at either end of the room. There is a large wooden table roughly center, and dough-mixers and various pieces of baking equipment are scattered willy-nilly. Everywhere there is bread. PIETRO, *a baker, is working at one of the ovens with a long wooden spatula.* RONNY *is at the other oven. He is just staring in the open door at the baking bread and burning coals. He's dressed in black jeans streaked with flour, a white restaurant shirt, white cotton gloves, with a red handkerchief around his neck. He is black haired, handsome, and intense.*

ROCCO: Ronny!

RONNY: What?!

ROCCO: Somebody here to see you.

(RONNY *turns and takes in* LORETTA.)

RONNY: Have you come from my brother?

LORETTA: Yes.

RONNY: Why?

LORETTA: I'm going to marry him.

RONNY: You are going to marry my brother?

LORETTA: Yes. Do you want . . .

RONNY: I have no life.

LORETTA: Excuse me.

RONNY: I have no life. My brother Johnny took my life from me.

LORETTA: I don't understand.

(*Everything in the oven room has stopped, and everyone is watching.*)

RONNY: And now he's getting married. He has his; he's getting his. And he wants me to come? What is life?

(RONNY *picks up the wooden spatula and slides it into the oven.*)

LORETTA: I didn't come here to upset you.

(RONNY *slides some loaves out of the oven on the spatula, turns them around, and slides them back in.*)

RONNY: They say bread is life. So I bake bread, bread, bread. (*He's picking up loaves of bread from one of the boxes on the floor and casually tossing them across the room.*) And the years go by! By! By! And I sweat and shovel this stinkin' dough in and outta this hot hole in the wall, and I should be so happy, huh, sweetheart? You want me to come to the wedding of my brother Johnny?!! Where is my wedding? Chrissy! Over by the wall! Gimme the big knife!

CHRISSY: No, Ronny!

(BARBARA *appears in the doorway and comes down the stairs into the room.*)

RONNY: Gimme the big knife! I'm gonna cut my throat!

LORETTA: Maybe I should come back another time.

RONNY: No, I want you to see this! I want you to watch me kill myself, so you can tell my brother on his wedding day! Chrissy, gimme the big knife!

CHRISSY: I tell you, I won't do it!

RONNY (to LORETTA): Do you know about me?

BARBARA: Oh, Mr. Cammareri!

RONNY: Nothing is anybody's fault, but things happen. (*Holds up his left hand to* LORETTA.) Look. (*He pulls off the glove. The hand is made of wood.*) It's wood. It's fake. Five years ago I was engaged to be married. Johnny came in here; he ordered bread from me. I put it in the slicer and I talked with him and my hand got caught 'cause I wasn't paying attention. The slicer chewed off my hand. It's funny 'cause— when my fiancé saw that I was maimed, she left me for another man.

LORETTA: That's the bad blood between you and Johnny?

RONNY: That's it.

LORETTA: But that wasn't Johnny's fault.

RONNY: I don't care! I ain't no freakin' monument to justice! I lost my hand, I lost my bride! Johnny has his hand, Johnny has his bride! You come in here, and you want me to put away my heartbreak and forget? (*He goes to the big table, which is floured and covered with bread. He sweeps everything off the tabletop.*) Is it just a matter of time till a man opens his eyes and gives up his one dream of happiness? Maybe. Maybe. All I have . . . have you come here, stranger, bride of my brother, to take these last few loaves from my table? All right. All right.

(*The table is bare.* RONNY *stares at it blankly. He wanders away, to the back room where the flour sacks are kept. We hear a single sob escape him from that room and then silence. Everyone in the oven room looks after him. Then* CHRISSY *approaches* LORETTA. CHRISSY *holds the big knife at her side.*)

CHRISSY: This is the most tormented man I have ever known. I am in love with this man. He doesn't know that. I never told him 'cause he can never love anybody since he lost his hand and his girl. (*She holds out the knife.*) Here. Why don't you just kill him? It would be so much more kind than coming here and inviting him to a wedding like he'll never have.

(LORETTA *considers* CHRISSY, *decides what she's going to do, and goes to the flour room.*)

INTERIOR: THE FLOUR ROOM. DAY.

Many fifty-pound bags of flour are stacked under a bare electric bulb. A rough stone staircase opposite is lit by daylight from above. RONNY, *quietly distraught, stands leaning, his forehead against a stack of flour.* LORETTA *approaches him. She feels for him.*

LORETTA: Where you live?

RONNY (pointing to the stone staircase): Upstairs.

LORETTA (touching his shoulder): Come on.

(RONNY *follows her up the stairs.*)

INTERIOR: THE PEACOCK CAFÉ. DAY.

It's a dark Italian coffee and dessert house. Reproductions of Roman statuary adorn grottos and alcoves. In the back is a glass case displaying various desserts, and behind the case is a big, burnished gold cappuccino machine. The place is almost empty.

Music: An album of Neapolitan folk songs is playing on the café's sound system.

The camera travels along the face of an exposed brick wall, discovering busts of Romans occasionally, and then it comes to the figure of COSMO. *He's sitting at a table that is set into a nook, so we cannot see who he's with.*

A dark nook in the café. At a little table away from prying eyes, COSMO *sits with* MONA, *his girlfriend.* MONA *is a pretty but overripe Italian woman in her late forties. She's all done up, and she looks at* COSMO *with adoration.*

COSMO: And then there is copper, which is the only pipe I use. It costs money. But it costs money because it saves money.

MONA: And what did they say?

COSMO: The man understood me. The woman wanted to be cheap, but the man saw that I was right.

MONA: You have such a head for knowing. You know everything.

COSMO: I brought you something. (*He takes out a small velvet box and hands it to her.*) It's a present.

(MONA *opens the box. It's a gold bracelet with a pattern of stars and birds.*)

MONA: Oh, Cosmo!

COSMO: They are little stars and birds. Birds fly to the stars, I guess.

EXTERIOR: RONNY'S APARTMENT BUILDING. DAY.

The apartment is a three-story walk-up above Cammareri's Bake Shop.

INTERIOR: RONNY'S APARTMENT. DAY.

It's a two-bedroom apartment. The decor reflects Ronny's love of the opera. The furniture is overstuffed, fringed in the colors of Italian passion. But it is all a bit faded, the remains of an old flamboyance. The walls are decorated with opera posters; and over the fireplace there is a painting depicting a scene from La Bohème: *Mimi standing in the snow.* RONNY *stares at the picture of Mimi in the* La Bohème *poster.* LORETTA *comes in from the kitchen and sets down a cup of coffee.*

LORETTA: You ready for the coffee?

(LORETTA *moves back into the kitchen.* RONNY *turns and watches as she walks down the hall.*)

RONNY: Loretta. What's that smell?

LORETTA: I'm making you a steak.

RONNY: You don't have to help me.

LORETTA: I know that. I do what I want.

RONNY: I like it well done.

LORETTA: You'll eat this bloody to feed your blood.

INTERIOR: RONNY'S APARTMENT. DINING ROOM. DAY.

Close-up of Ronny's artificial hand, holding a fork stuck in a steak. With his right he is cutting his steak. He switches hands and eats hungrily. LORETTA *watches.*

RONNY: This is good. Uhh . . .

LORETTA: Loretta.

RONNY: Where'd Johnny find you?

LORETTA: He knew my husband who died.

RONNY: How'd he die?

LORETTA: Bus hit him.

RONNY: Fast.

LORETTA: Instantaneous.

RONNY: When you get engaged?

LORETTA: Yesterday.

(RONNY *drops his knife and fork, and turns away.*
  LORETTA *is not surprised and doesn't move.*)

RONNY: Why?

LORETTA: Why what?

RONNY: I don't know.

LORETTA (smiles): So. Five years ago your hand got cut off, and your woman left you for another man. No woman since then?

RONNY: No.

LORETTA: Stupid.

RONNY: When your husband get hit by the bus?

LORETTA: Seven years ago.

RONNY: How many men since then?

LORETTA: Just Johnny.

RONNY: Stupid yourself.

LORETTA: No. Unlucky. I have not been lucky.

RONNY: I don't care about *luck*, you understand me? It ain't that.

LORETTA: What? Do you think you're the only one ever shed a tear?

RONNY: Why you talking to me?

LORETTA: You got any whiskey? How 'bout giving me a glass of whiskey?

EXTERIOR: STREET NEAR BAKERY. DAY.

Shot of COSMO *and* MONA *in the Buick. The car has just come to a stop.* COSMO *and* MONA *kiss. She exits the car.* COSMO *glances around with a slightly guilty look and pulls away.*

INTERIOR: RONNY'S APARTMENT. DINING ROOM. DAY.

LORETTA *and* RONNY *sit at the table with a bottle of whiskey.* RONNY *has poured himself a glass, and now he's pouring* LORETTA *a glass. He puts the bottle down.* LORETTA *picks up her glass and swallows a healthy dose.*

RONNY: She was right to leave me.

LORETTA: You think so?

RONNY: Yes.

LORETTA: You really are stupid, you know that.

(LORETTA *pours herself another shot.*)

RONNY: You don't know nothing about it.

LORETTA: I was raised that a girl is supposed to get married young. But I held out for Love. I didn't get married till I was twenty-eight. I met a man, I loved him, I married him! I got my way, right? And then we waited to have a baby till we were on our feet. And then he got hit by a bus! No baby, no love, no nothing! I was so smart! I knew everything! I didn't know that was my one chance. I didn't know that man was a gift I could not keep. I didn't know . . . you tell me a story, and you think you know what it means, but I see what the true story is, and you can't. (*She pours them both another drink.*) She didn't leave you! You can't see what you are. I can see everything. You are a wolf!

RONNY: I'm a wolf?

LORETTA: The big part of you has no words, and it's a wolf. This woman was a trap for you. She caught you, and you could not get away. (*She grabs his wooden hand.*) So you chewed off your foot! That was the price you had to pay to be free. (*Throws his hand down.*) Johnny had nothing to do with it. You did what you had to do, between you and you, and I know I'm right, I don't care what you say. And now you're afraid because you found out the big part of you is a wolf that has the courage to bite off its own hand to save itself from the trap of the wrong love. That's why there has been no woman since that wrong woman. You are scared to death what the wolf will do if you make that mistake again!

RONNY: What are you doing!

LORETTA: I'm telling you your life!

RONNY: Stop it!

LORETTA: No!

RONNY: Why are you marrying Johnny? He's a fool!

LORETTA: Because I have no *luck!*

RONNY (pounding on the table): He made me look the wrong way, and I cut off my hand. He could make you look the wrong way, and you could cut off your whole head!

LORETTA: I am looking where I should to become a bride!

RONNY: A bride without a head!

LORETTA: A wolf without a foot!

(RONNY *stiff-arms everything off the dining table and grabs* LORETTA. *They kiss passionately. He pulls her up on the table and over the table to him. They are in each other's arms. They are on fire.* LORETTA *pushes him away, gasping for air.*)

LORETTA (continuing): Wait a minute! Wait a minute!

(LORETTA *changes her mind and lunges into another kiss. They stop again after a long moment. They really haven't breathed. They both suck in air and look at each other in wonder and fear and passion.*)

RONNY: It's like I'm falling! It's like I'm in the ocean!

(*They kiss again. When they pull apart again,* LORETTA *is crying.*)

LORETTA: I have no *luck!*

(RONNY *picks her up in his arms.*)

RONNY: Son of a bitch!

LORETTA: Where are you taking me?

RONNY: To the bed.

LORETTA: Oh. Oh, God. I don't care about anything! I don't care about anything! Take me to the bed.

(RONNY *carries her away, into the bedroom.*
    Music: "O Soave Fanciulla," from La Bohème. *The music continues through the next scene.*)

INTERIOR: RONNY'S APARTMENT. BEDROOM.

RONNY *is laying her down on the bed. He is over her. They look into each other's eyes.*

RONNY: I can't believe what is happening.

LORETTA: Me neither.

RONNY: I was dead.

LORETTA: I was dead, too.

(*They kiss. When they part, there is a drop of blood on Loretta's lips.*)

RONNY: Your blood.

LORETTA: All my life I have never reached a man. I knew that I would reach my husband, but I took my time and he was dead. Ronny.

RONNY: Loretta.

LORETTA: I want to cut you open and crawl inside of you. I want you to swallow me.

RONNY: I've got you.

LORETTA: Get all of me. Take everything.

RONNY: What about Johnny?

LORETTA: You're mad at him, take it out on me, take your revenge on me! Take everything, leave nothing for him to marry! Hollow me out, so there's nothing left but the skin over my bones. Suck me dry!

RONNY: All right. All right. There will be nothing left.

(*Their eyes are boiling with fierce animal tears. They have opened their souls to each other, and they are coming together.*
    The music swells to a terrible triumph.)

EXTERIOR: THE CASTORINI HOUSE. NIGHT.

Dog whines.

INTERIOR: THE CASTORINI HOUSE. AN UPSTAIRS BEDROOM. NIGHT.

There are five beds for dogs. Four of the beds are empty, and on the fifth, Judas is whining. He looks around at the other beds. Where is everybody? He goes out the bedroom door.

INTERIOR: THE CASTORINI HOUSE. STAIRCASE. NIGHT.

Judas is running down the stairs and into the hall. We follow him down the hall. The hall is only dimly lit. He finds the four other dogs. They are crowded at a narrow doorway. A golden light comes from the doorway.

INTERIOR: THE CASTORINI HOUSE. DINING ROOM. NIGHT.

The pleased face of COSMO *through a veil of steam.*
    The camera pulls back.

COSMO *sits at the head of the table, a napkin tucked into his shirt.*
ROSE *has just laid down a massive platter of steaming baked fish.*
Already on the table is a platter of pasta, loaves of bread, a big bowl of
salad, two bottles of wine, and an appetizer plate of salami and
pimento. Seated at the table is COSMO, *the* OLD MAN, *and* RAYMOND *and*
RITA CAPPOMAGGI. RAYMOND *is rotund, moonfaced, bald, somewhere in his*
fifties. He has a pencil-thin mustache over his small mouth. His wife,
RITA, *looks very like him, except she has hair on her head and none*
over her lip. RAYMOND *is Rose's brother. There are two empty places at*
table, for ROSE *and* LORETTA.

COSMO: Where's Loretta? We're gonna start without her.

(*There is an accordion gate across one of the entranceways to the*
dining room. Behind the gate the five dogs stare at the people having
dinner.)

ROSE'S VOICE: She must be eating out.

RAYMOND'S VOICE: She don't know what she's missing.

ROSE'S VOICE: It's not like her not to call.

RITA'S VOICE: Well, she's got a lot on her mind.

(*At the dining table,* RITA *is loading up her plate.*)

RITA: I mean, can we talk about it, Rose? Everybody's heard. She's
getting married again.

COSMO: I don't wanna talk about it.

RAYMOND: Johnny Cammareri. I think it's great and about time. What's
she gonna do with the rest of her life, she don't get married?

COSMO: I don't wanna talk about it.

(*The* OLD MAN *has piled his plate high with food. Now he stands up, walks over to the dogs, and puts the plate down in their midst. The dogs attack the food and each other. The* OLD MAN *walks back to the table and sits down. He looks down at the empty place in front of him, a little sad.*)

COSMO (continuing): My father needs a plate.

(ROSE *gets another plate from a sideboard and puts it in front of the* OLD MAN. *He immediately, methodically begins to fill his new plate.* ROSE *goes to her place and sits down.*)

RAYMOND: Cosmo. Many years ago, when they told me you were marrying my sister, I was happy. When I told Rose I was marrying Rita, she was happy.

RITA: Marriage is happy news.

(*The* OLD MAN *laughs uproariously, subsides, goes back to filling his plate.*)

COSMO: Rose, pass the wine.

RAYMOND: I never seen anybody so in love like Cosmo back then! He'd stand outside the house all day and look in the windows. I never told you this 'cause it's not really a story. But one time I woke up in the middle of the night 'cause this bright light was in my face. Like a flashlight. I couldn't think a what it was. I looked out the window, and it was the moon! Big as a house! I never seen the moon so big before or since. I was almost scared, like it was gonna crush the house. And I looked down, and standing there in the street was Cosmo, looking up at the windows.

This is the funny part. I got mad at you, Cosmo! I thought you brought this big moon over to my house 'cause you were so in love and woke me up with it. I was half asleep I guess and didn't know no better.

COSMO: You were altogether asleep. You were dreaming.

RAYMOND: No. You were there.

(RAYMOND *stares at* COSMO, *nodding, remembering. There's a lull at the table, the sound of silverware.*)

COSMO: I don't wanna talk about it.

ROSE (suddenly angry): Well, what do you wanna talk about!

COSMO: Rita. Pass the wine.

ROSE: Why you drinking so much?

(The OLD MAN gets up with his newly filled plate and heads for the dogs.)

ROSE (continuing): Old Man, if you give another piece of my food to those dogs, I'm gonna kick you till you're dead!

(*The* OLD MAN *reverses direction and heads back to his chair. He sits down and starts to eat.*)

EXTERIOR: THE CASTORINI HOUSE. NIGHT.

Over the house is a great big full moon.

INTERIOR: THE CASTORINI HOUSE. MASTER BEDROOM. NIGHT.

The lights in the bedroom are still on. COSMO *is in bed, in his pajamas, asleep.* ROSE *comes in, wearing her nightgown. She looks at* COSMO. *He's snoring lightly.*

ROSE: Cosmo?

(COSMO *doesn't stir.* ROSE *goes to him and runs her hand through his hair.*)

ROSE (continuing): You drank too much and now you sleep too hard, and later you'll be up when you should be down.

(ROSE *kisses his cheek. Then she turns out the lights. When the electric lights go out, moonlight floods the room. She goes to the window and looks out through the curtains at the moon.* ROSE *puts her face in her hands and quietly cries.*)

EXTERIOR: SHOT OF MOON FROM CASTORINI HOUSE. NIGHT.

Rose's point of view: The moon is big and white, and seems very near.

INTERIOR: THE CASTORINI HOUSE. MASTER BEDROOM. NIGHT.

ROSE *is crying.*

INTERIOR: RONNY'S APARTMENT. BEDROOM. NIGHT.

The bedroom is flooded by moonlight. LORETTA *wakes up, a little alarmed.*

LORETTA: What's that?

(RONNY *wakes up, a little alarmed.*)

RONNY: What?

LORETTA: That light.

RONNY: I don't know. I think it's the moon.

(LORETTA *goes to the window wrapped in a white sheet from the bed. The window is glowing with moonlight. The moonlight strikes her, and she is caught in its spell.*)

LORETTA: Oh.

(RONNY *appears behind her, pulling on a robe. They speak in low voices, as if they were in church.*)

RONNY: It's so bright.

LORETTA: I've never seen a moon like that.

RONNY: It makes you look like an angel.

(LORETTA *turns and looks at him. They kiss. They break apart.* RONNY *looks up at the moon.*)

RONNY (continuing): Yeah. Looks like a big snowball.

EXTERIOR: THE CAPPOMAGGI HOUSE. NIGHT.

The moon is over the house.

INTERIOR: RAYMOND AND RITA CAPPOMAGGI'S BEDROOM. NIGHT.

There is a big window right by the bed, and in the window is the moon. RAYMOND *and* RITA *are in their bed, asleep.* RAYMOND *wakes up and sees the moon in the window. He's stunned and excited, but he too speaks in this low voice of respect.*

RAYMOND: Rita. Rita.

RITA (waking up): What? What?

RAYMOND: Look.

RITA: Oh.

RAYMOND: It's Cosmo's moon.

RITA: What are you talking about, Raymond? Cosmo can't own the moon.

RAYMOND: I mean, it's that moon I was talking about at dinner. (*Looks through the window, down into the street.*) Is he down there? No.

RITA: Is who down there?

RAYMOND: Cosmo.

RITA: What would he be doing down there?

RAYMOND: I don't know.

RITA: You know, in this light and with that expression on your face, you look about twenty-five years old.

(RAYMOND *smiles at her meekly.*)

EXTERIOR: THE CASTORINI HOUSE. NIGHT.

The great full moon is still over the house. The front door opens and out comes the OLD MAN *with the five dogs. The* OLD MAN *is in a greatcoat and a felt hat, and he's smoking a cigar. He stops on the top step and lets go a huge plume of cigar smoke. Then he starts off with the dogs down the street.*

EXTERIOR: EAST RIVER. NIGHT.

The moon and nothing else. Then a cigar is thrown into the moon and sends it shimmering. It was the moon reflected in water.
     Now the camera pulls back, and we see the OLD MAN *and the five dogs are standing on a ruined pier. The moon gleams up from the East River.*

OLD MAN (speaking to the dogs): All right now. Howl. Howl.

(*The dogs do not howl. So the* OLD MAN, *by way of demonstration, howls at the moon. He looks to the dogs to follow suit. They do nothing. He howls at the moon again.*

The dogs do nothing. The camera continues to pull back until we can see the whole pier, with the OLD MAN *and the dogs on it and the moon above them.*)

OLD MAN (frustrated, crying out): How long must I wait? *Quanto tempo devo aspettare!*

(*The dogs start to howl. The* OLD MAN, *pleased as the Mad Hatter he is, laughs and laughs.*)

EXTERIOR: EAST RIVER. DAWN.

Transition from the moon reflected in the water to dawn.

INTERIOR: RONNY'S APARTMENT. BEDROOM. DAY.

Morning sun floods the room. Close on LORETTA. *She wakes up.*

LORETTA: Oh, my God.

RONNY: What?

(LORETTA *jumps from bed, grabs her clothes to cover herself, and backs into the closet.*)

LORETTA: What? *What* have we done?

RONNY (perturbed): Take it easy.

LORETTA (from the closet as she hurriedly gets dressed): This time I was trying to do everything right.

RONNY (grabs a bathrobe, pulls it on, and moves toward the closet): Don't just become excited.

LORETTA: I thought if I stayed away from the city hall, I won't have that *bad luck* I had again.

RONNY: You're trying to make me feel guilty.

LORETTA: I'm marrying your brother!

RONNY: All right, I'm guilty. I confess!

LORETTA: You're invited to the wedding! It's in a few weeks. Why didn't you do like him and be with your dying mother in Palermo?

RONNY: She don't like me.

LORETTA: You don't get along with anybody!

RONNY: What did you do?

LORETTA: What did I do?

RONNY: You ruined my life!

LORETTA: That's impossible! It was ruint when I got here! You ruint my life!

RONNY: Oh no, I didn't!

LORETTA (emerging from the closet, tucking in her blouse): Oh yes, oh yes, you did! You've got those bad eyes like a gypsy! Why didn't I see it yesterday! *Bad luck!* Is that all I'm ever gonna have? Why didn't I just pick up a stone and kill myself years and years ago? I'm gonna marry him!

RONNY: What?

LORETTA: Last night never happened, you hear me? I'm gonna marry him anyway and last night never happened and you and I are gonna take this to our coffins!

RONNY: I can't do that!

LORETTA: Why not?

RONNY: I'm in love with you!

(LORETTA *stares at him in alarm, slaps his face, then studies his face to see the effect of the slap. She is dissatisfied and slaps him again.*)

LORETTA: Snap out of it!

RONNY: I can't!

LORETTA: All right. Then I must never see you again. The bad blood will have to stay there between you and Johnny for all time. You won't come to the wedding.

RONNY: I'll come to the wedding.

LORETTA: I'm telling you, you can't.

RONNY: But he wants me to come!

LORETTA: But that's 'cause he don't know!

RONNY: All right. I will not come. Provided one thing.

LORETTA: What?

RONNY: That you come with me tonight. Once. To the opera.

LORETTA: What are you talking about?

RONNY: I love two things. I love you and I love the opera. If I can have the two things that I love together for one night, I will be satisfied to give up the rest of my life.

LORETTA: All right.

RONNY: All right. Meet me at the Met.

LORETTA: All right. Where's the Met?

INTERIOR: A CATHOLIC CHURCH IN LITTLE ITALY. DAY.

Camera moves from stained glass windows to the confessional. LORETTA *is next in line of three sinners waiting to go into the confessional. A forgiven woman emerges from the curtained booth and walks off to say her penance.* LORETTA *goes into the booth.*

INTERIOR: CHURCH. CONFESSIONAL. DAY.

LORETTA *kneels. The slide opens, and an old priest's face can be seen in outline through the screen.*

LORETTA: Bless me, Father, for I have sinned. It's been two months since my last confession.

PRIEST: What sins have you to confess?

LORETTA: Twice I took the name of God in vain, once I slept with the brother of my fiancé, and once I bounced a check at the liquor store— but that was really an accident.

PRIEST: Then it was not a sin. But what was that second thing you said, Loretta?

LORETTA: I . . . a . . . slept with my fiancé's brother.

PRIEST: That's a pretty big sin.

LORETTA: I know.

PRIEST: You should think about this.

LORETTA: I know.

PRIEST: All right. This is your penance. Say two rosaries and . . . be careful, Loretta. Reflect on your life.

LORETTA: All right.

PRIEST: I absolve you in the name of the Father and of the Son and of the Holy Spirit, Amen.

INTERIOR: CHURCH. DAY.

LORETTA *comes out of the confessional and enters a pew. She crosses herself. Then she recognizes the back of a woman's head a few pews down. She gets up, walks down the aisle, and kneels down next to her mother,* ROSE.

LORETTA: Hi.

ROSE (looking up from her prayers): Where you been?

LORETTA: I don't wanna talk about it.

ROSE: Just like your father. I lied to him. He thinks you came home last night.

LORETTA: Thanks. What's the matter with you?

ROSE: Cosmo's cheating on me.

LORETTA: What! How do you know?

ROSE: A wife knows.

LORETTA: Then you don't know. You're just imagining it. He's too old.

(ROSE *starts to reply but then decides it's not worth the argument.*)

LORETTA (continuing): I won't be home for dinner.

(LORETTA *crosses herself quickly, gets up, and leaves.* ROSE *looks after, and then goes back to her prayer.*)

INTERIOR: CAMMARERI'S BAKE SHOP. DAY.

Feminine hands apply the final decorative touches of blue icing to a wedding cake. Then the hands set the plastic bride and groom on the pinnacle. The camera pulls back. BARBARA *is viewing her handiwork, a wedding cake on a stainless-steel wheeled cart. She's in the back part of the bakery.* BARBARA *is pleased with her creation. We travel with her as she rolls the cart out to the front of the store where* CHRISSY *is waiting on a huge man,* HARVEY. CHRISSY *hands him a tiny box, which he takes meekly.*

HARVEY: See you tomorrow, Chrissy.

CHRISSY: Okay, Harvey.

(HARVEY *lumbers off as* BARBARA *enters the front of the store with the cake on its cart.* BARBARA *calls Chrissy's attention to the cake.*)

BARBARA: So what do you think?

CHRISSY: About what?

BARBARA: The cake!

CHRISSY (without enthusiasm): It's big. Where's Ronny? How come he ain't come down?

BARBARA: How should I know?

(*The phone rings.* CHRISSY *answers it.*)

CHRISSY: Hello, Cammareri's? Hi. Uh-huh. Okay. (*She hangs up.*) That was Ronny. He don't feel good. He ain't gonna be down today.

(CHRISSY *comes out from behind the counter. She's staring at the cake.*)

BARBARA: What, is he still upset?

(*Without warning,* CHRISSY *whacks the little bride and groom off the cake and onto the floor.*)

CHRISSY: It's that bitch!

(BARBARA *looks at her, shocked.*)

EXTERIOR: CAPPOMAGGI'S ITALIAN PROVISIONS. DAY.

An Italian specialty store in Little Italy.

INTERIOR: CAPPOMAGGI'S STORE. DAY.

Provolones and salamis hang from above. To the one side is a deli counter; to the other, a series of tables displaying cheeses by the pound, packaged cakes, and other items. In the back are a few tables and a kitchen with a counter. Up front, behind the deli counter, stands RITA CAPPOMAGGI *in a blue apron. Out by the tables,* RAYMOND *unpacks some jars of olives. In the back a truck driver can dimly be seen eating his lunch.*

RAYMOND (to RITA): I feel great! I got no sleep, but I feel like Orlando Furioso!

RITA (looks around cautiously, then speaks): You were a tiger last night.

RAYMOND: And you were a lamb. As soft as milk.

RITA: Shut up. They'll hear you in the back.

RAYMOND: So what? The pleasure of marriage is you sleep with the woman, and then you don't worry about nothing. Hey, how 'bout a date tonight, Rita. Let's eat pasta and roll around!

RITA (scandalized): Raymond, Raymond, lower your voice! What's got into you?

RAYMOND: I don't know! That moon! That crazy moon Cosmo sent over!

(LORETTA *walks in.*)

LORETTA: Hi.

RAYMOND: Hey there, (*sings*) . . . *you with the stars in your eyes* . . .

LORETTA (to RITA): What's the matter with him?

RITA: You got me.

RAYMOND: You see that moon last night?

LORETTA (suspicious and guilty): What about the moon?

RAYMOND: Did you see it?

LORETTA (nervous, lying): No.

RAYMOND: Oh.

LORETTA: Listen, I gotta go. I'll take the deposit to the bank, but I'll do the books tomorrow. I gotta go.

RAYMOND: You gotta date?

RITA: What are you talking about, you fool? Her fiancé's in Palermo.

RAYMOND: Oh. Right.

LORETTA: I got things to do.

RITA: Sure you do. You got all that wedding stuff.

LORETTA: Right.

RAYMOND: Well, that's romantic, too. (*Sings.*) *Isn't it romantic* . . .

(RAYMOND *is walking toward the back now.*)

RAYMOND (shouting to somebody in the kitchen): Hey! Make me a bowl of minestrone.

(*The women are left alone.*)

RITA: What's the matter? You look crazy.

LORETTA: I got a lot on my mind, Aunt Rita.

EXTERIOR: A LITTLE GRAVEYARD BY A LITTLE CHURCH. DAY.

The OLD MAN *and his five dogs and two other old Italian men,* FRANCO *and* PIETRO, *stand regarding a new grave. The grave is covered with several small wreaths and bouquets of flowers.* FRANCO *and* PIETRO *wear big hats. The camera pans slowly from the dogs to the group. One of the dogs sniffs the grave and begins to pee.*

OLD MAN: *Basta, basta.* Don't do that. He's asleep.

FRANCO: Look at all the flowers Alphonso got.

OLD MAN: I can't. I can only see the things in my house. Things are very bad in my house.

PIETRO: My brother sent the blue ones.

OLD MAN: I don't know what to advise my son. I think he should pay for the wedding, but it is important that he don't look ridiculous.

FRANCO: Don't make yourself sick.

OLD MAN: Cosmo drank five glasses of wine at dinner.

FRANCO: Talk to him.

OLD MAN: I will. But I must find the right moment.

PIETRO: Did you see the moon last night?

(*The Old Man's eyes light up.*)

OLD MAN: *Si! La bella luna.* The moon brings the woman to the man!

(FRANCO *and* PIETRO *laugh and nod in agreement.*)

INTERIOR: CAPPOMAGGI STORE. DAY.

Eight neat stacks of money are being rubber-banded by a woman's hands. The last stack is topped with a filled-out deposit slip. The banded stacks are then stuffed into a night-deposit bag. The camera pulls back a bit to include a ledger. A last entry is made, and the ledger is shut. The camera pulls back more, and now we see LORETTA *reaching for her coat. She puts it on, picks up the deposit bag, and sees* RITA.

LORETTA: 'Bye, Aunt Rita.

RITA: Bye-bye, honey. See you tomorrow?

LORETTA: Yeah, I'll be in.

(LORETTA *goes out the door, with* RITA *looking after, thoughtful.*)

EXTERIOR: CINDERELLA BEAUTY SHOP. DAY.

LORETTA *walks down the street and comes to the Cinderella Beauty Shop, fidgets a moment, looks around to see if anybody is looking, and goes in.*
    We see her through the window talking to MILDRED, *who handles appointments.* MILDRED *nods, points, and* LORETTA *goes back into the store.*

INTERIOR: CINDERELLA BEAUTY SHOP. DAY.

An uneasy LORETTA *sits in a beauty chair with* BONNIE, *her hairdresser, about to start.* BONNIE *is a little bored.*

BONNIE: So? You want the usual?

LORETTA: I want you to get rid of the gray.

(*Music: transformational music starts here and continues through the following scenes. This music should convey that* LORETTA *is turning from a frumpy pumpkin into a sleek and beautiful coach.*)

BONNIE (waking up upon hearing this startling news and getting very excited): I've been wanting to do this for three years! Let me show you some magazines! You've got to get a manicure! And your eyebrows! Sheila! I'm gonna need help!

(PATRICE, *another beautician, joins* BONNIE, *and they both get very excited and start showing* LORETTA *and each other magazines. They argue merrily about what they should do, leaving* LORETTA *far behind. A manicurist joins them with her stuff and starts soaking Loretta's nails.*
    A montage follows:
    They're plucking Loretta's eyebrows.

They're cutting and dying Loretta's hair.
They're painting Loretta's nails.)

EXTERIOR: CINDERELLA BEAUTY SHOP. DAY.

LORETTA *comes out. Her hair is jet black and done in a much more styl-*
ish way. She looks great. She looks around as if she has committed a
crime, and walks off quickly.

EXTERIOR: A DOWDY DRESS SHOP. DAY.

LORETTA *looks in the window, is dissatisfied, and walks on.*

EXTERIOR: A BOLD DRESS SHOP. DAY.

A stylish dress shop called Insinuation. LORETTA *looks in the window, is*
intimidated, and walks on. A moment passes. She reappears. Tenta-
tively, she enters.

INTERIOR: INSINUATION. DAY.

LORETTA *approaches a young woman,* MER, *who works there.* MER *is about*
thirty, trendily dressed, and French. MER *and* LORETTA *greet and talk.*
LORETTA *makes vague gestures trying to convey what she wants, but the*
truth is she doesn't know what she wants. MER *takes the situation in*
hand.
     There follows a montage of MER *showing* LORETTA *various dresses,*
some outlandish, some beautiful, some incomprehensible. LORETTA *tries*
on several of the dresses in a big triple mirror. Some horrify her; some
frighten her because they're so sexy; one bores her. We don't see the
dress that she ultimately does buy.

EXTERIOR: INSINUATION. DUSK.

LORETTA *walks out with a big shopping bag. She walks away down the*
street.

We follow LORETTA *down the street. She comes to a bridal shop with a big bride dummy in the window. She stops and looks at the bride. She walks close to the window and stares in hard. Then she slowly backs up from the bride. Two nuns are walking by.* LORETTA, *backing up from the dummy, bumps into the nuns. She's flustered, makes a brief apology, and hurries away, casting a furtive last glance at the shop window.*
The transformational music comes to a close.

EXTERIOR: THE CASTORINI HOUSE. DUSK.

Night is falling. LORETTA *appears and enters the house.*

INTERIOR: THE CASTORINI HOUSE. FRONT HALL. NIGHT.

As LORETTA *enters, she drops her bag.*

LORETTA (taking off her coat and calling): Ma! Grandpa! No? Okay.

(*A single bark is heard from the top of the stairs.* LORETTA *looks up.*
A wooden accordion gate seals off the top of the stairs.
A couple of dogs are visible behind the gate.)

INTERIOR: THE CASTORINI HOUSE. KITCHEN. NIGHT.

LORETTA *goes through a door and into the kitchen. She opens the refrigerator and a cabinet, and makes herself a scotch on the rocks. She sips it and starts to hum in an understated way. She takes her drink and wanders out of the kitchen.*
LORETTA *walks into the living room. She walks to each lamp in the room and turns it on. There are many table and standing lamps throughout the room.*
LORETTA *is lighting the kindling that was already laid in the fireplace. It catches on nicely. She puts her drink down and gets a big standing antique mirror on rollers from its place against the wall. She wheels it to a central place in the room. Satisfied, she picks up her drink again, leaves the room for a moment, and then returns with her shop-*

ping bag. She throws it on a chair. Then she goes to the stereo and looks through the albums. She selects one and puts it on.
   Music begins.
   LORETTA *waltzs around in front of the mirror, flirting with herself in a very serious way. She starts to unbutton her blouse.*

EXTERIOR: THE CASTORINI HOUSE. NIGHT.

The moon is overhead as music continues to play. The camera soars up close to the moon until the moon completely fills the frame with its magic. The moon dissolves into:

INTERIOR: THE CASTORINI HOUSE. LIVING ROOM. NIGHT.

A close-up of Loretta's face as she puts the final touches on her makeup. Music continues to play. The camera pulls back. We see her full figure. She has changed into her evening dress and put on her heels. She's swaying to the music. The evening dress is sensational. She leans forward and kisses the mirror.
   We see the lipstick kiss on the mirror.
   In the mirror, the fire is reflected all around the kiss.

EXTERIOR: EAST RIVER. NIGHT.

The moon is reflected in the water as we see the dock of the night before.
   We can see New Jersey lit up across the river. But then something starts to replace New Jersey. It's a huge white liner coming down the river now, all of her lights burning, heading back out to sea. Flashbulbs go off along the deck. We watch the length of the great ship pass as the music plays.
   End of music.

EXTERIOR: LINCOLN CENTER PLAZA. NIGHT.

LORETTA *is emerging from a cab.*
   Loretta's point of view: Lincoln Center. Crowds of people in beautiful clothes fill the plaza created by the three great buildings. A glori-

ous fountain filled with lights forms the centerpiece. Behind the foun-
tain, grand and splendidly lit, is the magical Metropolitan Opera
House. Two huge Chagalls, one to the right and one to the left, inhabit
the face of the building, filling it with marvelous color.

LORETTA *comes to the fountain. The fountain is quiet and dark*
now. LORETTA *is puzzled. She remembers that it was going. While she*
looks, it lights up. Then small jets of water begin to appear, then larger
jets. Then with a roar the central shaft of water rises high, higher into
the night sky. She follows the column of water with her eyes up into
the sky. Right above the crest of the water, like a beach ball on a seal's
nose, is the moon.

From over Loretta's shoulder, we see the rushing water forming
an opaque wall before her. Then the fountain, for its next piece of
aquatic choreography, drops away to nothing quite suddenly. And
there, facing LORETTA, *on the opposite side of the fountain, is* RONNY.

RONNY *is looking incredibly handsome and dashing in a tuxedo*
and topcoat and, of course, gloves. He smiles slightly and raises a hand
in greeting. LORETTA, *caught off guard, smiles brilliantly at him. Then*
she remembers her situation and starts to put on her usual serious
expression. But the fountain has rushed up into the sky again, obscur-
ing from RONNY *her attempt at composure.*

RONNY *comes into view again, walking toward* LORETTA *around the*
fountain's perimeter. He comes close to her.

RONNY: Hi.

LORETTA: Hi.

RONNY: You look beautiful. Your hair . . .

LORETTA: I thought I'd try it. (*Grudgingly.*) You look good.

RONNY: Thank you.

(RONNY *goes to kiss her. She takes a step back.*)

LORETTA: I said I'd go to the opera with you. Nothing else.

(RONNY *immediately relents, gently takes her arm, and they walk off in the direction of the opera house.*

RONNY and LORETTA *look up at one of the Chagalls immediately in front of the Metropolitan Opera House.*)

LORETTA: Who painted that?

RONNY: Marc Chagall. A Russian.

LORETTA: Kinda gaudy.

RONNY: He was having some fun. Yeah, well, he's dead. (*He smiles.*) Come on, let's go in.

(RONNY *and* LORETTA *join the crowd streaming into the building.*)

INTERIOR: THE OPERA HOUSE ENTRANCE. NIGHT.

RONNY *and* LORETTA *enter, giving tickets to an usher.*

INTERIOR: THE OPERA HOUSE. COAT CHECK. NIGHT.

RONNY *and* LORETTA *are checking their coats. Ronny's coat is already off, and he's helping* LORETTA *take off hers. He hands her coat to the checker and pockets the check. Then he turns and sees* LORETTA *in her dress for the first time. He's stunned by her beauty. He's at a loss. He mumbles.*

RONNY: Thank you!

LORETTA: For what?

RONNY: I don't know. For your hair. For your beautiful dress. For . . . you know, I feel like a man again. You know I love the opera. You know it's been a long time since I've been to the opera.

(*His eyes are bright with tears.* LORETTA *is touched and starts to put her hand out to him, but she stops herself.*)

LORETTA: So. Where are we sitting?

RONNY: Come on.

(RONNY *takes her arm. They pass under the great chandelier and go into the house.*)

INTERIOR: THE OPERA HOUSE. NIGHT.

The camera picks out a series of couples.

The first couple is PEGGY *and* CLIVE, *a very distinguished pair of silver-haired lovers dressed magnificently. They are in their seats, delighted to be where they are, holding hands.*

Next is a celebrity couple. Maybe Jackie O and her son, John. They are seated, and people are looking at them.

The next couple is COSMO *and* MONA. COSMO *is helping* MONA *to sit down, something she could probably handle herself. He's wearing a good but old-fashioned suit. She is in a dress that makes her look like a big piece of hard candy.*

The last couple is RONNY *and* LORETTA. *They are sitting in the first row of the First Circle, in other words, very good seats. They are holding their programs.* LORETTA *opens her program.*

Loretta's point of view: the open program. The opera is La Bohème. *But then the page fades away into the dark as the house lights go down.*

We see RONNY *and* LORETTA *from behind.*

RONNY (leaning his head toward her and whispering): Here we go.

(*As the lights come up in the orchestra pit, the conductor takes his place. The audience applauds. He bows and turns to the orchestra. The Overture begins.*)

EXTERIOR: THE GRAND TICINO. NIGHT.

The Overture plays through this establishing shot and then fades away at the start of the next shot. We see ROSE *enter the restaurant.*

INTERIOR: THE GRAND TICINIO. NIGHT.

The dinner crowd is in, and most of the tables are occupied. The entranceway door opens, and ROSE *enters.*

She has got herself up very nicely. The host, JIMMY, *quickly approaches her. She's very dignified.*

JIMMY: Hello, Mrs. Castorini! Who's coming?

ROSE: It's just me. I want to eat.

JIMMY: Okay. I got a table for you right now.

(JIMMY *leads* ROSE *to a table for two against the wall.*)

JIMMY: This all right?

ROSE: Fine.

(JIMMY *seats her.*)

JIMMY: Enjoy your meal.

(JIMMY *breezes off. There's another table for two against the wall to Rose's front. From Rose's point of view, we see a woman's back and a pretty head of hair. This woman, whose name is* SHEILA, *is having an argument with the man across from her. But the man's face is blocked by Sheila's back and head, and the argument is too low to be made out.* BOBO *approaches Rose's table.*)

BOBO: Good evening, Mrs. Castorini. You eating alone tonight?

ROSE: Hello, Bobo. Yes. Let me have a martini, no ice and two olives.

BOBO: Very good.

(BOBO *heads off for the bar. The couple at the next table catches Rose's attention again, and their argument becomes a little louder.*)

SHEILA'S VOICE: I'm trying to explain to you how *I* feel. Every time I try to explain how I feel, you explain how *you* feel. I don't think that's really much of a response.

MAN'S VOICE: Well, it's the only response I've got.

(BOBO *reappears with the martini and serves it.*)

BOBO: You wanna see a menu?

ROSE: Not yet. I'll wave.

(BOBO *is gone.* ROSE *is mildly intrigued with the argument at the next table now. She tries to see past* SHEILA, *to see the man, but she can't without making too big a move. The argument goes on.*)

SHEILA'S VOICE: I really do hate it, though, when you take that tone with me. Like you're above it all and isn't it amusing.

MAN'S VOICE: But it is, isn't it?

SHEILA'S VOICE: Not to me! This is my life, no matter how damned comical it may seem to you. I don't need some man standing above the struggle while I roll around in the mud!

MAN'S VOICE: I think you like the mud and I don't. That's fair, isn't it? If I don't care to . . .

(SHEILA *stands up abruptly and flings a glass of water in the man's face. She pulls her coat off the back of her chair and stalks off. This whole operation takes about two seconds. When she stalks off, the face of the man becomes visible to* ROSE *for the first time. It's* PERRY, *the professor in his fifties who appeared and was treated in a similar way in the earlier scene in this restaurant. His face is covered with beads of water. He pats his face with his napkin and apologizes to customers at neighboring tables.)*

PERRY: Sorry about that, folks. She's a very pretty mental patient.

(The SHY WAITER arrives to assist PERRY in drying himself.)

PERRY (continuing): Don't mind about me. But could you do me a favor and clear her place and take away all evidence of her, and bring me a big glass of vodka?

SHY WAITER: Absolutely!

(*The* SHY WAITER *heads for the bar. For the first time* PERRY *notices* ROSE. *They are facing each other with no obstacles in the way now.)*

PERRY: I'm sorry if we disturbed you.

ROSE: I'm not disturbed. By you.

PERRY: My lady friend has a personality disorder.

ROSE: She was just too young for you.

(*The* SHY WAITER *serves* PERRY *his drink.)*

PERRY (to the SHY WAITER): Thanks, comrade.

SHY WAITER: It's nothing!

(*The* SHY WAITER *goes.)*

PERRY (Rose's comment strikes home): Ouch. Too young! I just got that. You know how to hurt a guy. How old are you?

ROSE: None of your business.

PERRY (dropping his posturing): Sorry. That was rude.

ROSE: Will you join me for dinner?

PERRY: Are you sure?

(ROSE *nods.*)

PERRY (continuing): Then I'd be delighted. I hate eating alone, and it's amazing how often I end up doing just that.

(ROSE *and* PERRY *are halfway through their dinner.*)

ROSE: What do you do?

PERRY: I'm a professor. I teach communications at NYU.

ROSE: That woman was a student of yours?

PERRY: Sheila? Yes, she was. Is. Was.

ROSE: There's an old saying my mother told me. Would you like to hear it?

PERRY: Yes.

ROSE: Don't shit where you eat.

PERRY (taken aback, then recovering): I'll remember that. What do you do?

ROSE: I'm a housewife.

PERRY: Then why are you eating alone?

ROSE: I'm not eating alone. Can I ask you a question?

PERRY: Go ahead.

ROSE: Why do men chase women?

PERRY (considers): Nerves.

ROSE: I think it's because they fear death.

PERRY: Maybe. Listen. You wanna know why I chase women? I find women charming. I teach these classes I've taught for a million years. The spontaneity went out of it for me a long time ago. I started off, I was excited about something and I wanted to share it. Now it's rote; it's the multiplication table. Except sometimes. Sometimes I'm droning along and I look up and there's this fresh, young, beautiful face, and it's all new to her and I'm this great guy who's just brilliant and thinks out loud. And when that happens, when I look out among those chairs and look at a young woman's face, and see *me* there in her eyes, *me* the way I always wanted to be and maybe once was, then I ask her out on a date. It doesn't last. It can go for a few weeks or a couple of precious months, but then she catches on that I'm just a burnt-out old gasbag and that she's as fresh and bright and full of promise as moonlight in a martini. And at that moment, she stands up and throws a glass of water in my face, or some action to that effect.

ROSE: What you don't know about women is a lot.

INTERIOR: THE OPERA HOUSE. LOBBY. NIGHT.

Intermission. Throngs of people are talking, talking, talking. They are piled up at the bars to get drinks.

INTERIOR: THE OPERA HOUSE. LOBBY OUTSIDE WOMEN'S BATHROOM. NIGHT.

Outside the women's bathroom, there is a huge line waiting to get in.

INTERIOR: WOMEN'S BATHROOM. NIGHT.

LORETTA *and three other women freshen their makeup before a mirror. The woman next to* LORETTA *leaves and is replaced by* MONA. MONA *and* LORETTA *stand side by side freshening their makeup.*

INTERIOR: THE OPERA HOUSE. LOBBY. NIGHT.

Many people are pressing to the bar to buy drinks. COSMO *and* RONNY *achieve the bar's perimeter at the same moment and start to order.*

INTERIOR: THE OPERA HOUSE. LOBBY. NIGHT.

A concessionaire is selling special glossy La Bohème *programs.*
      Elsewhere in the lobby during intermission, RONNY *and* LORETTA *are standing by a column holding drinks.* LORETTA *is looking around.*

LORETTA: They get some turnout for this stuff.

RONNY: It's the best thing there is.

LORETTA: I like parts of it, but I don't really get it.

(*In another part of the lobby during intermission,* COSMO *and* MONA *are sitting on a bench.*)

MONA: You haven't once said you like my dress.

COSMO: I like your dress. (*He thinks.*) It's very bright.

(COSMO *looks around.*)

MONA: Why you looking around so much?

COSMO: I don't know. I got a feeling.

MONA: I'm wearing your bracelet.

(COSMO *nods, still looking around.*)

(*Chimes sound throughout lobby, indicating the end of intermission. The audience starts to file back into the theater.*)

EXTERIOR: THE GRAND TICINO. NIGHT.

ROSE *and* PERRY *emerge from the restaurant.*

PERRY: May I walk with you a ways?

ROSE: Sure.

(*They set off to the left.*)

EXTERIOR: THE CASTORINI HOUSE. NIGHT.

The door opens, and the OLD MAN *comes out, in his greatcoat and hat, with the five dogs. He strikes off to the right.*

EXTERIOR: STREET I. NIGHT.

ROSE *and* PERRY *come around a corner and pass a store. They pause and look at the Christmas decorations in the window. They continue walking.*

EXTERIOR: STREET 2. NIGHT.

The OLD MAN *and the dogs have stopped by a big tree, which the dogs adore.*

EXTERIOR: STREET I. NIGHT.

ROSE *and* PERRY *are walking. They exit camera left.*

EXTERIOR: STREET 2. NIGHT.

The OLD MAN *drags the dogs away from the tree and sets off, camera right.*

EXTERIOR: STREET 1. NIGHT.

ROSE *and* PERRY *are walking to the left.*

EXTERIOR: STREET 2. NIGHT.

The OLD MAN *and the dogs are walking to the right.*

EXTERIOR: STREET 1. INTERSECTION OUTSIDE LAUNDROMAT. NIGHT.

ROSE *and* PERRY *are walking toward camera.* ROSE *stops short, stunned and alarmed by what she sees before them.*

EXTERIOR: STREET 2. INTERSECTION OUTSIDE LAUNDROMAT. NIGHT.

Aghast by what he sees before him, the OLD MAN *pulls up the dogs.*

EXTERIOR: STREET 3. INTERSECTION OUTSIDE LAUNDROMAT. NIGHT.

PERRY *and* ROSE *face the* OLD MAN *and the dogs.*
All remain in a silent standoff. PERRY *is puzzled but has the sense to say nothing. After a long moment the* OLD MAN *silently steers his dogs past them. He walks away, down the dark street, silently disappearing into the gloom.* PERRY *and* ROSE *never move but follow his slow progress until he disappears.*

PERRY: You knew that man?

ROSE: Yes.

INTERIOR: THE OPERA HOUSE. NIGHT.

The stage: the opera is in progress. It's the scene in which Mimi is standing in the falling snow. She sings to Rudolf. It is a beautiful, poignant moment. The snow is falling, falling. Mimi is singing her heartbreaking aria of farewell. The lighted tavern window is behind them, glowing with a golden light.

We see Ronny's face. He's staring intently at the stage with shining eyes. He wants to share this moment with LORETTA, *but he is timid, afraid that she will not feel as he does.*

We see Loretta's face. A single tear trails down her cheek. Otherwise, she is almost succeeding in hiding that the opera is moving her. She notices Ronny's hand creeping toward hers, but she makes no move toward it.

The stage: Mimi is still singing sadly in the snowfall. She and Rudolf join hands.

RONNY *and* LORETTA *grab each other's hand fiercely. At last, they look at each other. She is admitting that she is affected by the opera. He is grateful that she admits it.*

INTERIOR: THE OPERA HOUSE. AUDIENCE. NIGHT.

Audience exits.

INTERIOR: THE OPERA HOUSE. LOBBY. NIGHT.

The lobby overflows with the audience coming out.

INTERIOR: THE OPERA HOUSE. COAT CHECK. NIGHT.

RONNY *and* LORETTA *in line at the coat check.* LORETTA *dabs her eyes and blows her nose.*

LORETTA: That was just so . . . awful!

RONNY: Awful?

LORETTA: Beautiful. Sad. She died!

RONNY (giving the check to the checker): Yeah.

LORETTA: I couldn't believe it! I didn't think she was going to die. I knew she was sick . . .

(RONNY *gets the coats and helps her on with hers.*)

RONNY: She had TB.

(RONNY *is putting on his coat.*)

LORETTA: I know. She was coughing her brains out. And still, she had to sing all the time . . .

(LORETTA *has stopped suddenly, transfixed by the sight before her.*
LORETTA *and* RONNY *are standing face-to-face with* COSMO *and* MONA. MONA *is wearing a coat like a wrapper for hard candy.* COSMO *is wearing his coat and has his hat in his hand. Stunned at seeing* LORETTA, *he unconsciously puts his hat on. Then he thinks about it and takes it off again. He looks at* RONNY. *Then he looks at* MONA.)

LORETTA (continuing): Pop?

(RONNY *looks at* LORETTA. *He waits to follow her lead.*)

COSMO: Wait for me by the doors, Mona.

(MONA *obeys after looking curiously at* LORETTA.)

LORETTA: Pop? What are you doing here?

(COSMO *approaches* RONNY.)

COSMO: Excuse me.

(COSMO *takes Loretta's arm and steers her a distance away for a confidential exchange.*)

LORETTA: Mona?

COSMO: What d'you do to your hair?

LORETTA: I got it done.

COSMO: What are you doing here?

LORETTA: What are you doing here?

COSMO: Who is this man? You're engaged!

LORETTA: You're married.

COSMO: You're my daughter. I won't have you acting like a tramp!

LORETTA: You're my father.

COSMO: All right. I didn't see you here.

LORETTA: I don't know whether I saw you or not.

(COSMO *puts on his hat again. He glares at* RONNY. *He looks at* LORETTA, *but he's at a total loss. At last, he stalks off. Angry and disturbed,* LORETTA *looks after him.*

Loretta's point of view: COSMO *and* MONA *are going out the doors.*

Stricken, LORETTA *is looking after them.* RONNY *appears at her side, solicitous.*)

RONNY: Let's get outta here. I'll buy you a drink.

(LORETTA, *still looking after, slowly shakes her head.*)

LORETTA: That wasn't my mother.

EXTERIOR: THE CASTORINI HOUSE. NIGHT.

ROSE *and* PERRY *stand on a sidewalk under a streetlight dimly shining. About half a block away stands the Castorini house. They regard it. Over the house hangs the moon, cut through now with a sharp gray cloud. Rose's and Perry's voices can be heard.*

ROSE'S VOICE: That's my house.

PERRY'S VOICE: You mean the whole house?

ROSE'S VOICE: Yes.

PERRY'S VOICE: My God, it's a mansion!

ROSE'S VOICE: It's a house.

PERRY'S VOICE: I live in a one-bedroom apartment. What exactly does your husband do?

ROSE'S VOICE: He's a plumber.

PERRY'S VOICE: Well. That explains it.

(*The wind can be heard rising up.*
   Now we see ROSE *and* PERRY *close up.*
   The rising cold wind stirs their hair. They both shiver slightly.)

PERRY: Temperature's dropping.

ROSE: Yes.

PERRY: I guess you can't invite me in?

ROSE: No.

PERRY: People home.

ROSE: No. I think the house is empty. I can't invite you in because I'm married and because I know who I am. You're shaking.

PERRY: I'm a little cold.

ROSE: You're a little boy, and you like to be bad.

PERRY: We could go to my apartment. You could see how the other half lives.

ROSE: I'm too old for you.

PERRY: I'm too old for me. That's my predicament.

ROSE: Good night.

(ROSE *kisses him on the cheek.*)

PERRY: Good night. Can I kiss you on the cheek, too?

ROSE: Sure.

(PERRY *kisses her on the cheek.*)

PERRY: I'm freezing.

ROSE: Good night.

(ROSE *walks away, toward the house.* PERRY, *shivering, looks after.*)

INTERIOR: THE BOERUM CAFÉ, A BROOKLYN BAR. NIGHT.

RONNY *and* LORETTA *sit at the bar. They are just finishing a couple of old-fashioneds. The barman,* AL, *inspects their drinks.*

AL: Another old-fashioned?

RONNY: Loretta?

LORETTA: No, thanks.

RONNY (to AL): I think that's it.

(AL *nods and walks off.*)

RONNY (leaning forward toward LORETTA and continuing): What do you want to do now?

LORETTA: I wanna go home.

EXTERIOR: A COLD AND EMPTY STREET. NIGHT.

RONNY *and* LORETTA *are walking. Their breath is coming out in long plumes.*

LORETTA: It's really cold.

RONNY: Yeah. It smells like snow.

(*They walk in silence for a moment, then* LORETTA *speaks.*)

LORETTA: My mother guessed that my father was seeing somebody, and I told her she was crazy. She looked like a real piece of cheap goods. But who am I to talk?

(*Loretta's eyes are full of tears.*)

RONNY: What's the matter?

LORETTA: How can you ask me that?

RONNY: You're making me feel guilty again.

LORETTA: You are guilty. I'm guilty.

RONNY: Of what? Only God can point the finger, Loretta.

LORETTA: I know what I know.

RONNY: And what do you know? You tell me my life? I'll tell you yours. I'm a wolf? You run to the wolf in me, that don't make you no lamb! You're gonna marry my brother? Why you wanna sell your life short? Playing it safe is just about the most dangerous thing a woman like you could do. You waited for the right man the first time, why didn't you wait for the right man again?

LORETTA: He didn't come!

RONNY: I'm here!

LORETTA: You're late!

RONNY: We're here.

EXTERIOR: RONNY'S APARTMENT BUILDING. NIGHT.

LORETTA *looks. It's Ronny's building.*

LORETTA: This is your place.

RONNY: That's right.

LORETTA: This is where we're going!

RONNY: Yeah.

LORETTA: The deal was if I came to the opera with you, you'd leave me alone forever. (*Looks for his response. He makes none.*) I went with you. (*Pause. He says nothing.*) Now, I'm gonna marry Johnny, and you're gonna leave me alone. (*He says nothing.*) Right? (*Nothing.*) A person can see where they've messed up in their life, and they can change how they do things, and they can change their *luck*. Maybe my nature does draw me to you, but I don't haveta go with that. I can take hold of myself and say yes to some things and no to something that's just gonna ruin everything! I can do that. Otherwise, what is this stupid life that God gave us for, what? (*Pause, nothing.*) Ronny? Are you listening to me?

RONNY: Yeah.

LORETTA: I'm really afraid.

RONNY: Why?

LORETTA: I'm afraid of who I am.

RONNY: I was.

LORETTA: And you're not now?

(RONNY *shakes his head.*)

LORETTA (continuing): Why not?

RONNY: I don't know. Everything seems like nothing now against that I want you in my bed. I don't care if I burn in hell. I don't care if you burn in hell. The *past* and *future* is a joke to me now. I see that they're nothing, I see they ain't here. The only thing that's here is you. And me. I want you to come upstairs. Now. I tried to take everything last night, like you told me, but I couldn't. I couldn't take everything in a hundred years. It's the way we are. We compound each other.

LORETTA: Let me go home.

RONNY: No.

LORETTA: Let me go home.

RONNY: No.

LORETTA: I'm freezing to death.

RONNY: Come upstairs. I don't care why you come. No, that's not what I mean. Loretta, I love you. Not like they told you love is, and I didn't know this either. But love don't make things nice, it ruins everything, it breaks your heart, it makes things a mess. We're not here to make things perfect. Snowflakes are perfect. The stars are perfect. Not us. Not us! We are here to ruin ourselves and break our hearts and love the wrong people and die!

The storybooks are bullshit. Come upstairs with me, baby! Don't sell your life out to somebody else's idea of sweet happiness. Don't try to live on milk and cookies when what you want is meat! Red meat just like me! It's wolves run with wolves and nothing else! You're a wolf just like me! Come upstairs with me, and get in my bed! Come on! Come on. Come on.

(LORETTA *follows* RONNY *into his building.*
    Now we see the street.
    Just as the door shuts, a moment passes. Lights go on in Ronny's apartment. Out of a doorway on the opposite side of the street steps the figure of a woman. She walks to the middle of the deserted street and looks up at the lighted windows.
    Now we see the woman close up—it's CHRISSY *from the bakery. Her heart is about to break. She loves this man. She looks up at the lighted windows, her feelings hanging by one slender, slender thread.*
    Music: It's Mimi's aria from the snow scene in La Bohème.
    We see the street with the figure looking at the lighted window above. Mimi's aria plays. This tableau reminds us of the scene in the

opera where Mimi stands in the snow. The music plays, and the singer holds a note for a long moment. Then the lights in the apartment go out. CHRISSY *shudders almost imperceptibly. Her heart has broken. She hangs her head. Then she lifts her head and slowly walks away down the street.)*

EXTERIOR: KENNEDY INTERNATIONAL AIRPORT. RUNWAY. NIGHT.

With a great and abrupt roar, a big jet is landing.

INTERIOR: KENNEDY INTERNATIONAL AIRPORT. TERMINAL. NIGHT.

Passengers are pouring into the terminal from the plane. Most of them are Italians or Italian Americans. Suddenly, MR. JOHNNY *appears out of the shifting crowd, up very close to the camera. He looks alert, determined, geared up for action.*
    MR. JOHNNY *is at the luggage carousel. He pulls his two suitcases off the carousel with one quick, powerful jerk.*

EXTERIOR: KENNEDY INTERNATIONAL AIRPORT. TERMINAL. NIGHT.

MR. JOHNNY *sticks out his hand, and a cab immediately rushes to him.*

INTERIOR: CAB. NIGHT.

MR. JOHNNY *leans forward to the driver.*

MR. JOHNNY (in a very definite, determined way): Nineteen Cranberry Street.

EXTERIOR: KENNEDY INTERNATIONAL AIRPORT. NIGHT.

The cab rushes off into the night.

EXTERIOR: THE CASTORINI HOUSE. NIGHT.

The cab pulls up to the Castorini house. The living room windows are all lit up. Vicki Carr can be made out singing "It Must Be Him." MR.

JOHNNY *gets out of the cab, gets his luggage, and heads for the front door. He rings the bell. The door opens. It's* ROSE. *Music floods out around her.*

MR. JOHNNY: Hello. I'm sorry to call so late . . .

(ROSE *is a little tipsy.*)

ROSE: Moving in?

MR. JOHNNY: I came right from the airport.

ROSE: Come on in.

(ROSE *holds the door open for him, and he goes in past her, carrying his suitcases. She closes the door.*)

INTERIOR: THE CASTORINI HOUSE. FRONT HALL. NIGHT.

MR. JOHNNY: Can you wake up Loretta? I need to talk to her.

ROSE: She's not home yet. Take off your coat, and come in the living room. I'll make you a drink. I wanna talk to you.

INTERIOR: THE CASTORINI HOUSE. LIVING ROOM. NIGHT.

ROSE *comes in with two scotches on the rocks.* MR. JOHNNY *takes one.*

MR. JOHNNY: Thank you.

(ROSE *turns off the stereo and then sits down across from him.*)

ROSE: So.

MR. JOHNNY: Where is she?

ROSE: Out. I don't know where. I was waiting up for my husband.

MR. JOHNNY: It's late.

ROSE: Yes.

(*There's a pause.* MR. JOHNNY *is uncomfortable with it.*)

MR. JOHNNY: Maybe I should go?

ROSE: What are you doing here? You're supposed to be in Palermo.

MR. JOHNNY: That's what I came to tell Loretta. There's been a miracle.

ROSE: A miracle. Well, that's news.

MR. JOHNNY: My mother's recovered.

ROSE: You're kidding?

MR. JOHNNY: The breath had almost totally left her body. She was as white as snow. And then she completely pulled back from death and stood up and put on her clothes and began to cook for everyone in the house. The mourners. And me. And herself! She ate a meal that would choke a pig!

ROSE: That's incredible.

MR. JOHNNY: Yes.

(*The front door can be heard slamming, out of view, and then dogs can be heard barking.* MR. JOHNNY *and* ROSE *look to the entranceway. The* OLD MAN *appears there, holding the five dogs.*)

ROSE: Hello, Pop.

(*The* OLD MAN *looks at* ROSE. *He is a specter. He stares, and then he makes a long, low accusing noise. Then he disappears.*)

MR. JOHNNY: Who was that?

ROSE: That was my father-in-law, who has a wrong idea in his head. Listen, Johnny, there's a question I want to ask you. And I want you to tell me the truth if you can. Why do men chase women?

MR. JOHNNY: Well. There's the Bible story. God took a rib from Adam and made Eve. Maybe men chase women to get the rib back. When God took the rib, he left a hole there, a place where there used to be something. And the women have that. Maybe a man isn't complete as a man without a woman.

ROSE: But why would a man need more than one woman?

MR. JOHNNY: I don't know. Maybe because he fears death.

(ROSE *leaps up, very excited.*)

ROSE: That's it! That's the reason!

MR. JOHNNY: I don't know.

ROSE: No, that's really it. Thank you for answering my question.

(*The front door slams again.* MR. JOHNNY *and* ROSE *look to the entrance-way.* COSMO *appears there.*)

COSMO: Hi. (*Taking in* MR. JOHNNY.) Hi.

MR. JOHNNY: Hello, Mr. Castorini.

ROSE: Where you been?

COSMO: I don't know, Rose. I don't know where I've been, and I don't know where I'm going. (*To* MR. JOHNNY:) You should have your eyes opened for you, my friend.

MR. JOHNNY: I have my eyes open.

COSMO: You do, huh? Stick around. Don't go on any long trips.

MR. JOHNNY: I don't know what you mean.

COSMO: I know you don't. That's the point. I'll say no more.

MR. JOHNNY: You haven't said anything.

COSMO: And that's how much I'm saying.

ROSE: Cosmo?

COSMO: What?

ROSE: I just want you to know. No matter what you do. You are going to die, just like everybody else.

COSMO: Thank you, Rose.

ROSE: You're welcome.

COSMO: I'm going to bed now.

(MR. JOHNNY *stands up.* COSMO *walks off, out of view.*)

MR. JOHNNY: I'm going.

COSMO'S VOICE (from top of stairs): Good!

ROSE (to MR. JOHNNY): He doesn't like you. Thank you for answering my question.

MR. JOHNNY: You don't know where Loretta is?

ROSE: No idea.

MR. JOHNNY: Then tell her I'll come by in the morning. We need to talk.

ROSE: Okay, I'll tell her.

INTERIOR: RONNY'S APARTMENT. EARLY MORNING.

RONNY *is sitting alone in the early morning light. The operatic music fills the apartment. He sits listening, then gets up and goes for his coat and exits. The music continues to play over the empty apartment.*

EXTERIOR: THE CASTORINI HOUSE. MORNING.

The front door opens, and the OLD MAN *and the dogs come out. He has got them on their leashes, and over his head, he carries the black umbrella. He walks off toward the park and disappears.*

EXTERIOR: STREET. DAY.

LORETTA *is walking along a sidewalk a couple of blocks away. She is a wreck. She's still in her clothes of the night before. She hasn't slept. Her hair is a bit funny. And she's tormented by the complications in her life. And, at the same time, she looks great. She looks like she has been loved up and down. She has a hickey on her neck. Her eyes are dreamy, and her walk is slow, utterly careless, and sexual. She's carrying, crunched in her hand, her program from* La Bohème. *She starts singing. We follow her as she sings and walks.*

We watch LORETTA *walking from the back now. She's still muttering. She comes to a tin can. She kicks it. She comes to it again. She kicks it again.*

EXTERIOR: THE CASTORINI HOUSE. DAY.

LORETTA *appears kicking her can. She abandons the can and enters the house.*

INTERIOR: THE CASTORINI HOUSE. KITCHEN. DAY.

ROSE *is at the stove. The kitchen is filled with steam and sunlight.* ROSE *is stirring a pot filled with oatmeal. Another range has the coffeepot heating.* LORETTA *shuffles into the kitchen, goes to the tin table, and sits down. There are red roses on the table.* ROSE *sees* LORETTA.

ROSE: What the hell happened to you?

LORETTA: Well. I don't really know where to start.

ROSE: Your hair's different.

LORETTA: Everything's different.

ROSE: Are you drunk?

LORETTA: No. Are you drunk?

ROSE: No. But I have a hangover.

LORETTA: Where's Pop?

ROSE: Upstairs. Johnny Cammareri showed up last night.

LORETTA (suddenly electrified): What?! He's in Sicily!

ROSE: No more he's not.

LORETTA: He's with his dying mother!

ROSE: She recovered.

LORETTA: What!! She was dying!

ROSE: It was a miracle.

LORETTA: A miracle? This is modern times! There ain't supposed to be miracles anymore!

ROSE: I guess it ain't modern times in Sicily. He came right from the airport. He wanted to talk to you. You got a love bite on your neck. He's coming back this morning.

(*With a long low moan,* LORETTA *lowers her head to the table.*)

EXTERIOR: STREET. DAY.

RONNY *is walking along the same stretch of sidewalk as* LORETTA *just was. He looks like hell, too. His hair is wild, and he hasn't slept. He has thrown on an old leather jacket and brown leather gloves. He has a love bite on his neck, too. He starts to sing "O Soave Fanciulla." He sings it any old way, occasionally getting a good attack, occasionally just muttering his way through. He sings as much of it as he remembers, which is a lot.*
    We watch RONNY *walking from the back now. He's singing away, carelessly sauntering along. He passes an Italian couple of middle age. They smile as they recognize what he is singing. They start to sing along with him. They sing till they get to the ceiling of the aria and to a resting place a little beyond. Then they nod to each other appreciatively and go on their ways,* RONNY *turning his back to the camera and they walking into it.*

EXTERIOR: THE CASTORINI HOUSE. DAY.

RONNY *appears and approaches the door. He knocks, waits, and then rings the bell.* ROSE *answers the door and invites him in.*

INTERIOR: THE CASTORINI HOUSE. KITCHEN. DAY.

ROSE *walks in with* RONNY *behind her. There's no one in the kitchen.*

ROSE (calling out): It's not Johnny.

(LORETTA *comes out of a closet, where she was hiding. She's very surprised to see* RONNY.)

LORETTA: Ronny!

RONNY: Is Johnny here?!

LORETTA: He's coming.

RONNY: Good! We can get this out on the table. (*To* ROSE:) I'm Ronny, Johnny's brother.

(RONNY *shakes her hand.*)

ROSE: I'm Rose Castorini.

RONNY: Nice to meet you.

ROSE: Nice to meet you. You've got a love bite on your neck. Your mother's recovered from death.

RONNY: Oh. Good. We're not close. I'm not really moved.

LORETTA: You've gotta get outta here.

RONNY: No, I'm gonna wait.

LORETTA (arguing with RONNY): Ronny, please . . .

ROSE: Would anyone like some oatmeal?

(LORETTA *continues arguing.*)

RONNY (ignoring LORETTA): Yes, I would like some oatmeal.

(RONNY *and* LORETTA *sit down, and* ROSE *serves them oatmeal.*
    COSMO *walks in dressed for business. He regards the trio, puts on his hat in shock, and then takes it off again.*)

ROSE: Cosmo, this is Ronny, Johnny's brother.

COSMO: His brother.

(COSMO *sits down.* ROSE *puts a bowl of oatmeal in front of him. He absently begins to eat it. A silence reigns. Then he puts down his spoon.*)

COSMO (continuing): You're Johnny's brother?

RONNY: Yeah.

(COSMO *picks up his spoon, and they all eat silently once more. The sound of dogs barking comes up and then fades away.*
    The OLD MAN *walks in. He looks at the assemblage. The assemblage looks at him. He points at* ROSE. *Then his pointing drifts to* COSMO, *and his hand opens in a gesture of supplication.*)

OLD MAN: I am old. The old are not wanted. And what they say has no weight. But, my son, I must speak. You should pay for the wedding of your only daughter. You are breaking your house through pride. There. I've said it.

COSMO: It's okay, Pop. If she gets married, I'll pay for the whole thing.

(*The* OLD MAN *lets go a great noise of relief, sits down at the table, and waits.* ROSE *brings him a bowl of oatmeal. He is content now and eats his oatmeal with great relish. The others eat with a more meaningful silence.* ROSE *puts down her spoon. She looks at the table, but she is speaking to* COSMO.)

ROSE: Have I been a good wife?

COSMO: Yes.

ROSE: I want you to stop seeing her.

(*Everyone stops eating. A tremendous silence falls. An old wall clock goes tick, tick, tick. Suddenly* COSMO *smashes his fists to the table and stands. He doesn't look at* ROSE *during this. Then, slowly, he sits down.*)

COSMO: Okay.

ROSE: And go to confession.

COSMO (still not looking at her): A man . . . understands one day . . . that his life is built on nothing. And that's a bad, crazy day.

ROSE: Your life is not built on nothing. *Ti amo.*

(ROSE *puts her hand across the table to him.*)

COSMO: *Ti amo.*

(COSMO *slides his hand out and takes her hand. Slowly he lifts his eyes. Their eyes meet. It's the first time he has been able to hold her gaze in this whole story. The doorbell rings.*)

LORETTA (in a fatalistic tone): It's Johnny. I'll get it.

RONNY: I'll get it.

(ROSE *gets up.*)

ROSE: I'll get it.

(ROSE *goes to answer the door.*)

RONNY (going for the door): No, I'll tell him.

LORETTA: No, I'll tell him. (*To her father*.) What am I going to tell him?

COSMO: Tell him the truth, Loretta—they find out anyway.

LORETTA (looking at COSMO): I love you, Pop.

(*It's a private moment.*
     But who appears at the kitchen door is not JOHNNY *but* RITA *and* RAYMOND CAPPOMAGGI. *They have their coats on, and they look very serious and concerned and timid.*)

RITA: Hi, Loretta.

LORETTA: Hi.

RAYMOND: Hi, Loretta.

LORETTA: Hi. Why ain't you at the store?

RITA: Is there anything you want to tell us, honey?

LORETTA: You? No.

RAYMOND: We just come from the bank.

LORETTA: The bank. OH, MY GOD, I FORGOT TO MAKE THE DEPOSIT!

RITA (to RAYMOND): She's got it.

RAYMOND: I knew she had it.

(LORETTA *runs out of the kitchen and reappears with her everyday bag. She takes out the night-deposit bag and hands it to* RAYMOND.)

RITA: We didn't know what to think. You were so weird yesterday, and then this morning, we go to the bank and no bag.

RAYMOND (a sudden outburst to LORETTA): WE NEVER SUSPECTED YOU!

(RAYMOND *covers his face to hide his emotion.* ROSE, *meanwhile, is clearing the oatmeal bowls.*)

ROSE: Listen. Who wants coffee?

(*There is a general acknowledgment. Everybody wants coffee.* ROSE *passes out white mugs and begins pouring steaming drafts of coffee.* RAYMOND *and* RITA *stand. The rest sit.*)

RITA: So what are we doing?

ROSE: We're waiting for Johnny Cammareri.

(RITA *nods. A silence.*)

RONNY: I'm his brother.

RITA (taking and shaking his hand): Nice to meet you. I'm Rita Cappomaggi.

RAYMOND (taking and shaking his hand): I'm Raymond Cappomaggi. I'm Rose's brother.

RONNY: Nice to meet you.

(*A silence.*)

OLD MAN (erupting): Somebody tell a joke!

(*The doorbell rings and rings again. Everyone is frozen for a moment, then* RITA *mobilizes.*)

RITA: I'll get it.

(RITA *goes.* LORETTA *puts down her coffee and deep breathes, preparing herself.*)

LORETTA: I'm getting palpitations!

(LORETTA *pushes away her coffee.*)

RAYMOND: I thought he was in Palermo.

(RITA *appears with* MR. JOHNNY *in tow.* RITA *continues into the room, leaving* MR. JOHNNY *in the doorway. He is in a dark, vested suit. He is a little bewildered by the crowd of people but succeeds in hiding most of his discomfort.*)

RITA: It's Johnny Cammareri.

LORETTA: Johnny.

MR. JOHNNY: Loretta . . .

RONNY: Johnny . . .

MR. JOHNNY: Ronny! Our mother has recovered from death!

RONNY: Good.

MR. JOHNNY: Have you come to make peace with me?

RONNY: Well. Yeah. You may not want to.

MR. JOHNNY: Of course I want to.

LORETTA: I don't know. But, Johnny, how did your mother recover? She was dying.

MR. JOHNNY: We should talk alone.

LORETTA: I can't. I need my family around me now.

MR. JOHNNY: Well. I told my mother that we were to be married. And she got well. Right away.

RONNY: I'm sure she did.

MR. JOHNNY: It was a miracle!

LORETTA: Johnny, I have something to tell you.

MR. JOHNNY: I have something to tell you. But I must talk to you alone.

LORETTA: I have no secrets from my family.

MR. JOHNNY: Loretta, I can't marry you.

LORETTA: WHAT?

MR. JOHNNY: If I marry you, my mother will die.

(*The* OLD MAN *laughs a loud, sudden laugh, which then subsides.*)

LORETTA: What the hell are you talking about? We're engaged.

RONNY: Loretta, what are *you* talking about?

LORETTA: I'm talking about a promise. You proposed to me!

MR. JOHNNY: Because my mother was dying! But now she's not.

RONNY: You're forty-two years old, Johnny, and Mama is still running your life.

MR. JOHNNY: And you are a son who doesn't love his mother!

LORETTA: And you're a big liar! I've got your ring here!

MR. JOHNNY: I must ask for that back.

(LORETTA *struggles and pulls off the ring.*)

LORETTA: Here! Take your stupid pinky ring. (*She throws it at* JOHNNY.) Who needs it? The engagement's off.

(MR. JOHNNY *retrieves the ring.*)

MR. JOHNNY: In time, you will see that this is the best thing.

LORETTA: In time, you will drop dead, and I will come to your funeral in a red dress!

RONNY: Loretta?

LORETTA: What!

RONNY: Will you marry me?

MR. JOHNNY: What?

LORETTA: Where's the ring?

RONNY (looking to MR. JOHNNY a little sheepishly): Could I a . . . borrow that ring?

(MR. JOHNNY, *in shock, hands it over to* RONNY.)

RONNY (continuing): Thanks. (*He kneels down before* LORETTA. *He presents the ring to her.*) Will you marry me, Loretta Castorini Clark?

LORETTA: Before all these people, yes, I will marry you, Ronny Cammareri!

(*She takes the ring.* RONNY *and* LORETTA *kiss.*)

ROSE: Do you love him, Loretta?

LORETTA: Yeah, Ma, I love him awful.

ROSE: Oh God, that's too bad.

(RONNY *and* LORETTA *enter into a long kiss. The* OLD MAN *starts to cry.* COSMO *leans forward to the* OLD MAN *solicitously.*)

COSMO: What's the matter, Pop?

OLD MAN (lifts his head and cries out): I'M CONFUSED!

(LORETTA *pushes* RONNY *away, breaking the kiss. They have both neglected to breathe the whole time they were kissing. They are both gasping for air, especially* LORETTA.)

LORETTA: Wait a minute! Wait a minute!

(*But then* LORETTA *looks at* RONNY *and lunges back to him, diving into another kiss like a mermaid diving into the bluest ocean.*
Music: "O Soave Fanciulla" from La Bohème, *comes up and engulfs the lovers, the family, the world.*
We see the faces of the lovers swirl away into a golden and diamond light, and dissolve into:
Eight full champagne glasses glistening in sunlight on the white tabletop. A lump of sugar is being dropped into each. A recently employed bottle of bitters sits nearby with its cap off (like a respectful peasant in aristocratic company). And the roses are in the center of the table.
Now the camera pulls back. We see the table is surrounded. COSMO *drops the last of the sugar cubes in the last glass of champagne.* ROSE *is*

by him. RITA *and* RAYMOND *are side by side, as are* RONNY *and* LORETTA. *The* OLD MAN *sits, staring at his son, intent and approving. But where is* MR. JOHNNY?)

COSMO: Everybody take a glass.

(*Everybody takes a glass. The* OLD MAN *takes one and gets up.*)

OLD MAN (to COSMO): Wait.

(*The* OLD MAN *takes the glass and walks over to a corner of the kitchen where* MR. JOHNNY, *deeply disturbed and somewhat catatonic, sits on a stepladder.*)

OLD MAN (to MR. JOHNNY, offering the glass): Here.

MR. JOHNNY: I don't want it.

(*But the* OLD MAN, *wise and merry and tough, presses the glass on* MR. JOHNNY, *who takes it.*
    COSMO, *the head of the family now, lifts his glass.*)

COSMO: To . . . the family. Right? *Ti amo.*

(*They all lift their glasses.*
    A close-up of Rose's face.)

ROSE: *Ti amo.*

(*A close-up of* RAYMOND *and* RITA.)

RAYMOND: That's right.

(RITA *nods.*
    A close-up of RONNY *and* LORETTA *drinking their champagne and looking into each other's eyes.*

A close-up of the OLD MAN, *who knocks back his drink lustily and then with a glittering eye looks away from the table.*

The Old Man's point of view: MR. JOHNNY *sits without moving, holding his glass. A long moment passes.* MR. JOHNNY *is thinking. Then he nods to himself.*

MR. JOHNNY (lifting his glass and murmuring): To family.

(*A close-up of the* OLD MAN *looking away from* MR. JOHNNY.

The OLD MAN *laughs his laugh. This laugh could kill him. The camera pulls back a little. He pounds the table and knocks over the roses.*

A close-up of the red roses on the white tabletop.

Closing black credits roll against the white background.

FADE OUT

THE END

Joe versus the Volcano

The cast of *Joe versus the Volcano* includes:

Joe Banks	Tom Hanks
Dede/Angelica/Patricia	Meg Ryan
Graynamore	Lloyd Bridges
Dr. Ellison	Robert Stack
Chief of the Waponis	Abe Vigoda
Mr. Waturi	Dan Hedaya
Luggage Salesman	Barry McGovern
Dagmar	Amanda Plummer

Casting	Marion Dougherty
Music	Georges Delerue
Costume Designer	Colleen Atwood
Production Designer	Bo Welch
Editor	Richard Halsey
Director of Photography	Stephen Goldblatt
Executive Producers	Steven Spielberg, Kathleen Kennedy, and Frank Marshall
Producer	Teri Schwartz
Writer	John Patrick Shanley
Director	John Patrick Shanley

GRAY SCREEN:

The title appears in white letters: JOE VERSUS THE VOLCANO.

Music: The stormy part of Borodin's "Polovtsian Dances," performed by the Chicago Symphony Orchestra, begins to play.

The credits roll. The credits have that depressing, shitty, this is going to be one of those lousy black-and-white movies from the 1950s look. This is going to be one of those cheap teen sci-fi movies about a creature.

Music: When the female star's name appears, Borodin's theme, which will later become adapted into "Strangers in Paradise," plays. Then the stormy part returns, subsiding as the credits end.

The following legend appears on the field of gray:

You only live twice.
Once when you're born,
Once when you look death in the face.
—James Bond

The legend remains, but the field of gray turns to a rich texture of solid gold.

The music starts as the field turns from gray to gold. The music is "The Girl from Ipanema," sung by the likes of Tom Waits, sung like it was the downest blues song anybody ever croaked out just before the final curtain. The music plays on.

EXTERIOR: AMERICAN PANASCOPE CORPORATION. DAY.

We're in color now, but it's a gray world. It's an ugly building about
the size of a city block, and it's a couple of stories high. It's surrounded
by a hurricane fence topped with barbed wire. Outside the fence is a
muddy parking lot. On the fence is a sign that reads:

AMERICAN PANASCOPE CORP.

A SUBSIDIARY OF

ACHI

The sign also has an abstract logo; a sort of German expressionist's
version of a lightning bolt. Another sign reads: HOME OF THE RECTAL PROBE.

It's a gray winter morning. It's raining or snowing or it just has
or it's about to. There's a guard at a gate, nodding workers inside the
fence. They trail listlessly past him and continue on their way to the
building's entrance. Most of them carry or are using gray or black
umbrellas. Since they are coming from the parking lot and since the
entrance to the building is still almost a city block away once inside
the fence, this straggling line of workers stretches hundreds of yards.
Some of the workers wear hats.

We see the line of workers from high overhead.

The line is in the same shape as the lightning-bolt logo.

One of these workers is JOE BANKS. JOE *is in his early thirties. He's*
wearing a beat-up black trench coat; under the trench coat, he's got
on a cheap and square jacket and tie. This is a depressed man. You
can see where he could be cool, where he could have something on
the ball. But he's way too beaten down and depressed to be cool. JOE
steps in a puddle. He pulls his shoe out of the water. He notices the sole
is coming loose from the shoe. This depresses him further. He walks
on. The sound of the water squishing in his shoe can be heard.

INTERIOR: PANASCOPE BUILDING. DAY.

JOE *is shuffling down the main walk in the building. On his left are*
doors leading to offices. On his right is the factory, which has the feel
of an airplane hangar. The factory is separated from the walk on which
JOE *progresses by a heavy wire fence twelve feet high.* JOE *passes by a*

sign on this fence that says SHIPPING. *This area is filled with thousands of brown cardboard boxes; a shipping clerk among these boxes pulls a lever on a device; the device spews out several feet of wet brown tape.* JOE *continues on. He passes a sign on the fence that says* CANTEEN. *This area contains a row of vending machines and two long tables. A guy who looks as if he's going to die is sitting at one of the tables, eating pink Hostess Snowballs; he eats them in a slow, dismal way, as if they were giant sleeping pills.* JOE *continues. He passes a sign on the fence that says* QUALITY CONTROL. *This is the biggest area; it's filled with workers in shower caps and worn white jackets. They work a distance apart from each other, at long tables; they are inspecting terrifying medical instruments. One of these workers, a middle-aged woman,* SALLY, *attaches a catheter to an air pump. The catheter inflates and finally explodes.* SALLY *seems satisfied.* JOE *continues, his shoe distantly squishing. He stops at one of the office doors on his left. The lettering on the door reads:* ADVERTISING DEPARTMENT.

JOE *opens the door and goes in. The song ends.*

INTERIOR: ADVERTISING DEPARTMENT. DAY.

The place is lit with those totally draining, deadening fluorescent lights. DEDE, *a secretary in her late twenties, is sitting at her desk, typing. She's pretty, maybe a little hard.*

She types like an automatic weapon. Her makeup doesn't really work under these lights. She nods briefly to JOE, *and goes on with her typing.* JOE *tries to hang up his hat, but it keeps falling off the hook. He is endlessly patient. It's the sound of the typewriter that makes him miss. At last he succeeds. Behind* DEDE, *at a bigger desk, is* MR. WATURI. *He's leaning back in an executive chair, talking on the phone. He's middle-aged, olive skinned, in a dark suit that shows up his significant dandruff. His teeth are yellow as rancid butter. And there's enough grease shining on his forehead to coat a skillet. He's talking into the phone.*

MR. WATURI: Yeah, Harry, but can he do the job? I know he can get the job, but can he do the job? I'm not arguing that with you. I'm not arguing that with you. I'm not arguing that with you . . . (*He waves absently at* JOE *and goes on talking into the phone.*) Who told you that? No. I told you that. Me. What? Maybe. Maybe. Maybe.

(JOE *hangs up his coat on the coatrack and goes to the coffee setup at the rear of the office. He snaps a disposable plastic coffee cup into a permanent plastic holder. He puts a spoonful of instant coffee in the cup. Then a spoonful of powdered creamer. Then two spoonfuls of sugar. He takes a plastic stirrer and stirs the powders. He pours in the hot water and stirs. Little clumps of undissolved stuff rise to the top.* JOE *tries to break them up with the stirrer and partially succeeds. He feels the glands in his throat. Maybe they're a little swollen. He rubs his eyes. They're burning a little. He takes his coffee and walks past* MR. WATURI *and into his own office.*)

INTERIOR: ADVERTISING LIBRARY. JOE'S OFFICE. DAY.

The same fluorescent lighting. There's a small wooden desk, which has on it an old electric typewriter and an out-of-place lamp; it's a lamp JOE *brought from home. The rest of the office is almost entirely taken up with gray industrial shelving. On these shelves are brochures depicting various medical instruments. Samples of each brochure are taped to the appropriate shelf. Behind Joe's desk is a pipe that runs floor to ceiling and is painted fire engine red.*

In the center of this pipe is a big wheel valve. Hanging from this valve is a printed metal sign that reads: THE MAIN DRAIN. *Another sign reads:* DO NOT TOUCH. JOE *turns on the lamp, which casts a small ring of golden light, and sits down with his coffee. He takes off his shoe and examines it. He tries to huddle close to the lamp, like a cold creature trying to get warm.* DEDE *comes in.*

JOE: Good morning, Dede.

DEDE: Hi, Joe. What's with the shoe?

JOE: I'm losing my sole.

DEDE: Yeah. How you doin'?

JOE: I'm a little tired.

DEDE: Yeah. (*She hands him some labels.*) Here. Each one gets sent five catalogs.

JOE: Can't do it.

DEDE: Why not?

JOE: I only got twelve catalogs left altogether.

DEDE: Okay.

(DEDE *leaves.* JOE *puts his shoe back on.* MR. WATURI *comes in.* JOE *cowers. He's threatened by* MR. WATURI.)

MR. WATURI: How you doin', Joe?

JOE: Well. I'm not feeling very good, Mr. Waturi.

(MR. WATURI *chuckles.*)

MR. WATURI: So what else is new? You never feel good.

JOE: Yeah. Well. That's the problem. Anyway, I got the doctor's appointment today.

MR. WATURI: Another doctor's appointment?

JOE: Yeah.

MR. WATURI: Listen, Joe. What's this Dede tells me about the catalogs?

JOE: I've only got twelve.

MR. WATURI: How'd you let us get down to twelve?

JOE: I told you.

MR. WATURI: When?

JOE: Three weeks ago. Then two weeks ago.

MR. WATURI: Did you tell me last week?

JOE: No.

MR. WATURI: Why not?

JOE: I don't know. I thought you knew.

MR. WATURI: Not good enough, Joe! Not nearly good enough! I put you in charge of the entire advertising library . . .

JOE: You mean, this room . . .

MR. WATURI: I gave you carte blanche how to deal with the materials in here . . .

JOE: You put the orders into the printer, Mr. Waturi, not me. That's how you wanted it.

MR. WATURI: You're not competent to put the orders into the printer! That's a very technical . . .

JOE: I thought you were going to explain it to me.

MR. WATURI: I was going to do better than that. I was going to make you assistant manager. I want to make you assistant manager. But you, you're not flexible! You're inflexible.

JOE: I don't feel inflexible.

MR. WATURI: You're inflexible. Totally. And this doctor appointment! You're always going to the doctor!

JOE: I don't feel good.

MR. WATURI: So what! Do you think I feel good? Nobody feels good. After childhood, it's a fact of life. I feel rotten. So what? I don't let it bother me. I don't let it interfere with my job.

JOE: What do you want from me, Mr. Waturi?

MR. WATURI: You're like a child. What's this lamp for? Isn't there enough light in here?

JOE: These fluorescent lights affect me. They make me feel blotchy, puffy. I thought this light would . . .

MR. WATURI: Get rid of the light. This isn't your bedroom, this is an office. Maybe if you start treating this like a job instead of some kind of welfare hospital, you'll shape up. And I want those catalogs.

JOE: Then please order them.

MR. WATURI: Watch yourself, Joe. Think about what I've said. You've gotta get yourself into a flexible frame, or you're no place. (*He starts to leave, but stops and looks back.*) Take that light off your desk.

JOE: I will.

MR. WATURI: Take it off now.

(JOE *unplugs the light and takes it off his desk.*)

MR. WATURI: Good.

(MR. WATURI *leaves.* JOE *sits at his desk, shrinking in the fluorescent light. He sips his coffee. The phone rings and he answers.*)

JOE (answering the phone): Advertising library. Fifty? I'm sorry, we don't have that many in stock. I don't know why. The catalog is a thing . . . I don't know. It's here and it's gone. I can't explain. It's a mystery.

(JOE *hangs up the phone.* DEDE *has quietly come in. She's looking at him. She speaks to him in a low voice.*)

DEDE: Why do you let Waturi talk to you like that?

JOE: Like what?

DEDE: What's wrong with you?

JOE: I don't . . . feel very good.

(DEDE *looks at him. She's frustrated with this guy. This is somebody who she could go for, but he's just lying there like a dog waiting to be kicked.* JOE *looks at her. If he had the strength, if he were feeling a little better, he would make a play for this woman. But he's helpless. He just doesn't feel very good. Absently, he feels the glands in his throat.*)

DEDE: What's the matter with you?

JOE: I don't know.

(DEDE *stares at him. She's angry, frustrated. She turns and walks out. Joe's eyes are shining with tears that will not fall. He is powerless to help himself. He mutters to himself, fierce and impotent.*)

JOE: I don't know.

(JOE *presses the heels of his hands into his eyes.*)

INTERIOR: DOCTOR'S WAITING ROOM. DAY.

We discover JOE *with the heels of his hands pressed into his eyes. This room is fluorescently lit, too, and perhaps at first we don't realize we have gone somewhere else.*

NURSE (offscreen): Mr. Banks? Mr. Banks?

(JOE, *startled, takes his hands from his eyes. The camera pulls back, and we see we're in a doctor's waiting room. And now we see the* NURSE. *She is a very conservative, WASP* NURSE.)

JOE: Yeah?

NURSE: Dr. Ellison will see you now.

INTERIOR. DR. ELLISON'S OFFICE. DAY.

The lighting in the doctor's office is the first warm, relaxing light we've seen. It comes from lamps and a little frosted window. The office itself is full of old wood and books. DR. ELLISON *sits in a comfortable chair, at an old desk. He is the last word in doctors. He's a large, respectable, distinguished, gray-haired MD. He's a specialist. You get the feeling he may be a genius.*

ELLISON: How are you feeling, Mr. Banks?

JOE: Pretty much the same. I feel puffy, blotchy. I never seem to have very much energy. I get these little sore throats. I just don't feel good.

ELLISON: And how long have you felt this way?

JOE: Well. Pretty much since I left the Fire Department. On and off. But since then. 'Bout eight years.

ELLISON: What did you do in the Fire Department?

JOE: Well, ah, you know, I put out fires.

ELLISON: Was it dangerous?

JOE: Yeah. Ahm, pretty rough stuff. But I came out of it okay. The hard part was not feeling good all the time. I started not feeling good all the time. So I hadda quit.

(ELLISON *nods*.)

ELLISON: Yes. I've gotten the results of your tests.

JOE: I've got cancer.

ELLISON: No.

JOE: This new venereal . . .

ELLISON: No.

JOE: Is there something wrong with my blood or urine or? . . .

ELLISON: No, they're fine. But there is something.

JOE: Tell me.

ELLISON: You have a brain cloud.

JOE: A brain cloud.

ELLISON: There's a black fog of tissue running right down the center of your brain. It's very rare. It will spread at a regular rate. It's very destructive.

JOE: And it's incurable.

ELLISON: Yes.

JOE: How long?

ELLISON: Six months. You can pretty much count on it being about that. It's not painful. Your brain will simply fail. Followed abruptly by your body. You can depend on at least four and a half or five months of perfect health.

JOE: But what are you talking about, Doctor? I don't feel good right now.

ELLISON: That's the ironic part, really. Mr. Banks, you're a hypochondriac. There's nothing wrong with you that has anything to do with your symptoms. My guess is your experiences in the Fire Department were extremely traumatic. You experienced the imminent possibility of death. Several times? (JOE *nods numbly.*) You survived. But the cumulative anxiety of those brushes with death left you habitually fearful. About your physical person.

JOE: I'm not sick? Except for this terminal disease?

ELLISON: Which has no symptoms. That's right. It was only because of your insistence on having so many tests that we happened to discover the problem.

(JOE *laughs, a little maniacally, then stops abruptly.*)

JOE: What am I going to do?

ELLISON: Well, if you have any savings, you might think about taking a trip, a vacation?

JOE: I don't have any savings. A few hundred bucks. I've spent everything on doctors.

ELLISON: Yes. Perhaps you'll want a second opinion?

JOE: A brain cloud. I knew it. Well, I didn't know it, but I knew it.

ELLISON: Yes.

JOE: What am I going to do?

ELLISON: You have some time left, Mr. Banks. You have some life left. My advice to you is: Live it well.

JOE: I've got to go. I'm on my lunch hour, which is over.

(JOE *gets up, and* ELLISON *follows suit, putting out his hand.*)

ELLISON: I'm sorry for what I had to tell you. I wish the news had been better.

(JOE *doesn't take his hand.*)

JOE: Yeah.

(JOE *leaves.* ELLISON *starts to sit down.* JOE *comes back in.*)

JOE: I'm sorry I didn't shake your hand.

(JOE *takes the doctor's hand and shakes it. Then he drops it and exits abruptly.* ELLISON *sits there a moment, not moving. Then he opens a drawer in his desk and takes out a flask. He pours himself a drink and begins to drink it.*)

EXTERIOR: MEDICAL LEAGUE BUILDING. DAY.

This is the building Ellison's office is in. Joe's car is parked out front. JOE *comes slowly out. It's still overcast, but lighter and dryer than it was earlier. As* JOE *walks down the steps, an elderly woman approaches with her dog, Molly, a mutt.* JOE *sees the dog and stops, fixed on it. He pats the dog on the head. The elderly woman thinks this is nice.*

Then JOE *embraces the dog and, kneeling down, hugs it intensely. The elderly woman is alarmed and pulls the dog away.* JOE *looks after them.*

Then he gets in his car, which is beat-up and beige. He drives off.

EXTERIOR: AMERICAN PANASCOPE CORPORATION PARKING LOT. DAY.

JOE *drives into frame. He gets out, and we follow him as he approaches the* GUARD *at the gate. The* GUARD *nods him in.* JOE *starts to walk past. Then he goes back to the* GUARD.

JOE: What's your name?

GUARD: Fred.

JOE: Fred.

(JOE *thinks that over and then goes on his way.*)

INTERIOR: PANASCOPE BUILDING. DAY.

JOE *stands outside the door marked* ADVERTISING DEPARTMENT. *He is thoughtful. He goes in.*

INTERIOR: ADVERTISING DEPARTMENT. DAY

JOE *comes in.* DEDE *is typing away.* MR. WATURI *is on the phone.* JOE *hangs up his coat. He misses with the hat again because of Dede's typing. He leans over and switches the typewriter off. Then he picks up his hat, dusts it off and throws it in the garbage can.*

MR. WATURI (on the phone): No. No. You were wrong. He was wrong. Who said that? I didn't say that. If I had said that, I would've been wrong. I would've been wrong, Harry, isn't that right?

(*Mr. Waturi's attention is split between his call and* JOE, *who is walking around the office like a tourist.*)

MR. WATURI: Listen, let me call you back, I've got something here, okay? And don't tell him anything till we finish our conversation, okay?

(MR. WATURI *hangs up the phone.* JOE *is looking at the coffee setup.*)

MR. WATURI: Joe?

JOE: Yeah?

MR. WATURI: You were at lunch three hours.

JOE: About that.

(JOE *wanders away, into his office.* MR. WATURI *looks after.*)

INTERIOR: JOE'S OFFICE. DAY.

JOE *is staring at the big wheel valve sporting the sign that says* THE MAIN DRAIN. MR. WATURI *comes in as* JOE *moves forward and, with great effort, rotates the wheel to its opposite extreme. This scares* MR. WATURI.

MR. WATURI: Joe, what are you doing?

JOE: I'm opening, or closing, the main drain.

(*Nothing happens.*)

MR. WATURI: You shouldn't be touching that.

JOE: Nothing happened. Do you know how long I've been wondering what would happen if I did that?

MR. WATURI: What's the matter with you?

JOE: Brain cloud.

MR. WATURI: What?

JOE: Never mind. Listen, Mr. Waturi. Frank. I quit.

(JOE *starts to take some stuff out of his desk. He looks at his lamp, gets the cord, plugs it in, and turns it on.*)

MR. WATURI: You mean, today?

JOE: That's right.

MR. WATURI: That's great. Well, don't come looking for a reference.

JOE: Okay, I won't.

MR. WATURI: You blew this job.

(JOE *takes in the little room.*)

JOE: I've been here for four and a half years. The work I did I probably could've done in five, six months. That leaves four years leftover.

(JOE *has been filling up a shopping bag with stuff from his desk: three books* (Romeo and Juliet, Robinson Crusoe *and* The Odyssey), *an old ukulele, and his lamp. Now he's finished. He walks out of the room without even looking at* MR. WATURI. MR. WATURI *goes after him as he exits.*)

INTERIOR: ADVERTISING DEPARTMENT. DAY.

JOE *is walking toward the front door.* MR. WATURI *follows him in.* JOE *stops at Dede's desk. She's typing. He looks at her. She stops typing.*

JOE: Four years. If I had them now. Like gold in my hand. Here. This is for you. (*Gives* DEDE *the lamp.*) Bye-bye, Dede.

DEDE: You're going?

(JOE *nods*.)

MR. WATURI: Well, if you're leaving, leave. You'll get your check. And, I promise you, you'll be easy to replace.

JOE: I should say something.

MR. WATURI: What are you talking about?

JOE: This life. Life? What a joke. This situation. This room.

MR. WATURI: Joe, maybe you should just . . .

JOE: You look terrible, Mr. Waturi. You look like a bag of shit stuffed inna cheap suit. Not that anyone would look good under these zombie lights. I can feel them sucking the juice outta my eyeballs. Three hundred bucks a week, that's the news. For three hundred bucks a week I've lived in this sink. This used rubber . . .

MR. WATURI: Watch it, mister! There's a woman here!

JOE: Don't you think I know that, Frank? Don't you think I'm aware there's a woman here? I can taste her on my tongue. I can smell her. When I'm twenty feet away, I can hear the fabric of her dress when she moves in her chair. Not that I've done anything about it. I've gone all day, every day, not doing, not saying, not taking the chance for three hundred bucks a week, and, Frank, the coffee stinks, it's like arsenic, the lights give me a headache, if the lights don't give you a headache you must be dead, let's arrange the funeral.

MR. WATURI: You better get outta here right now! I'm telling you!

JOE: You're telling me nothing.

MR. WATURI: I'm telling you!

JOE: And why, I ask myself, why have I put up with you? I can't imagine, but I know. Fear. Yellow freakin' fear. I've been too chickenshit afraid to live my life, so I sold it to you for three hundred freakin' dollars a week! You're lucky I don't kill you! You're lucky I don't rip your freakin' throat out! But I'm not going to, and maybe you're not so lucky at that. 'Cause I'm gonna leave you here, Mister Wa-a-Waturi, and what could be worse than that?

(JOE *opens the door and leaves.* MR. WATURI *and* DEDE *are frozen. The door reopens, and* JOE *comes halfway back in.*)

JOE: Dede?

DEDE: Yeah?

JOE: How 'bout dinner tonight?

DEDE: Yeah, uh, okay.

(JOE *smiles for the first time since we've met him and closes the door again.*)

DEDE: Wow. What a change.

MR. WATURI: Who does he think he is?

INTERIOR: THE SPANISH ROSE RESTAURANT. NIGHT.

JOE *and* DEDE *are sitting at a table, steaming plates of food before them. They are drinking red wine.* JOE *is caught up in a big idea.* DEDE *is mesmerized.*

JOE: I mean, who am I? That's the real question, isn't it? Who am I? Who are you? What other questions are there? What other questions are there, really? If you want to understand the universe, embrace the universe, the door to the universe is you!

DEDE: Me?

JOE: You. Me.

DEDE: You are really intense.

JOE: Am I? I guess I am. I was.

DEDE: What do you mean?

JOE: I mean, a long time ago. In the beginning. I was, you know, full of piss and vinegar. Nothing got me down. I wanted to know!

DEDE: You wanted to know what?

JOE: Everything! But then, I had some experiences . . . I was talking to this guy today, he says I got scared.

DEDE: Scared of what?

JOE: Have you ever been scared?

DEDE: I guess so. Sure.

JOE: What scared you?

DEDE: A lot of things. At the moment, you scare me a little bit.

JOE: Me?

DEDE: Yeah.

(*Across the room, at another table, three guys with guitars, in traditional Spanish costumes, sing a happy Castilian song.* DEDE *and* JOE *turn and take in the singers.*)

JOE: Why would I scare you?

DEDE: I don't know. There's something going on with you. This morning you were like a lump, and now you're . . . how you feel?

JOE: I feel great.

DEDE: See? You never feel great.

JOE: No, I never do.

(JOE *laughs.*)

DEDE: What's funny?

JOE: I do feel great. And that is very funny!

DEDE: Where are you?

JOE: I'm right here.

DEDE: I wish I was where you are, Joe.

JOE (nodding): No, you don't. Did I ever tell you that the first time I saw you, I felt like I'd seen you before?

(DEDE *shakes her head.*)

JOE: Wait a minute.

(JOE *gets up, goes over to the three guys with guitars, slips them a fin, confers briefly, and returns to the table.*)

DEDE: What'd you do?

JOE: I bribed them to sing a song that would drive us insane and make our hearts swell and burst.

(*Whereupon the three guys with guitars arrive at the table and launch into an extremely passionate Castilian love song. The song makes conversation impossible.* JOE *pours* DEDE *some more red wine. They toast, looking into each other's eyes. The scene ends, but the song continues through the following.*)

EXTERIOR: THE SPANISH ROSE. NIGHT.

A sailor in uniform leans against a slightly tilting lamppost. JOE *and* DEDE *emerge from the restaurant and get in his beat-up car. The car pulls away. The song continues through the following.*

EXTERIOR: STATEN ISLAND FERRY. JOE'S CAR. NIGHT

The ferry pulls away from the shore. JOE *and* DEDE *go to the railing and look back at Manhattan, all lit up, receding. They kiss and look again. The song continues through the following.*

EXTERIOR: STATEN ISLAND. THREE-FAMILY HOUSE. NIGHT.

Joe's car pulls to a stop in front of it, and he and DEDE *get out. There are some steps. He kisses her and carries her up the steps. Then he puts her down to open the door. The song ends.*

INTERIOR: JOE'S APARTMENT. FOYER. NIGHT.

JOE *throws open the door with one hand. He has got* DEDE *on his arm. They kiss passionately.* JOE *reluctantly ends the kiss.*

JOE: Listen.

DEDE: What happened to you?

JOE: Huh?

DEDE: What happened to you that you're . . . so alive? I can see it.

JOE: The doctor told me I've got this thing wrong with my brain. It's not catching. But I've just got five or six months to live.

DEDE: What?

JOE: I'm gonna die. And it's made me . . . very appreciative of my life.

(DEDE *shrinks from him, clutching her coat, suddenly cold.*)

DEDE: I've gotta go.

JOE: Please don't.

(JOE *reaches for her.* DEDE *steps back.*)

DEDE: I've gotta go home. You may've quit, but I got the job in the morning.

JOE: Dede, I really want you to stay.

DEDE: You're gonna die?

JOE: Yeah, but so what? Stay! Just tonight. Tomorrow'll take care of itself.

(DEDE *hesitates on the brink of staying, lifts her hands to say yes, but her courage fails her.*)

DEDE: I can't handle it, Joe. (*She drops her hands, grabs the doornob, and opens the door.*) Sorry.

(DEDE *quickly goes, slamming the door after her.* JOE *looks after her blankly. Then he takes off his coat, tie, and jacket, and throws them on the floor. He walks off down the hall.*)

INTERIOR: JOE'S KITCHEN. PREDAWN.

JOE *is making some real coffee. He has changed into his bathrobe. He has got a little lamp on, not the overhead light. He opens the refrigerator and takes out a loaf of white bread. He puts a couple of slices in the toaster. Then he looks at his little tin dining table and at the window. The window is so dirty, it's opaque. You would have to open it to see out. He pulls the table over to the window. Then he pulls a chair over to face the window. The window looks out on a long, little street. At the end of the street is a brightness where the sun will be. He brings his coffee to the table, and a napkin, and a spoon. He hears the toast pop. He gets it, puts it on a plate, butters it, and brings it to the table. He sits down. He takes a sip of coffee and a bite of toast. He looks out the window. The sun is just starting to come up. He looks at the coffee, at the little plume of steam rising from the cracked cup. The crack is in the shape of the ACHI logo. He looks at the toast with one bite missing and at the butter melting into the golden bread. He looks at the sun's splendid red rim. These things are so beautiful. His eyes well up. He takes another bite of the toast and another sip of the coffee, and looks at the rising sun. It's so great that he's here to experience these things and so sad that he's leaving. He goes back to the refrigerator and takes out the loaf of bread. He puts a couple more slices in the toaster and leaves the almost full loaf of bread next to the almost full pot of coffee.*

INTERIOR: JOE'S KITCHEN. MORNING. A COUPLE OF HOURS LATER.

The loaf of bread is almost gone, and the pot of coffee is empty. Now we pull back and see JOE *sitting by the window with his feet up, some crusts of toast lying on the plate next to him. The sun has risen a goodly bit and can no longer be seen by us. But* JOE *is dappled with sunlight.*

He is no longer in the thrall of a big emotion, but he is extremely deep in thought. The doorbell rings. JOE *doesn't move. It rings again. Did he hear the doorbell? It rings again. He is now satisfied the doorbell is ringing. He gets up and goes out into the foyer.*

INTERIOR: JOE'S FOYER. DAY.

The doorbell starts to ring again as JOE *opens the door. In the hallway is a powerful, glittering-eyed old man of seventy,* MR. GRAYNAMORE. *He's wearing a long, black cashmere overcoat, a dramatic but not silly black fedora, and cowboy boots. He carries a vacuum-sealed can of Planters Peanuts in his pocket. He has got a cane with a duck's head.*

GRAYNAMORE: Joe Banks? Mr. Joe Banks?

JOE: Yeah?

GRAYNAMORE: Have I come at a bad time?

JOE: Yeah. No. I don't know how to answer that question.

GRAYNAMORE: Can I come in? Can we talk?

(JOE *throws the door open. He's in his bathrobe.*)

GRAYNAMORE: You're not dressed?

JOE: No.

GRAYNAMORE: Doesn't bother me if it doesn't bother you.

(GRAYNAMORE *strides past* JOE *into Joe's living room.* JOE *looks after, in a bit of a daze. Then he follows.*)

INTERIOR: JOE'S LIVING ROOM. DAY.

It's modest, to say the least. It's messy and cheaply furnished. An enormous crack runs up the wall and across the ceiling. GRAYNAMORE *takes the room in.*

GRAYNAMORE: Not a nice place you have here, Joe. Mind if I call you Joe?

JOE: No.

(GRAYNAMORE *smacks a hole in the wall with his cane.*)

GRAYNAMORE: Dingy, shabby, dinky, not much.

(GRAYNAMORE *rips off his coat with gusto and tosses it away. He sings a little of "Someone's in the Kitchen with Dinah."*
    He's a rich man from out West, and that's what his clothes look like. He seems to be enjoying himself very much. He sticks out his hand to JOE.)

GRAYNAMORE: I see it as a sign of tremendous sophistication that you haven't demanded my name or asked me what I'm doing here. My name is Samuel Harvey Graynamore.

(*They shake hands.*)

JOE: Joe Banks.

GRAYNAMORE: I know. (*Stares into Joe's face.*) I'm trying to see the hero in there.

JOE: What do you mean?

GRAYNAMORE: You dragged two kids down a six-story burning staircase. That was brave. But then you went back up for the third. That was heroic. C'mon, you're a hero.

JOE: That was a long time ago.

GRAYNAMORE: Yes, it was.

(GRAYNAMORE *opens the nuts and dumps them on the table.*)

JOE: How do you know my name?

GRAYNAMORE: I know all about you. As much as I could learn in twenty-four hours, anyway. Peanuts?

JOE: No.

GRAYNAMORE: Quit your job, huh?

JOE: Yeah.

GRAYNAMORE: Well, sounded like a dumb job. No family?

JOE: No.

GRAYNAMORE: Good for you. Families are a pain in the neck. What do you know about superconductors?

JOE: Nothing.

GRAYNAMORE: Me neither. But I own a huge company that dominates the world market for superconductors.

JOE: Really.

GRAYNAMORE: Yes. Sit down. (*He sits down, suddenly grounded and serious.*) I got a call from Dr. Ellison. You were at his office yesterday?

(JOE *nods.*)

GRAYNAMORE: He told me your news. I hope you won't be angry with him. He thought you and I might be able to help each other. Got any whiskey?

(JOE *shakes his head.* GRAYNAMORE *produces a pipe.*)

GRAYNAMORE: I want to hire you, Joe Banks. I want you . . . (*striking an enormous match and lighting up*) to jump into a volcano.

(JOE *jumps up.*)

JOE: I do have some whiskey.

(JOE *pulls a bottle of cheap scotch out of a cabinet, along with two glasses. He pours them both a drink and sits down.* GRAYNAMORE *downs his whiskey, which makes his eyes glitter all the more.*)

GRAYNAMORE (leaning forward and speaking with great intensity): There's an island in the South Pacific called Waponi Woo. The name means "the little island with the big volcano." The Waponis are a cheerful people who live a simple existence, fishing in the lagoon and picking fruit. They have one fear. That's a big volcano, they call it the Big Woo. They believe an angry fire god in the volcano will sink the island unless, once every hundred years, he is appeased. It's been ninety-nine years, eleven months, and eleven days since the fire god got his propers, and the Waponis are scared.

JOE: How's the god appeased?

GRAYNAMORE: Of his own free will, a man's got to jump into the volcano. Now, as you might imagine, none of the Waponis are anxious to volunteer for the honor of jumping into the Big Woo. And the problem is that whoever does it gotta do it of his own free will, so what do you do?

JOE: What do you do?

(GRAYNAMORE *gets up and starts to move around the room.*)

GRAYNAMORE: You do some tradin'. There's a mineral on that island, Mr. Banks. It's called *bubureau*. I don't know anywhere else on the planet where you can find more than a gram of this stuff, and believe me, I've looked. Because without *bubureau* I can't make my superconductors. I've tried to get the mineral rights from the Waponis, but I don't seem to have anything they want. But they do want a hero, Mr. Banks. And they'll give me the mineral rights if I find them one.

JOE: Why would I jump into a volcano?

(GRAYNAMORE *moves behind* JOE.)

GRAYNAMORE: From your exploits in the Fire Department, I think you've got the courage.

JOE: You do?

GRAYNAMORE: Does it take more guts to twice traverse a staircase in flames or to make a onetime leap into the mouth of a smoking volcano? Damned if I know, *Kemo sabe*. All I know is, when you're making those kind of calls, you're up in the high country. From your doctor, you know you're on your way out anyway. You haven't got any money. I checked. (*Grabs* JOE *by the shoulders.*) Do you want to wait it out here, in this apartment? That sounds kinda grim to me. It's not how I'd wanna go, I'll tell you that.

(GRAYNAMORE *lets go of Joe's shoulders. He takes out his wallet and lays out four credit cards on the stereo console: Diners Club, Visa Gold, Gold MasterCard, and American Express gold card. The cards have "Joseph Banks" printed on them.* JOE *looks at the cards. We hear Graynamore's voice as we look at the cards.*)

GRAYNAMORE (offscreen): These are yours if you take the job. It'd be twenty days from today before you'd have to actually jump in the

Big Woo. You could shop today, get yourself some clothes, you know, for an adventure. Then tomorrow a plane to L.A., first class, naturally. You'll be met. Stay in the best hotel. Then the next day, you board a yacht. My competitors sometimes watch the airports. The yacht's a real beauty. (*Produces a wallet photo of the yacht.*) It belongs to me. Gourmet chef. You sail to the South Pacific. Ten, fifteen days. The Waponis come out to meet you, a total red carpet situation, you're a national hero. You're Charles Lindbergh. It's wine, women, and song in the sweetest little paradise you ever saw. Then you jump in the volcano. Live like a king, die like a man, that's what I say. What do you say?

(JOE *slowly picks up the credit cards and looks at them. Then he looks at* GRAYNAMORE.)

JOE: All right. I'll do it.

GRAYNAMORE: Here's my card and your plane ticket. American, noon out of Kennedy tomorrow.

(GRAYNAMORE *picks up his coat and hat and heads for the door.*)

JOE: Mr. Graynamore?

GRAYNAMORE: Yes?

JOE: What if I use the cards and take the plane and go on the yacht and party on the island, and then I change my mind and don't jump in the volcano?

GRAYNAMORE: Why, then I'd kill you in a very slow and painful way. But you'll jump.

(GRAYNAMORE *laughs in a warm and wonderful way, goes to the front door, opens it, and leaves.* JOE *stands there, looking after him for a moment, and then pulls out the Yellow Pages. He flips through, finds what he wants, and dials the number.*)

JOE: Hi, I'd like to rent a limousine and driver for the day, please? Thank you. Yes, I do. American Express. The Gold Card. Can I have a white limousine?

(JOE *smiles, looking at the card in his hand.*)

EXTERIOR: WHITE LIMOUSINE IN LOWER MANHATTAN. DAY.

The car has just emerged from Staten Island Ferry traffic. We see the friendly face on the front grill of the limousine. It is a slightly overcast day.

INTERIOR: LIMOUSINE. DAY.

JOE *is sitting in the back, idly plucking his ukulele, looking out the windows, stretching his legs. The driver,* MARSHALL, *is a middle-aged black man. He's wearing a jacket and tie and sunglasses. He seems reserved and efficient.*

MARSHALL: So where would you like to go?

JOE: Excuse me?

MARSHALL: Where would you like to go, sir?

(JOE *thinks for a moment.*)

JOE: I thought I might like to do some shopping.

MARSHALL: Okay. Where would you like to go shopping?

JOE: I don't know.

(MARSHALL *is disgruntled but hides it behind his reserve.*)

MARSHALL: All right.

JOE: Where would you go shopping?

MARSHALL: For what? What do you need?

JOE: Clothes.

MARSHALL: What kind of clothes? What is your taste?

JOE: I don't exactly know.

(MARSHALL *pulls the car over and stops.*)

JOE: Why'd you stop?

MARSHALL: I'm just hired to drive the car, mister. I'm not here to tell you who you are.

JOE: I didn't ask you to tell me who I am.

MARSHALL: You were hinting around about clothes. It happens that clothes are very important to me, Mr. . . .

JOE: Banks.

MARSHALL: Banks. Clothes make the man. I believe that. You say to me you wanna go shopping, you wanna buy clothes, but you don't know what kind. You leave that hanging in the air, like I'm going to fill in the blank, that to me is like asking me who you are, and I don't know who you are, I don't wanna know. It's taken me my whole life to find out who I am, and I'm tired now, you hear what I'm sayin'? What's your name?

JOE: Joe.

MARSHALL: My name's Marshall, how you do?

(They shake hands quite seriously.)

MARSHALL: Wait a minute. I'm coming back.

(MARSHALL gets out of the driver's seat, goes back, and gets in next to JOE.)

MARSHALL: Now what's your situation? Explain your situation to me.

JOE: I'm going away on a long trip.

MARSHALL: Okay.

JOE: I've got the opportunity to buy some clothes today.

MARSHALL: Yes.

JOE: Money's no object.

MARSHALL: Good. Where you going?

JOE: Well. I'm going out tonight in the city.

MARSHALL: Nice places?

JOE: I hope so. Then tomorrow I'm flying to L.A.

MARSHALL: First class?

JOE: Yeah.

MARSHALL: Good.

JOE: Then I'm getting on a yacht and sailing to the South Pacific.

MARSHALL: Hawaii?

JOE: No. A really unknown little island.

MARSHALL: No tourists?

JOE: I don't think so.

MARSHALL: Good.

JOE: Then I'll be on the island a couple of weeks, then that's it.

MARSHALL: And what do you got in the way of clothes now?

JOE: Well, I've got the kind of clothes I'm wearin'.

MARSHALL: So you've got no clothes. We'll start with basics. We'll start with underwear. We'll start with Dunhill.

(MARSHALL *gets out of the car and heads back for the driver's seat.* MARSHALL *puts the car in gear and pulls away from the curb.*)

EXTERIOR: DUNHILL. DAY.

The white limousine pulls up. Two dog bars bracket the entrance to Dunhill with two big matching dogs, probably Great Danes, drinking at each of the dog bars. The dogs are held on leashes by a man in a business suit and a woman in a pretty coat.

INTERIOR: LIMOUSINE. DAY.

JOE *is getting ready to get out.*

JOE: So just socks and underwear?

MARSHALL: Conservative underwear is the only way to go. White cotton broadcloth boxers. Silk shorts make you feel like a whore, so none of that. But with the T-shirts, Egyptian cotton, all right?

JOE: All right.

(JOE *gets out of the car and goes in.*)

INTERIOR: DUNHILL. UNDERWEAR COUNTER. DAY.

A conservative UNDERGARMENT SALESMAN *is helping* JOE.

UNDERGARMENT SALESMAN: How many pairs of boxer shorts would you like, sir?

JOE: How many does a man need?

(*The* UNDERWEAR SALESMAN *pauses and thinks.*)

UNDERGARMENT SALESMAN: Eight pairs.

EXTERIOR: DUNHILL. DAY.

MARSHALL *is leaning against the limousine, reading a copy of* Scientific American.
    A WOMAN *appears dressed as the Statue of Liberty. She looks at* MARSHALL. *He returns the glance. She has a tin can in her hand.*

MARSHALL: What?

WOMAN: How about a dollar for the way I look?

MARSHALL: Shoot. How 'bout a dollar for the way I look? (*He gives her a dollar.*) Yeah.

(*The* WOMAN *exits.* JOE *comes out of the store with a shopping bag.* MARSHALL *opens the door for him.*)

JOE: They've got a changing room. I'm wearing the underwear.

MARSHALL: I knew that. I could see it on your face.

INTERIOR: LIMOUSINE. AT CURB BY BROOKS BROTHERS. DAY.

MARSHALL: What else you need?

JOE: Ah, well, some kind of overcoat. I don't know, maybe like a English trench coat.

MARSHALL: English trench coat? That's foul weather wear, man. You're goin' *west*!

JOE: What would you get?

MARSHALL: You're a sexual man?

JOE: Yeah?

MARSHALL: Not that I mean to be crude, but I'm trying to express something. *Armani*. That's what you want. And how 'bout a haircut?

JOE: What's wrong with my hair?

MARSHALL: I can't express it. It looks like freedom without choice. It looks wrong. (*While he's talking, he picks up the car phone and punches some numbers. He speaks into the phone:*) Salon Salon, please. (*He breaks the connection and dials again.*) Hi, gimme Cassie Cimorelli, please. Hello, Cassie? It's Marshall, how you? Good. Listen, I got somebody who needs you today, can you help me out? Two-thirty? Great, good, thanks. (*He hangs up. He puts the car in gear and pulls away.*) We gotta get moving.

EXTERIOR: GIORGIO ARMANI. DAY.

The white limousine pulls up.

INTERIOR: LIMOUSINE. DAY.

JOE: So what do I ask for?

MARSHALL: This is too complicated. I gotta come in with you. If I getta ticket, it can't be helped.

EXTERIOR: LIMOUSINE OUTSIDE GIORGIO ARMANI. DAY.

JOE *and* MARSHALL *get out and go in.*

INTERIOR: GIORGIO ARMANI. DAY.

JOE *is standing on a fitting stool in a beautiful suit. He's being ministered to by an Italian* TAILOR *while* MARSHALL *supervises.* MARSHALL *murmurs to the* TAILOR.

MARSHALL: I still think the full break over the shoe is the way to go.

TAILOR: No more than half this year, I swear to you. (*To* JOE:) You can take it off now, sir.

(*The* TAILOR *points the way to* JOE *and walks off.*)

MARSHALL: Hey, Joe, how about a tux?

JOE: What for?

MARSHALL: Something'll come up. There's nothing a man looks better in.

JOE: I'll get one if you get one.

MARSHALL: I can't be buying no Armani tux. I'm a working man.

JOE: You're getting paid to drive the car. Nobody's paying you to give me all this advice. Let me buy you the tux, and we'll call it even.

(MARSHALL *thinks it over.*)

INTERIOR: GIORGIO ARMANI. DAY. TEN MINUTES LATER.

MARSHALL *is standing on the fitting stool in an Armani tuxedo. The* TAILOR *is doing his cuffs.*

MARSHALL: Gimme the full break over the shoe, Pietro. It's my preference.

TAILOR: Whatever's your pleasure, sir.

EXTERIOR: GIORGIO ARMANI. DAY.

JOE *and* MARSHALL *emerge.* MARSHALL *opens the door to the limousine for* JOE *and urges him to speed it up.*

MARSHALL: Come on, kid! We're on a roll! (*As he walks around to the driver's side.*) Didn't even get a ticket.

(MARSHALL *gets in, starts it up, and pulls away.*)

EXTERIOR: THE HORN OF AFRICA. LIMOUSINE OUTSIDE. DAY.

Two tiki heads bracket either side of the entrance.

INTERIOR: THE HORN OF AFRICA. DAY.

JOE *is trying on a safari jacket. Two salesmen stand by.* JOE *nods. Now one of the salesmen puts a particularly dashing safari hat on* JOE. *He looks in a mirror. He really, really likes it.*

INTERIOR: SALON SALON. DAY.

It's a large, bustling beauty center in Midtown. There must be fifteen hairdressers spread out over a spacious, well-windowed area. It's a festive place with glossy magazines and coffee and water running and blow dryers going. Happy Brazilian music is playing on the sound system.

Now we zero in on Cassie's corner. CASSIE *is in her thirties, with a short, fetching up-to-the-minute haircut. She also has a terrific personality; she's the salt of the earth. And she's cutting Joe's hair.* MARSHALL *sits on a nearby chair. He's reading B, a trendy magazine.*

JOE: How you making me look?

CASSIE: I'm undoing this cut from before. This is some piece of geography. Where'd you get this?

JOE: In one of those subway barber shops.

CASSIE: It has that reality. Grim. You're a very handsome guy—I'm just gonna bring that out. Marshall, which one is that?

MARSHALL: It's the in and out issue.

CASSIE: That's the best! What's in?

MARSHALL: Carrie Fisher, Barcelona, African Americans, happy endings, the *New York Daily News,* tomato salads, God, garlic, wristwatches you have to wind up, and true love.

CASSIE: Did you say Carrie Fisher?

MARSHALL: You don't like Carrie Fisher?

CASSIE: I love Carrie Fisher! I can't believe it! So intelligent! So dry! That's a totally great list. What's out? Read it slow.

MARSHALL: Kafka, CDs . . .

CASSIE: That's true. I've had it with Kafka. Those little eyes . . . so full of misery.

MARSHALL: Stand-up comedy . . .

CASSIE: Stand-up comedy makes me nervous.

MARSHALL: All restaurants that haven't been in existence for at least thirty years . . .

CASSIE: Yes.

MARSHALL: Paloma Picasso.

CASSIE: No, I don't agree with that. I love Paloma Picasso. Those lips! So red, so big!

MARSHALL: New money *and* old money . . .

CASSIE: Okay.

MARSHALL: All camp, all trash, all trivia . . .

CASSIE: Oh c'mon, take a risk.

MARSHALL: And the *New York Times.*

CASSIE: Finally somebody said it! What a rag!

(CASSIE *finishes cutting Joe's hair. It's a great cut.*)

CASSIE: Very gratifying. Thank you, Marshall. Well, here you are.

JOE: I look good.

MARSHALL: You're coming into focus, kid! I can see you now.

(MARSHALL *nods approval.* CASSIE *and* JOE *exchange a smile.*)

EXTERIOR: HAMMACHER SCHLEMMER. DAY.

The limousine pulls up. JOE *goes in.* MARSHALL *stays in the car.*

INTERIOR: HAMMACHER SCHLEMMER. DAY.

Angle on the indoor golfing practice green. JOE *putts a golf ball into the hole.*

JOE: I'll take it.

SALESWOMAN: Yes, sir.

(JOE *walks out of frame. Close-up pan across the glass countertop revealing a Swiss army knife, a world-band travel radio, shaving kit, lantern, and a violin case that doubles as a bar, until we come to a large light-colored umbrella pointed at us. The umbrella closes, revealing* JOE.)

JOE: I'll take this, too.

SALESMAN: Will that be all?

(JOE *walks away.*
    Cut to: picture cutout of a woman demonstrating the walk-on-water shoes. JOE *approaches. The* SALESWOMAN *appears as well.* JOE *is really looking at the shoes.*)

SALESWOMAN: Does that interest you?

JOE: You mean you can walk on water?

SALESWOMAN: With a little help. Yes.

JOE: I'll take a pair.

SALESWOMAN: All right. Very good, sir. Thank you.

JOE: Thank *you.*

INTERIOR: WHITE LIMOUSINE IN FRONT OF GIORGIO ARMANI. DAY.

Two uniformed attendants from Armani are handing the last of the boxes to JOE, *who's now sitting in front with* MARSHALL.
   The back of the car is completely loaded with stuff. The attendants head back to the entrance, where they stand at parade rest on either side of the door.

JOE (calling after): Thanks!

(MARSHALL *pulls away from the curb.*)

MARSHALL: You know what you need?

JOE: What else could I need?

MARSHALL: How you gonna carry this stuff? You need luggage!

JOE: I didn't think of that.

INTERIOR: SMALL EXCLUSIVE LUGGAGE STORE (J. RUSS). DAY.

It's as quiet as a church. A few pieces of extremely high-quality leather luggage are on display. The LUGGAGE SALESMAN, *a small neat man in a quiet suit, is the store's representative. He's talking with* JOE. *He's a very serious, understated man.*

LUGGAGE SALESMAN: Have you thought much about luggage, Mr. Banks?

JOE: No, I never really have.

LUGGAGE SALESMAN: It's the central preoccupation of my life. You travel the world, you're away from home, perhaps away from your family, all you have to depend on is yourself and your luggage.

JOE: I guess that's true.

LUGGAGE SALESMAN: Are you traveling light or heavy?

JOE: Heavy.

LUGGAGE SALESMAN: Flying?

JOE: Flying. And by ship.

LUGGAGE SALESMAN: An ocean voyage?

JOE: Yes.

LUGGAGE SALESMAN: Ah. Yes. So. A real journey.

JOE: And then I'll be staying on this island, I don't even really know if I'll be living in a hut or what.

LUGGAGE SALESMAN: Very exciting.

JOE: Yeah.

LUGGAGE SALESMAN: As a luggage problem. I believe I have just the thing.

(*The* LUGGAGE SALESMAN *rolls out an absolutely gorgeous steamer trunk of dark, wine-colored leather, with brass fittings.*)

JOE: Wow.

(*The* LUGGAGE SALESMAN *opens it. It has hangers, drawers, a mirror, the works.*)

LUGGAGE SALESMAN: This is our premier steamer trunk. All handmade, only the finest materials. It's even watertight, tight as a drum. If I had the need and the wherewithal, Mr. Banks, this would be my trunk of choice. I could face the world with a trunk like this by my side.

(JOE *is moved.*)

JOE: I'll take four of them.

(*This is the classiest thing the* LUGGAGE SALESMAN *has ever heard.*)

LUGGAGE SALESMAN: May you live to be a thousand years old, sir.

(*Not normally a demonstrative man, the* LUGGAGE SALESMAN *slowly raises his hand, offering it to* JOE. JOE *takes it and they shake.*)

EXTERIOR: STREET OUTSIDE LUGGAGE STORE. DAY.

MARSHALL *and* JOE *have just finished securing the four trunks to the top of the white limousine. They get in the car.*

INTERIOR: LIMOUSINE. DAY.

MARSHALL *starts it up.*

JOE: I'm through shopping.

MARSHALL: Fair enough. Where to? Back to Staten Island?

JOE: Yeah, I guess so. No. A really good hotel. The Plaza?

MARSHALL: The Plaza's nice.

JOE: Where would you go?

MARSHALL (lighting up): The Pierre!

EXTERIOR: THE PIERRE HOTEL. DUSK.

Seven bellboys and bellgirls are unloading the white limousine and carrying its contents into the hotel. They wear classic bellboy uniforms and caps. MARSHALL *and* JOE *are watching.*

JOE: Marshall?

MARSHALL: Yeah?

JOE: I wonder if you'd want to have dinner with me tonight?

MARSHALL: Can't do it. I got my wife and kids at the end of the day, you know?

JOE: Yeah.

HEAD BELLMAN (informing JOE): Everything's at check-in when you're ready, sir.

(*The* HEAD BELLMAN *departs within.*)

MARSHALL: Listen, ain't you got nobody?

JOE: No. But there are certain times in your life when I guess you're not supposed to have anybody, you know? There are certain doors you have to go through alone.

MARSHALL: You're gonna be all right.

(JOE *shrugs. He and* MARSHALL *shake hands. They look at each other.* MARSHALL *gets in the limousine and pulls away.* JOE *looks after him, then turns and goes into the hotel.*
    Music: A instrumental jazz version of "Do You Know the Way to San Jose" plays through the following scenes.)

INTERIOR: SUITE IN THE PIERRE HOTEL. NIGHT.

JOE *has one of his trunks open. He's hanging his tuxedo up in it. He has been taking stuff out of boxes and packing it into the trunks. He opens another box and takes out his new suit. The music continues.*

INTERIOR: MAIN RESTAURANT IN THE PIERRE HOTEL. NIGHT.

This is an incredibly beautiful, quiet restaurant. JOE *is discovered, sitting alone at a table. The Pierre waiter is just walking away.* JOE *is sipping a glass of wine, his entrée before him. The music continues.*

EXTERIOR: CENTRAL PARK SOUTH. NIGHT.

JOE *is walking along. As he approaches The Plaza Hotel, two cabs pull up, and eight theatergoers from out of town disembark. They are all middle-aged, wearing their best clothes, having a good time. They cross in front of* JOE *on their way into the hotel. He watches them go by and disappear. It makes him smile, and it makes him feel alone. He goes on. The music continues.*

EXTERIOR: DEPARTMENT STORE WINDOW. NIGHT.

JOE *walks by and stops, struck by the contents of the window. It's a female dummy, dressed as* PATRICIA *will be on the yacht. A photomural of the yacht is behind the dummy.*

INTERIOR: TUESDAY'S (JAZZ BAR). NIGHT.

We've arrived at the place where the music is coming from. JOE *sits at a little table, listening to a good jazz quartet. They are a pasty-faced English quartet. Everyone in the club is black except* JOE, *the bartender, and the band, which is playing "Do You Know the Way to San Jose." Everyone is drinking martinis. The martinis form a straight line down the bar, each with a giant green olive in it.* JOE *finishes a martini and waves for the check. The music continues.*

EXTERIOR: FIFTH AVENUE. THIRTY FEET FROM THE PIERRE HOTEL. NIGHT.

JOE, *weaving ever so slightly, walks up the street and approaches the hotel. The music concludes.*

INTERIOR: THE PIERRE HOTEL. JOE'S SUITE. NIGHT.

The lights are out. JOE *is in bed, staring at the ceiling. We look down on him. It's very, very silent. Finally, he closes his eyes and turns his head.*

EXTERIOR: AMERICAN AIRLINES PLANE IN FLIGHT. DAY.

INTERIOR: AMERICAN AIRLINES FLIGHT. FIRST-CLASS CABIN. DAY.

On the flight to Los Angeles, JOE *is sitting on the aisle. Next to him is a gray-haired, wholesome priest,* FATHER CONROY. *The clergyman is almost through with his drink, wrapped up in his own thoughts.* JOE *is deeply aware that he's sitting next to a priest; he's uneasy, shifting in his chair. The* STEWARDESS *notices* JOE *and approaches.*

STEWARDESS: Can I get you anything, sir?

JOE: No, thank you. No, I changed my mind. Some club soda, please.

STEWARDESS: All right.

(FATHER CONROY *catches her eye and slightly raises his almost empty drink.*)

FATHER CONROY: I think I'll have one more.

STEWARDESS: All right.

(*The* STEWARDESS *heads off, down the aisle.* JOE *catches the priest's eye.*)

JOE: Have you ever been to California before?

FATHER CONROY: Oh, many times.

JOE: I've never been anywhere.

FATHER CONROY: I was a chaplain there, years ago. For the Marines. Camp Pendleton.

JOE: I don't believe in God.

FATHER CONROY: Okay.

JOE: I did when I was a kid, but I lost my faith in high school.

FATHER CONROY: Uh-huh.

JOE: And then, when I was in danger—I was a fireman—in the middle of the fire, I never like turned around and fell to my knees and started praying.

FATHER CONROY: No?

JOE: No. There are atheists in foxholes.

FATHER CONROY: I'm sure there are.

JOE: But I've come to a place in my life where I've come face-to-face with the facts of life and death. I mean, it's a chance happening I'm alive, it's a miracle, I'm so lucky! And it's not going to last. It's like a shooting star. So beautiful, so fleeting, make a wish before it's gone, you know? I'm so moved. But cutoff. If there is a God, if there is some kind of music going through everything, I can't hear it. I'm alone. I really feel I'm alone. I'm walking down this little path by myself.

FATHER CONROY: Yes.

JOE: Can you help me?

(*The* STEWARDESS *has returned with their drinks.*)

STEWARDESS: Hi. I have your drinks.

JOE: Oh, yeah. Thank you.

(*The* STEWARDESS *serves* FATHER CONROY *a little bottle of bourbon and a glass of ice. He gives her his old glass.*)

FATHER CONROY: Thank you.

(JOE *is still focused on* FATHER CONROY. *The good priest carefully pours the little bottle of bourbon over the ice.* JOE *is very intense.*)

JOE: Can you help me?

FATHER CONROY: Do you see an analyst of some kind?

JOE: I don't need an analyst. That's not the kind of problem I have.

(*Inspirational light shines through the cabin window.*)

FATHER CONROY: If you need a guide. If you're a seeker and you need a guide, someone to counsel you, so you can find your way forward into a spiritual realm. And you're on an airplane. Don't look in first class.

(FATHER CONROY *raises his glass of bourbon in a little toast to* JOE, *and then takes a healthy swallow.*)

EXTERIOR: L.A. AIRPORT. RUNWAY. DAY.

The American flight lands.

INTERIOR: L.A. AIRPORT TERMINAL. DAY.

JOE *and his fellow travelers are just entering the terminal proper. A commercial airplane presses its nose inquisitively against a visible window. It is surrounded by orange trees.* JOE *is surrounded by blond California guys as he gets off the plane. We see a homemade banner* WELCOME TO L.A. ST. DYMPHNA'S GIRLS' ACADEMY. *Of the six people waiting, five of them look like Brezhnev. The sixth is* ANGELICA. *She is holding aloft a sign which reads* JOSEPH BANKS. *She looks like* DEDE. JOE *does a take; he goes to her. Several Catholic schoolgirls run by.*

JOE: Hi.

ANGELICA: Hi, are you Joe Banks?

JOE: Yeah. Who are you?

ANGELICA: I'm the daughter of the guy who hired you. Angelica Graynamore.

(JOE *shakes her hand.*)

JOE: Nice to meet you. Again.

ANGELICA: What?

(JOE *shakes his head.*)

ANGELICA: Daddy told me to tell you that I don't know what he hired you for, and not to tell me. That I'm totally untrustworthy. I'm a flibberti-gibbet. C'mon, let's get outta here.

JOE: I've got some luggage.

EXTERIOR: TAXI FULL OF STEAMER TRUNKS. DAY.

The taxi is going along a highway. We leave the taxi and move forward to a red convertible. In the red convertible are ANGELICA *at the wheel and* JOE *beside her. They are driving alongside the blue ocean. Green palm trees wave overhead. All is beautiful and fresh.*

JOE: I've never been to L.A. before.

ANGELICA: What do you think?

JOE: It looks fake. I like it.

EXTERIOR: SHANGRI-LA HOTEL. SUNSET.

The red convertible pulls up to the entrance.

ANGELICA (offscreen): Daddy wanted to put you up in Bel Air, but I said no way! Shangri-la, Shangri-la!

(*The taxi pulls up behind them.* ANGELICA *gets out of the car and goes back to the cab. She gives the* DRIVER *money.*)

ANGELICA: Thanks. That's for you. And put everything on the curb, please.

DRIVER: Thank you.

(JOE *gets out of the convertible. Two porters emerge from the hotel with luggage carriers, and assist the* DRIVER *in transferring the trunks.* ANGELICA *jumps back in her car and calls to* JOE.)

ANGELICA: Check in, fresh up, I'll be back for you at seven. We'll have dinner.

(ANGELICA *drives off.* JOE *looks after, then turns and goes into the hotel.*)

INTERIOR: CHINOIS. NIGHT.

A fancy fun restaurant. A big platter of Dungeness crabs is being carried through the restaurant. It's placed on the table at which JOE *and* ANGELICA *are sitting. There are already two other platters of exotic food on the table. Now we see the waiter, a slick blond named* RALPH, *and the waitress, a redhead named* RITA.

RITA: Black bread with sour cream and golden caviar.

RALPH: The Dungeness crabs.

(JOE *looks at this dish with alarm.* RALPH *and* RITA *depart.*)

ANGELICA: What's the matter?

JOE: Nothing.

ANGELICA: They do look like little monsters or something. (*Picks one up and attacks it.*) But they're good little monsters.

(JOE *tentatively takes one and small portions of the other dishes.*)

ANGELICA: What'd you do before you signed on with Daddy?

JOE: I was an advertising librarian for a medical supply company.

ANGELICA: Oh. I have no response to that.

JOE: What do you do?

ANGELICA: Why do you ask?

JOE: Uh, I don't know.

(ANGELICA *produces and takes two pills. Suddenly she gets very defensive.*)

ANGELICA: I'm a painter. And a poet.

JOE: Really?

ANGELICA: Yes. Does that bother you?

JOE: No. .

ANGELICA: People from New York usually look down on painters. And poets.

JOE: I didn't know that.

ANGELICA: They think if you live in L.A. and you say you're an artist, you really do nothing!

JOE: Why?

ANGELICA: You don't think I do nothing?

JOE: No.

ANGELICA: You believe me when I say I'm a painter?

JOE: And a poet. Sure.

ANGELICA: Well, you're right. There's a painting of mine right there.

(*Cut to: painting of a car in a yellow pool of light, overlooking a lit-up city below.*
    Cut back to: JOE *and* ANGELICA *looking.*)

JOE: It's terrific. Where you get your ideas?

ANGELICA: I'll show you.

(*Cut back to: painting.*
    Dissolves into:)

EXTERIOR: HILL WITH STREETLIGHT. NIGHT.

The streetlight casts a pool of light just like the one in the painting, and the city glitters below. When Angelica's car pulls into the pool of light and stops, the picture is complete.

JOE: Nice view. It's like looking down at the stars.

(ANGELICA *takes two more pills.*)

ANGELICA: Do you want to hear one of my poems?

JOE: Sure.

ANGELICA: Long ago, the delicate tangles of his hair,
        Covered the emptiness of my hands.
(*To* JOE:) Do you wanna hear it again?

JOE: Okay.

ANGELICA: Long ago, the delicate tangles of his hair,
        Covered the emptiness of my hands.

(ANGELICA *has tears in her eyes.* JOE *looks at her, concerned.*)

JOE: What's the matter?

ANGELICA: Did you ever think about killing yourself?

JOE: What? Why would you do that?

ANGELICA: Why shouldn't I?

JOE: Some things take care of themselves. They're not your job. Maybe they're not even your business. I like your poem.

ANGELICA: I'm a grown woman, and I live on my father's money. That restaurant that had my painting up, that's my father's restaurant.

JOE: Why are you telling me?

ANGELICA: I don't know. (*Making a joke out of it.*) I'll tell anybody who'll listen. (*Dropping it.*) No, that's not true. I don't know why I'm telling you.

JOE: Listen to me. If you have a choice between killing yourself and doing something you're scared of doing, why not take the leap and do the thing you're scared of doing?

ANGELICA: You mean stop taking money and leave L.A.?

JOE: You see? You know what you're afraid of doing. Why don't you do it? See what happens?

(*Inspired by him,* ANGELICA *hesitates on the brink of courage. For a moment she finds it and lifts her hands to say yes, but her courage fails her. She gets a chill.*)

ANGELICA: You must be tired. (*She starts up the car.*) Thanks for listening, but I'm a little high, and you don't know me from Adam, I mean, I guess, Eve. Anyway, forget it.

JOE: I don't mind talking.

ANGELICA (suddenly very angry): Well, I do! This is one of those typical conversations where we're all open and sharing our innermost thoughts, and it's all bullshit and a lie, and it doesn't cost you anything!

JOE: Look. I don't know you. I don't think I know anybody. You're angry. I can see that. (*He quietly gets upset.*) I'm very troubled. I'm not ready to . . . there's only so much time, and you wanna use it well. So I'm here talking to you, I don't wanna throw that away. Time. I can feel it going by. Like when I was a kid on a sled going down a hill. I wanna drag my feet to slow it down, it's so scary. But you're gone, you know? You're born, and you're on the move, you're on the sled, and you're going down the hill. Fast. Fast as life. I'm doing the best I can. Angelica. I like your name. I didn't tell you that. Maybe you better take me back to the hotel.

(*Joe's eyes are shining.* ANGELICA *looks at him. She puts the car in gear and pulls out.*)

EXTERIOR: SHANGRI-LA HOTEL. NIGHT.

The red convertible pulls up. JOE *gets out.*

ANGELICA: You want me to come in? I could come up with you?

JOE: No.

ANGELICA: All right. Will you have breakfast with me? I'm supposed to get you to the boat by ten, but I could meet you for breakfast.

JOE: Okay.

ANGELICA: I told you I was a flibbertigibbet.

(ANGELICA *drives off.* JOE *turns to go into the hotel, changes his mind, and walks out into the street. We follow him. He dodges a lone car and makes it to the other side, where the palm trees grow.*)

EXTERIOR: AMONG PALM TREES. NIGHT.

JOE *is making his way through some greenery. He parts some tall grass, and we see what he sees.*

EXTERIOR: BEACH AND OCEAN. NIGHT.

Joe's point of view: A couple of stars vaguely twinkle overhead. There's the dull boom of the surf.

EXTERIOR: WHERE BEACH MEETS OCEAN. NIGHT.

JOE *arrives at this spot and sits down in the sand. He looks out at the ocean, at the horizon, where the night presses down on the water. Time passes. The sky gets lighter.*

Music: The vague beginnings of something magical and very, very big are heard.

A band of golden light hits JOE *in the back of the head. He turns around, and it's in his eyes. We see the fake sun rising over a row of palm trees. Just a touch of red on the horizon.*

The magical music ceases, but the sun continues to rise and rise until it clears the horizon and is a discreet orange-blue disk in the morning sky.

INTERIOR: SUNNY RESTAURANT. DAY.

The sun turns into an orange-yellow yolk of a sunny-side-up egg. The camera pulls back. JOE *and* ANGELICA *are eating breakfast.* JOE *is dressed like a jungle explorer.*

ANGELICA: I'm so tired. You take that stuff, it just ruins your sleep. I'm sorry I was so abusive, immature, hostile, and needy last night.

JOE: You were fine.

ANGELICA: I disappointed you. So, what did Daddy hire you to do?

JOE: It's real complicated.

ANGELICA: Okay. I don't even know where you're going on the boat. Patricia won't tell me.

JOE: Who's Patricia?

ANGELICA: She's my half sister. She's the one who's sailing you wherever you're going.

JOE: She is?

ANGELICA: You didn't know?

JOE: No.

ANGELICA: Daddy loves a secret almost as much as he loves money. Can I ask you something?

JOE: What?

ANGELICA: Why are you dressed like Jungle Jim?

JOE: You think this is inappropriate? For the boat?

ANGELICA: No, it's fine. We'd better get going. I gotta guy dropping your trunks off at the marina, who may or may not have understood my travel directions.

(*They get up to go.*)

EXTERIOR: BIG MARINA. MANY BOATS LIKE RESTLESS HORSES. DAY.

At the end of a long, narrow dock is a yacht about seventy-five feet long. It dwarfs all the other vessels. We hear a car door slam and hear Angelica's voice.

ANGELICA (offscreen): Here we are.

(ANGELICA *and* JOE *approach the dock and start walking down it. We see them from the back and hear them talking.*)

JOE: Is that it?

ANGELICA: Yeah.

JOE: It's big.

(*They approach the yacht, which is called* The Tweedle Dee. *It has on its hull a single, arrogant eye that looks haughtily at* JOE. *The four steamer trunks are on the dock by the yacht. A magnificent, athletic, truly feminine, blond, blue-eyed woman in her late twenties sits on a piling, staring balefully at the trunks. This is* PATRICIA. *On* The Tweedle Dee *two boat boys,* MIKE *and* TONY, *ready the yacht for departure; they are young and shining and strong.* JOE *and* ANGELICA *arrive at the slip.* PATRICIA *looks just like* DEDE *and* ANGELICA. JOE *does a take.*)

JOE: (to ANGELICA): You say this is your *half* sister?

ANGELICA: Yeah.

PATRICIA: What's the trunks, Felix?

JOE: They're my . . . my name's not Felix, it's Joe.

PATRICIA: I know. (*Calling out:*) Mike! Tony! Find a place for these boxes.

(MIKE *and* TONY *jump off the yacht and proceed to load the trunks.*)

PATRICIA: That outfit's wearing you, Felix.

JOE: Why are you calling me Felix? My name's Joe.

PATRICIA: I'm calling you Felix because I do what I want. Hello, Angelica.

ANGELICA: Hello, Patricia.

PATRICIA and ANGELICA: (simultaneously): Do you know where Daddy is?

PATRICIA (to JOE): We never know where our father is and we always suspect that the other one knows. But it's all phone calls and telegrams, hey, Angelica?

ANGELICA: Well, you're in a rotten mood.

PATRICIA: It's the sunshine. It gets me down.

(*The boat boys have finished bringing aboard the last trunk.*)

ANGELICA: Where are you going?

PATRICIA: Can you believe it? Dad said not to tell you. Goes with my theory. Power makes you paranoid.

MIKE (calling out from the yacht): All set.

(PATRICIA *hops off the piling.*)

PATRICIA: Well, get ready to heave, Felix.

(JOE *gets angry.*)

JOE: My name is Joseph or Joe.

(PATRICIA *deflates a bit.*)

PATRICIA: All right. Joe. Get ready. We're leaving.

(JOE *turns to* ANGELICA.)

JOE (speaking to her privately): 'Bye.

ANGELICA: 'Bye.

JOE: Listen. Don't take drugs.

ANGELICA: Okay.

JOE: Wish me luck.

ANGELICA: Good luck.

(JOE *takes her hand and gives her a little kiss on the cheek. She notes his hand. She's puzzled.*)

ANGELICA: You're shaking.

(JOE *smiles, examining his hand.*)

JOE: Am I? A little. (*Looks at the land in the distance behind her.*) Yeah.

(JOE *runs up the gangway.* PATRICIA *has already boarded the boat. The boat boys are casting off.* PATRICIA *takes the wheel. But we are still with* ANGELICA *on the dock. She stands there. Slowly, as the yacht pulls away, she waves.* JOE *stands at the railing, the sails still furled behind him. He waves back.*

Now we are with JOE *on the yacht, at the railing. He waves a little, and then his eyes rove the shore.*

Joe's point of view: shore. JOE *looks at the flag on the stern of* The Tweedle Dee. *He looks up from the flag at his departing homeland. A ghost image of the flag follows his glance up, so that he sees the following through that image. He sees* ANGELICA *on the dock and then the boats behind her and then the parking lot behind the boats. And then the hills in the distance off to his left. And the rich people's houses off to his right. And cars on roads. And a smokestack. He sees all this through the ghost image of that American flag. He sees his homeland. Receding. He's leaving his homeland. He will never see it again. And now we see again:*

JOE *is at the rail, staring, moved, determined. His clothes are a bit much, but he almost fills them in this moment. A wind comes up and sweeps his safari hat off his head, into the ocean. He flinches slightly at the loss.*

His hat swirls away into the wake.

But now we see JOE *again: And after a glance, he gives up the hat without regret. He continues to look after the receding land. Without the hat he looks great. His hair blows in the wind, and he stares and stares.)*

EXTERIOR: YACHT. FROM A FEW HUNDRED YARDS AWAY. DAY.

The Tweedle Dee *has cleared the harbor, and the boat boys have started unfurling the sails. The huge, snowy sails fill with a rich wind.*

INTERIOR: *THE TWEEDLE DEE.* GALLEY. DAY.

The chef, a German named DAGMAR, *is laying out lovely Niçoise salads.* TONY *awaits Dagmar's pleasure.*

DAGMAR: Have you put out the sunflowers yet?

TONY: Yeah.

DAGMAR: Good! Go.

(TONY *picks up the salads and exits.)*

EXTERIOR: *THE TWEEDLE DEE.* DINING TABLE. SUNSET.

The table is shaded by a canopy. JOE *and* PATRICIA *sit at the table. Place settings, white wine, and glasses are on the table.* TONY *serves their plates and goes.*

JOE: Looks delicious.

PATRICIA: We eat well aboard *The Tweedle Dee.*

JOE: *The Tweedle Dee?*

PATRICIA: That's the name of this boat.

JOE: Oh.

PATRICIA: So we're going to the island of Waponi Woo.

JOE: I guess so.

PATRICIA: Why?

JOE: You don't know?

PATRICIA: No.

JOE: Have you ever been there?

PATRICIA: No. All I know about Waponi Woo is that the name means "the little island with the big volcano," and that the people, the Waponis, like orange soda.

JOE: They like orange soda.

PATRICIA (producing a book called *History of Polynesia*): Yeah. But here! I've got a book. "Eighteen hundred years ago, a Roman galley, with a crew of Jews and Druids, got caught in a huge storm off Carthage. They were swept a thousand miles off course, and ended up on the wrong side of the Horn of Africa. Thinking they were returning to Rome, they sailed deep into the South Pacific and finally ended by colonizing a lightly populated, Polynesian island which they named Waponi Woo. Thus was born the Waponi culture—a mixture of Polynesian, Celtic, Hebrew, and Latin influences. The Waponis are known throughout Polynesia as having a peculiar love of orange soda and no sense of direction."

JOE: Why'd you talk to me so snotty back on the dock?

PATRICIA: Because you work for my father. And I'm angry with my father. But he's not around to give him a shot. So you work for him, I give you a shot.

JOE: Why you angry with him?

PATRICIA: Because he's never around.

JOE: If you're angry with him and he's never around, why are you working for him?

PATRICIA: I don't work for him. My transport of you is strictly a favor.

JOE: You do favors for people you're mad at?

PATRICIA: I don't work for him!

JOE: All right.

PATRICIA: He said he'd give me this boat if I took you.

JOE: Wow.

PATRICIA (defensive): He's got two of them. This is *The Tweedle Dee*. There's a *Tweedle Dum*, too. (*She gets up. She's flustered.*) I've got the wheel tied up, which is not good sailing. Excuse me.

(PATRICIA *goes toward the stern.* JOE *is left alone to finish his supper.*)

EXTERIOR: *THE TWEEDLE DEE*. DAY.

The yacht is cutting through the blue. The sun is setting.

EXTERIOR: *THE TWEEDLE DEE*. NIGHT.

The yacht is anchored and lit up. It's a dark and starless night.

INTERIOR: *THE TWEEDLE DEE*. CABINS. NIGHT

PATRICIA *is showing* JOE *his berth. The whole interior of the boat is made of beautiful wood.*

PATRICIA: Is this okay for you?

JOE: Sure.

PATRICIA: The boys like to sleep in the hull. Dagmar sleeps on deck when the weather's good. So you've pretty much got things to yourself. I'm in the little stateroom.

JOE: Great.

(*But* PATRICIA *lingers.*)

PATRICIA: I'm sorry I was so rude on the dock.

JOE: That's okay.

(PATRICIA *has finished, but still she lingers, awkward.*)

PATRICIA (finally blurting out): Did you sleep with my sister?

JOE: No.

PATRICIA: Actually, she's my half sister.

JOE: No, I didn't.

PATRICIA: Okay. (*Again she's awkward.*) Do you like to fish?

JOE: Sure.

PATRICIA: Maybe tomorrow we'll do some fishing. (*She goes to the entranceway and fingers a switch on the wall.*) This is the light switch. Did Mike show you how to work the bathroom?

JOE: Yeah.

PATRICIA: Good. Do you want me to turn off the light while I'm going?

JOE: Okay.

(PATRICIA *turns off the light. Only the light from the entranceway illuminates her now, and* JOE *is not visible.*)

PATRICIA: I love my sister. I know she's screwed up. I love my father, even though I never see him and he's not so great when I do see him. I'm very nervous about this trip. My father didn't tell me anything, and you don't seem to be telling me anything. But it's more than that. I've always kept clear of my father's stuff since I got out on my own. Now he's pulled me back in. He knew I wanted this boat and he used it and he got me working for him, which I swore I would never do. I feel ashamed because I had a price. He named it. And now I know that about myself. I don't know who you are. I don't know anything about you. But you're working for him, too, and that makes us two of a kind. I could treat you like I did back on the dock, but that would be me kicking myself for selling out. Which isn't fair to you and doesn't make me feel any better. I don't know what your situation is. But I wanted you to know what mine is. Not just to explain some rude behavior. But because we're on a little boat for a while and I'm soul sick and you're gonna see that. Like my sister. She's soul sick, too. And if you'd slept with her, I would've known something about you. But you didn't. You didn't. I believe you.

JOE: I'm glad you believe me.

PATRICIA: Have you ever slept on a boat before?

JOE: No.

PATRICIA: It really affects your dreams. I look forward to it. Even though, sometimes, the dreams really shake me up. Okay. Good night.

JOE: Good night.

(PATRICIA *departs through the entranceway. The light goes out, and it's dark and quiet.*)

EXTERIOR: STERN OF *THE TWEEDLE DEE*. DAY.

It's a really beautiful sunny day. TONY *is at the wheel, the sails are full, and* JOE *and* PATRICIA *are sitting in two chairs hard by the stern. They both are holding deep-sea fishing rods; they're trolling.*

Music: "The Girl from Ipanema," the famous recording by Getz and Gilberto, is playing now.

PATRICIA *reels in her line. A beautiful fish is flapping on the end of it.* JOE *reels in his line. Nothing. He watches as* PATRICIA *unhooks her catch and tosses it in a hamper.* DAGMAR *appears, looks in the hamper, and nods approvingly. Then she looks at* JOE. *Where's Joe's fish? Then she walks away again.* JOE *casts again while* PATRICIA *rebaits her hook. Then* PATRICIA *casts again.* MIKE *arrives with a beer for* PATRICIA, *who accepts it.* MIKE *leaves.* PATRICIA *gets another strike, asks* JOE *to hold her beer, which he does. She reels in another beautiful fish. She unhooks it and throws it in the hamper.* DAGMAR *appears, looks in the hamper, nods approvingly, and then looks at* JOE. *Where's Joe's fish?* JOE *looks at* DAGMAR *and then ignores her.* DAGMAR *departs.* JOE *goes back to fishing. Now* JOE *gets a strike. It's a big one! The line goes burning out of his reel.* PATRICIA *notices. She offers to help him. He waves her off.* DAGMAR *appears. She offers some advice. But* JOE *is completely focused on his rod. The rod, which is substantial, starts to bend.* MIKE *comes back to watch. The rod is almost bent double. Then it goes madly to the left. Offers of help are made, but* JOE *shouts them back. Then the rod goes madly to the right.* DAGMAR *runs out of view and reappears with an enormous gaff, which she brandishes excitedly. A sudden powerful tug almost pulls* JOE *off the back of the boat, but* MIKE *grabs him just in time.* JOE *is a man possessed. He reels and pulls with superhuman determination. Without warning, a huge head, the head of a hammerhead shark, appears at the stern. Its eyes turn inboard and look at* JOE. *Everybody drops everything and runs away.*

EXTERIOR: *THE TWEEDLE DEE*. DINING TABLE. TWILIGHT.

The sun has just sunk beneath the horizon's rim, so there's still all that setting sunlight in the sky. The first evening star has appeared. JOE *and* PATRICIA *are the last left at the dinner's end. The bones of the fish* PATRICIA *caught earlier are on a platter at the table's center.* MIKE *appears and removes the platter and a couple of stray plates, and disappears into the galley. There are balloon glasses by Joe's and Patricia's places and, by* PATRICIA, *a bottle of cognac.*

PATRICIA: Do you like cognac?

JOE: I guess so.

PATRICIA: I make a point of not knowing about certain things. One of them's cognac. I like cognac. But I don't want the accepted wisdom about cognac, you know what I mean? I mean I want glimpses of the myth about it. You see people drink it out of these big glasses, and smelling it forever. That's interesting to me, that sight of them doing that. But I don't want them to talk to me about it, you know what I mean? I want to figure it out based on what I've seen from other people, and what I personally get from it.

JOE: Cognac?

PATRICIA: Yeah. (*She opens the bottle and pours them both some.*) So this is what I've got. So far. To say about this: Most cognac is French. It's very volatile. Like gasoline or model airplane glue. And when you taste it, in my opinion, it tastes like gasoline or model airplane glue. That's because it's for smelling, really. And I figure that's because the French, physically, tend to have big noses. They get the pleasure of the cognac through the nose.

You could really just smell it and pour it down the sink. But this isn't French cognac. This is Italian cognac. It's probably generally considered inferior. But the news is, it tastes good. Maybe it doesn't smell as good—it smells okay—but it tastes good. And, when I came to that fork in the road, between the nose and the tongue, I chose the tongue. So, here's to the tongue.

(*They toast.*)

JOE: To the tongue.

(*They drink a little.*)

JOE: It's good. Don't the Italians have big noses, too?

PATRICIA: Yeah. And that really messes up my theory.

EXTERIOR: *THE TWEEDLE DEE*. NIGHT. AN HOUR AND A HALF LATER.

The yacht bobs gently on the sea. Many stars are coming out, some waxing quite bright. A half-moon, pale and small, hangs in the western sky.

EXTERIOR: *THE TWEEDLE DEE*. DINING TABLE. NIGHT.

JOE *and* PATRICIA *have been talking and sipping cognac for an hour and a half.* PATRICIA *is quite mellow, as is* JOE.

PATRICIA: So my understanding, as far as I understand it, is I'm leaving you on this island.

JOE: That's right.

PATRICIA: How long are you going to stay there?

JOE: For the rest of my life.

PATRICIA: Really.

JOE: Yeah.

PATRICIA: I can't imagine that.

JOE: I couldn't have imagined any of this. (*He looks at the stars.*) Are you used to this?

PATRICIA: What?

JOE: The ocean, the stars.

PATRICIA: You never get used to it. Why do you think I want this boat? All I want to do is sail away.

JOE: Where would you go?

PATRICIA: Away from the things of man.

JOE: Do you believe in God?

PATRICIA: I believe in myself.

JOE: What's that mean?

PATRICIA: I have confidence in myself.

JOE: I've done a lot of soul-searching lately. I've been asking myself some tough questions. You know what I've found out?

PATRICIA: What?

JOE: I have no interest in myself. I think about myself, I get bored out of my mind.

PATRICIA: What does interest you?

JOE: I don't know. Courage. Courage interests me.

PATRICIA: You're going to spend the rest of your life on a tiny island in the South Pacific?

(PATRICIA *pours them both a drink.*)

JOE: Well, up till now, I've lived on a tiny island called Staten Island, and I've commuted to a job in a shut-up room with pumped-in air, no sunshine, despicable people, and now that I've got some distance from that situation, that seems pretty unbelievable. Your life seems unbelievable to me. All this like, life, seems unbelievable to me. Somewhat. At this moment.

PATRICIA: My father says almost the whole world's asleep. Everybody you know, everybody you see, everybody you talk to. He says only a few people are awake. And they live in a state of constant total amazement.

(*They think about that for a while.*)

JOE: I have less than six months to live. The Waponis believe they need a human sacrifice or their island's going to sink into the ocean. They have a mineral your father wants. He's hired me to jump in their volcano.

PATRICIA: What?

JOE: You're not going to make me say that again, are you?

PATRICIA: No.

(*A silence falls.*)

JOE: Aren't you going to say anything?

PATRICIA: I don't know what to say. You tell me you're dying, you tell me you're jumping into a volcano, my mind is a blank.

JOE: I can understand that.

PATRICIA: Is this disease catching?

JOE: No.

(PATRICIA *gets up*.)

PATRICIA (as she leaves): Good night. I'll see you in the morning.

INTERIOR: *THE TWEEDLE DEE*. SLEEPING BERTHS. NIGHT.

JOE *enters, undresses to his new underwear, and climbs into the berth. Then he remembers the light, gets up, turns it off, and climbs back into his berth. It's dark. We see his face. He thinks for a moment and then goes to sleep. And he has a dream.*

DREAM SEQUENCE.

In utter darkness JOE *describes his dream.*

JOE (voice-over): So I fell asleep, and I had this dream. I dreamed I was a cowboy in the wilderness. I dreamed I was a cowboy, and I saved this girl . . .

(*Everything goes dead black. There is the sound of wind. Then Joe's face suddenly lifts up out of the dream into a close-up. Startled, he bangs his head. He has awakened from his dream.*)

END OF DREAM SEQUENCE.

INTERIOR: *THE TWEEDLE DEE*. DAY.

JOE *in his berth. It's the morning although you can't see that in here. The boat is rocking* JOE *in his berth. He looks around, bewildered. He realizes he was dreaming. Then he realizes the boat is rocking a lot. He starts to get up.*

INTERIOR: *THE TWEEDLE DEE.* GALLEY AREA. DAY.

PATRICIA *is trying to get the weather on the radio, but there's nothing but static. She puts on a set of headphones and adjusts the dial again; the radio is silent now, only she can hear it.* JOE *comes into the galley, his hair still rumpled from sleeping on it.*

JOE: Little weird today, huh?

(PATRICIA *waves for him to be quiet. She listens at the headphones another moment, adjusting the dial. She hears something. She's glad. She listens. Her face darkens. She tears off the headphones angrily.* DAGMAR *appears in the hatchway. She greets* JOE.)

DAGMAR: There's a typhoon warning. Good morning, Mr. Banks.

JOE: Good morning.

DAGMAR: Looks like we're in for a blow.

(JOE *exits.*)

EXTERIOR: *THE TWEEDLE DEE'S* FORWARD DECK. DAY. OVERCAST.

The ocean, which until now has been blue, turns green. MIKE *is tying up the sails, which have all been taken in.* PATRICIA *comes up and starts to assist him. A wind comes up.* PATRICIA *looks in the direction of the wind.* JOE *appears on the forward deck, near* PATRICIA.

JOE: Can I help?

PATRICIA: Yeah. You could tie that up. It feels dead, doesn't it?

JOE: Yes. It does.

PATRICIA (yelling): Mike, get below! Start the engine. Tell Tony to head us into the wind and keep us into the wind!

MIKE: Okay.

(MIKE *runs off to do her bidding.*)

JOE: There isn't any wind.

PATRICIA: There will be.

JOE: Are you worried?

(PATRICIA *looks in the direction the wind is coming from.*)

PATRICIA: I think we'll be all right. The hatches are down, the sails are down; we're ahead of the game.

(*Patricia's point of view: storm is coming. It's dark and it's big.*
        PATRICIA *is still staring at the storm.* JOE *looks where she is looking. The engine cranks up.*)

JOE: What exactly is a typhoon?

PATRICIA: You know, Joe, I think you're going to find out.

(*The shadow of the coming storm comes down the deck from forward and envelopes them.*)

EXTERIOR: *THE TWEEDLE DEE.* DAY.

The yacht is on the unhappy sea. The sea has turned very dark, perhaps even black. The storm breaks with a rising wind, a great boom of thunder, and a flash of lightning. It starts to rain, for a moment thinly and then heavily. Whitecaps appear. The Tweedle Dee begins to ride up and down the high waves. Its eye now has a frightened look.

EXTERIOR: *THE TWEEDLE DEE.* WHEEL. IN THE STORM.

MIKE *and* TONY *wrestle with the wheel to keep the bow into the wind. They are pummeled by the rain and wind.*

INTERIOR: *THE TWEEDLE DEE.* GALLEY. IN THE STORM.

PATRICIA *is trying to send a distress signal on the radio.* JOE *watches.* DAGMAR *is absent.*

PATRICIA: Mayday, Mayday, Mayday, latitude ten degrees, eight minutes south, longitude approximately 150 degrees, eighteen minutes west. We are in severe distress. Mayday, Mayday, latitude ten degrees, eight minutes south, longitude approximately 150 degrees, eighteen minutes west.

JOE: What should I do?

PATRICIA: Don't go on deck! Check on Dagmar. She went forward to look at the engine.

INTERIOR: *THE TWEEDLE DEE.* HALLWAY. IN THE STORM.

DAGMAR *has just finished lifting the floorboards, and she's checking the gauges on the engine with a flashlight.* JOE *approaches.*

JOE: Everything okay?

DAGMAR: Looks good, but I'm going to stay with it.

JOE: Okay.

(JOE *departs. A little water drips on* DAGMAR. *She looks up.*)

EXTERIOR: *THE TWEEDLE DEE.* WHEEL. IN THE STORM.

A huge wave engulfs MIKE *and* TONY. *They disappear within the wall of the water and then reappear, still hanging on to the wheel. This happens a second time. They withstand the onslaught. Then* MIKE *sees some-*

thing forward and points it out to TONY. *He leaves* TONY *at the wheel and starts to crawl forward. Lightning flashes nearby.*

INTERIOR: *THE TWEEDLE DEE.* GALLEY. IN THE STORM.

PATRICIA *is still trying to get through on the radio.*

JOE *looks out the cabin window and sees a fish swimming. He is uneasy but says nothing.*

PATRICIA: Mayday, Mayday! Latitude ten degrees, eight minutes south, longitude approximately 150 degrees, eighteen minutes west. Severe distress! Severe distress!

(PATRICIA *drops the mike as* JOE *enters.*)

PATRICIA: No way is anybody getting this. How's Dagmar?

JOE: She's fine.

PATRICIA: Good.

(*The hatch bursts open.* MIKE *falls in amidst water and the roar of the storm. He and* JOE *struggle to close the hatch.*)

MIKE: The main boom doesn't look secure!

PATRICIA: *What?!*

MIKE: I think it's gonna bust loose.

(*Without another word,* MIKE *goes out the hatch again.* JOE *shuts it behind him.* PATRICIA *rips open a cabinet and pulls out a coil of nylon rope.*)

JOE: What are you doing?

PATRICIA: It's my boat.

(PATRICIA *goes out the hatch.* JOE *follows her.*)

EXTERIOR: *THE TWEEDLE DEE.* IN THE STORM.

In severe distress in the storm, PATRICIA *and* JOE *crawl along the deck, battered by the raging typhoon.* PATRICIA *looks up.*
    Patricia's point of view: main boom. There's too much play in it. It's swinging from side to side. If it swings much longer, it's going to snap its stays.
    PATRICIA *and* JOE *continue to crawl toward it.* PATRICIA *is clutching the coil of rope. Lightning flashes.*

EXTERIOR: *THE TWEEDLE DEE.* WHEEL. IN THE STORM.

MIKE *and* TONY *are wrestling with the wheel and are inundated with water.*

INTERIOR: *THE TWEEDLE DEE.* HALLWAY. IN THE STORM.

DAGMAR *is at the engine. A little steady stream of water is splashing on* DAGMAR, *which she ignores. She's adjusting the timing of the engine with a fat screwdriver.*

EXTERIOR: *THE TWEEDLE DEE.* ERRANT BOOM. IN THE STORM.

With Joe's help, PATRICIA *starts to secure the boom, but a sudden roll of the boat throws them back, pinning them against a cabin wall.*
    Another angle: JOE *and* PATRICIA *are pinned against the wall. The rain pours over their faces. They are close, looking at each other, panting, illuminated by lightning. They lunge toward each other, careless of danger, and passionately kiss. The kiss ends. They look at each other. The boat rolls the other way, breaking the spell. They are thrown toward the boom again.*

At this moment, the boom breaks free. JOE *has fallen to the deck while* PATRICIA *is still standing. The boom swings over* JOE *and slams into* PATRICIA, *knocking her unconscious and into the raging sea.* JOE *stands up and, still holding the coil of rope, dives into the ocean after her with a slow-motion stylized leap.*

In the raging sea JOE *looks for* PATRICIA *in the storm. He dives under the water once, twice, but he doesn't find her. He looks around, desperate. He sees something.*

Joe's point of view: Patricia's hand is disappearing under the waves, illuminated by a single flash of lightning.

JOE *swims and dives. He pulls her up, so her head is above the surface of the water. She's unconscious and battered. A flash of lightning catches Joe's attention. He looks.*

EXTERIOR: *THE TWEEDLE DEE.* IN THE STORM.

Joe's point of view: Lightning forks around the ship once, twice, and then the third time, it strikes. A massive bolt sunders the yacht. It's the same German expressionist's bolt as at the beginning of the story: ACHI's logo.

Joe's stunned face is illuminated by the great flash. He is holding the unconscious PATRICIA.

Joe's point of view: The Tweedle Dee *is sinking in the storm.* The Tweedle Dee *'s eyes have turned to Xs. The yacht swamps and disappears beneath the swirling waves.*

JOE *is getting tired, but continues to hold Patricia's head above water. He accidentally swallows a gulletful of seawater, chokes, splutters, and recovers himself. But he's panting. How long can he hold on? But then he sees something!*

Joe's point of view: one of the steamer trunks bobbing.

JOE, *towing* PATRICIA, *starts swimming for the trunk.*

Another angle: JOE *reaches the trunk. He grabs on to it gratefully, recovers his breath, and then hoists* PATRICIA *as high up on it as he can. He takes the nylon rope and lashes her to the trunk. Then he gets a good grip on the trunk himself, and braces against the storm.*

EXTERIOR: TRUNK. DAY. LIGHTLY FOGGY.

JOE *and* PATRICIA *are on the trunk.* PATRICIA *is still unconscious, and* JOE *is asleep, exhausted. The storm is over, and the sky is overcast.* JOE *blinks and wakes up. He tries to wake* PATRICIA.

JOE: Patricia? Patricia?

(PATRICIA *is out cold. He looks around. He sees something*
   Joe's point of view: the other three steamer trunks. The sun shines through a crack in the clouds and lands, sparkling, on the three other trunks, which are floating in the same area. They are all that survived the sinking.
   JOE *lights up upon seeing his trunks. He tentatively moves a little away from* PATRICIA *on her trunk and, satisfied that she's not going to go under, he swims off.*
   Another angle: JOE *arrives at one of the other trunks, grabs it by the handle, and starts towing it back toward Patricia's trunk.*
   Another angle: JOE *arrives at Patricia's trunk with the second. He lets it go and swims back for another.*
   Another angle: JOE *is towing the fourth trunk into the proximity with the others. He takes out his Swiss army knife and cuts some rope from the lash holding* PATRICIA. *He uses it to tie two of the trunks together.*
   Another angle: twenty minutes later, JOE *with three trunks tied together. He is easing Patricia's unconscious body onto the three ganged-together trunks. Having accomplished this, he slides the fourth trunk into position with the other three and begins to secure it with the remaining rope. The four trunks together make up a raft of ten feet square.* JOE *crawls onto the raft, totally exhausted, reaches out a hand to the still form of* PATRICIA, *and passes out. The fog begins to thin. A few shafts of sunlight dapple the raft.*
   The sun sets into the South Pacific, and night begins to fall.)

EXTERIOR: LITTLE RAFT. NIGHT.

Under the stars, JOE *and* PATRICIA, *he asleep and she unconscious, lie unknowing under an enormous canopy of stars. The universe is great and they are small.*

EXTERIOR: LITTLE RAFT. DAY.

The little raft in bright, fresh sunlight: JOE *stirs and wakes. He tries to wake* PATRICIA *but to no avail. He looks in all directions: nothing but blue horizon. After a moment's thought, he opens one of the trunks. But it's the wrong one. He secures it and opens another. He takes out a violin case and opens it; it's a bar masquerading as a violin case, the one he bought at Hammacher Schlemmer. It contains two bottles of Moët champagne, two champagne glasses, and two bottles of Pellegrino water.* JOE *takes out one of the bottles of water and closes the case. Then he gets his little world-band radio out of the trunk and sets it down. He opens the Pellegrino water and starts to drink. But then he thinks. He looks at* PATRICIA. *Her lips are a little parched. He looks up at the sun.*

Joe's point of view: The sun looks powerful.

JOE *looks again at the bottle of water. He decides not to drink any. He pours a little into the bottle cap and presses the cap to Patricia's lips. He repeats the process and then, satisfied, screws the cap on the bottle again and puts it away in the case. Then he puts the case back in the trunk and fastens the lid. He turns on the radio. Static. He turns the dial. The voice of a German announcer speaks confidentially.* JOE *turns the dial. A Japanese announcer's voice solemnly intones a short statement in Japanese ending with "Elton John."* JOE *immediately switches the station. The song "Good-bye, Cruel World" begins to play.* JOE *sits listening for what seems a long time.*

EXTERIOR: LITTLE RAFT. NIGHT.

JOE *is discovered with his ukulele, looking at the sky. He is staring at the millions of stars overhead. He is full of wonder. He is singing "The Cowboy Song."*

JOE: Ee he o he-o cowboy
    Ee he o he-o oooo

Ee he o he-o cowboy, cowboy, cowboy
Under the moon.

I was ridin' my horse
By the Rio Grand-ee
And all the coyotes singin'
In a prairie symphony.
I was ridin' my horse
Down by the Rio Grand-ee
When I seen me a cowboy, cowboy, cowboy
Ridin' towards me.

Ee he o he-o cowboy
Ee he o he-o oooo
Ee he o he-o cowboy, cowboy, cowboy
Under the moon.

He was twirling his guns
And he had a guitar
And we sang us up a sweet old song about love
Under the stars.

Ee he o he-o cowboy
Ee he o he-o oooo
Ee he o he-o cowboy, cowboy, cowboy
Under the moon.

Giddyup.

EXTERIOR: LITTLE RAFT. DAY.

JOE *is chipping golf balls on his Hammacher Schlemmer practice green,
occasionally making a shot, occasionally hitting one into the water.
One of the golf balls gets tossed back onto the raft.* JOE *looks. There is a
mischievous dolphin, who laughs and then submerges.*

JOE: Thank you.

EXTERIOR: LITTLE RAFT. NIGHT.

JOE *sits on the raft, listening to the radio. A Hawaiian disk jockey,* PETE, *comes on.*

PETE (voice-over): This is KRU, Honolulu, speakin' ta ya from the shadow of the Koolau mountains. And here's one that was a hit when I was a kid. "Sukiyaki."

(*The song "Sukiyaki," which became a pop hit in America, even though it's sung in Japanese, begins to play.* JOE *is satisfied and lies back to listen.*)

EXTERIOR: LITTLE RAFT. DAY.

The radio is off. JOE *is trying out his aquatic shoes. Just trying his first tentative steps, he accidentally punctures one of his shoes, so it deflates. He topples over to one side. He swims back to the raft, abandoning his shoes. He turns the radio on, but it's only giving out a little static now. He checks on* PATRICIA *but gets no response. He tries to get something on the radio, but the batteries are too weak now. He turns it off. He notices he's sweating. He shifts, knocking the radio in the ocean. Irritated, he looks up.*

Joe's point of view: The sun looms down, hot and white and huge.

JOE *looks at the sun with concern. He gets out the violin case. He gets the water out and fills the cap and ministers to* PATRICIA. *His lips are parched, but he takes none for himself. He takes off his now well-seasoned safari jacket and puts it over* PATRICIA *to protect her from the sun. We hear a sound, like the hiss of something being seared in a skillet.*

EXTERIOR: LITTLE RAFT. NIGHT.

Again the sky is ablaze with stars. They are even brighter than before. JOE *is looking at them. He's shaking. He has got a fever. He closes his eyes and then opens them again. He looks at the stars again. And shakes his head in disbelief.*

Joe's fevered point of view: stars. What's this? The stars are all connected by little, pale blue lines, and over that are boldly visible the astrological signs: the flying horse, the archer, the twins, and others.

JOE *shakes his head, bewildered and amazed. He blinks and looks again.*

Joe's point of view: starry night. All of the lines and pictures are gone.

JOE *looks and looks. But, no, they are gone. It's just a starry night. He relaxes, closes his eyes, and quakes with fever.*

EXTERIOR: LITTLE RAFT. DAY.

JOE, *very ill with fever, checks the water supply. There's a little less than half a bottle of water left. His lips are deeply cracked. But still he takes no water for himself. He looks up at the sun. The sound of sizzling.*

The sun burns down, bright and big.

JOE *pours a capful of water and gives it to* PATRICIA. *She is still unconscious, but she looks pretty good. It's* JOE *that's really going down the tubes.*

EXTERIOR: LITTLE RAFT. NIGHT.

We come in on Joe's face. JOE *quakes with fever. Then he sees something.* JOE *is entranced by what he sees.*

JOE*'s point of view: night sky. The astrological signs have appeared in the sky again as they did the night before.*

JOE *stares. He's half mad with fever. What is he seeing?*

Joe's point of view: night sky. The dome of astrological signs begins to rotate from horizon to horizon, so that the full panoply of the ancient mythology is revealed.

JOE *is frightened, moved. His eyes fill with tears.*

The signs continue to turn.

JOE *rubs his eyes and looks again.*

Night sky: The sky has become ordinary again.
JOE *wonders if he really saw the astrological signs.*

EXTERIOR: LITTLE RAFT. DAY.

Another scorching day under the sun. JOE *looks very bad. He has got a fever. He's slowly dying of thirst. He gets out the bottle, gives a capful to the still unconscious* PATRICIA, *and then looks at the water level. There's a quarter of a bottle left. He puts the bottle away. He crawls to the raft's edge and plunges his head in the sea. A dolphin sticks his head out of the water and looks at* JOE. JOE *lifts his head out of the water and finds himself looking at the dolphin, who is looking at him. Man and dolphin are just a few feet apart. They regard each other.*

JOE: Hello. My name is Joe.

(*The dolphin makes sounds. It could be talking.*)

JOE: I'm dying. Ahead of schedule.

(*The dolphin disappears back beneath the water.* JOE *lowers his head and lies still.*)

EXTERIOR: LITTLE RAFT. NIGHT.

Again it is a great, starry night. JOE, *weak and sick and bleary-eyed, looks up at the stars. He closes his eyes. He opens them again. Again he is astonished.*
    Joe's point of view: the heavens. All the lines and astrological signs are back, brilliant and splendid.
    JOE *rouses himself, crawling to his knees to look. He stares in utter wonder.*
    The signs begin to rotate again.
    Music: Earlier, in Los Angeles, JOE *stared at the horizon, just before dawn, and big, magical music began to play. But then it*

stopped prematurely. That music begins to play now, but this time it does not stop. It's the big, dramatic pas de deux music from the Nut-cracker Suite.

The astrological signs melt away into Disney dust as a light appears at the horizon.

Another angle on horizon: A light appears at the horizon's edge.

An enormous moon, with slow majesty, rises from the glittering sea, directly to Joe's front.

JOE *and his little raft are utterly dwarfed by this great heavenly body.*

JOE *is on his raft. It is still night. Although he is on the verge of utter collapse, he is so moved by what he sees he clambers his way to his shaky feet and raises his arms over his head in complete reverence. He is dwarfed. He's a bug. The raft is a mote in the eye of God.* JOE *is deeply moved, humbled, awestruck. The moon continues to ascend up and up and out of view.*

JOE *looks at the stars that are simply stars. Sinking to his knees, he presses his hands to his breast.*

JOE: Dear God, whose name I do not know, thank you for my life. I forgot how big . . . thank you for my life.

(JOE *slowly crumbles, physically crumbles from thirst and fever and exhaustion. His eyes dim.*

Joe's point of view: stars. We watch the stars dissolve, and blackness closes in.

Then the blackness starts to fade, to become rosy. We hear the sound of labored breathing, water being poured, someone coughing a little, choking a little, and then recovering. Then we hear Patricia's voice.)

PATRICIA (offscreen): Joe? Joe? Didn't you drink any water for yourself? Joe?

(Joe's point of view: day; light fog. The fog begins to clear. And there, above him, ministering to him, is PATRICIA. *She has the bottle of water, and she's giving him a little to drink at a time.*

Joe's head is cradled in Patricia's arm. She has the bottle at his lips. He pushes it away, croaking weakly.)

JOE: That's for you.

PATRICIA: How long have I been unconscious?

JOE: I don't know. Days. You woke up.

PATRICIA: I guess I did.

JOE: Good.

*(*PATRICIA *gives some more water, over his weak resistance. The bottle has one more sip in it.)*

PATRICIA: Finish this.

JOE: No. You need it.

PATRICIA: I feel pretty good. You look like shit.

JOE: It's good to hear you talking.

PATRICIA: C'mon, drink it. Don't you wanna be in good shape for the Waponis?

JOE: I'll never make it.

PATRICIA: What are you talking about? Look.

*(*PATRICIA *points.* JOE *looks where she points.)*

EXTERIOR: LITTLE RAFT. DAY.

Joe's point of view: An island sporting a big volcano. A little, steady stream of smoke issues from the volcano's mouth. We hear Patricia's voice.

PATRICIA (offscreen): It's a miracle. We must've just lucked into the right tidal current.

(PATRICIA *looks at* JOE. *She makes him take the last sip of water.*)

PATRICIA: What happened to the yacht?

JOE: Struck by lightning.

PATRICIA: No sign of Dagmar or the boys?

JOE: Everything went under.

PATRICIA: Except your trunks.

JOE: Except my trunks. (*He takes a look at the island.*) So that's Waponi Woo.

(*Joe's point of view: island.*

Another angle: We fly over the surface of the ocean to the island, to one hill on the island, on which stands a lookout, EMO. EMO *is scanning the sea with an old telescope on a stand. In his free hand he holds a can of orange soda called Jump. He sips from this with great relish. Then he spots something with the telescope. It's the raft! He carefully puts town his soda, cups his hands, and lets out with a mighty formal cry.*)

EMO: Ah bey!

(*Fifty voices answer from all over the island.*)

VOICES (offscreen): Ho!

EMO: Ah bey!

VOICES (offscreen): Ho!

EMO: Kimo Sabby Sah!

VOICES (offscreen): Ha-ha-ha-ha-ha-ha!

EXTERIOR: LITTLE RAFT. DAY.

JOE *and* PATRICIA *hear the cries and look at each other.*

JOE: What's that?

PATRICIA: I think we've been spotted.

EXTERIOR: ISLAND. LONG STRETCH OF BEACH. DAY.

Outrigger canoes lie along the shore. The excited cries of running natives are heard approaching. And now we see them. It's the Waponis! They are a motley lot, used to the good life. They sport big orange dots on their foreheads. They carry fruit, garlands of flowers, and cans of Jump. They leap into their canoes and head out toward the raft. Their eyes are enhanced with eyeliner.

EXTERIOR: LITTLE RAFT. DAY.

As the canoes reach the raft, the leader of the welcoming group, BAW, *calls out to* JOE.

BAW (in a formal way): Whooa! Are you Joe?

JOE: Yeah.

WELCOMING GROUP (impressed): Whooa!

BAW: Are you Joe Banks?

JOE: Yeah.

BAW (to group): Pelica beeble bum bum!

(*The* WELCOMING GROUP *goes crazy, showering the little raft with a thou-sand flowers.* JOE *and* PATRICIA *exchange a look through the shower of flowers.*)

PATRICIA: I guess they're glad to see us.

(*They are both handed cans of Jump. Natives grab the pop-tops with their teeth and rip them off, smiling.* JOE *and* PATRICIA *drink from the cans of Jump. All the natives cheer. Then hands reach out and pull them gently off their raft and into the canoes. Another canoe's occupants get a grass rope and tie it to the raft.*

Now we see whole flotilla of canoes. JOE *and* PATRICIA *and the whole* WELCOMING GROUP, *covered with flowers and drinking Jump, head for the island, with the raft of trunks in tow. The* WELCOMING GROUP, *led by* BAW, *sing a Polynesian song of greeting that sounds strangely like "Havah Nagilah."*)

EXTERIOR: SHORE OF ISLAND. DAY.

The canoes arrive. Upon reaching the shore JOE *and* PATRICIA *are hoisted onto the shoulders of the natives and carried inland. Then other natives hoist the trunks onto their shoulders and follow. Everybody is sing-ing. Two Waponi men hoisting an enormous spool of handmade red carpet on a wooden yoke lead the way into the jungle.*

EXTERIOR: STRETCH OF JUNGLE. DAY.

The red-carpet unrollers run through a stretch of jungle, unrolling the carpet as they run. Through a thin veil of greenery we see the red-carpet unrollers pass by, on a jungle path. After a second they are followed by JOE *and* PATRICIA *and the full, happy entourage.*

EXTERIOR: CENTER OF VILLAGE. DAY.

Exhausted, the carpet men, their spindle all but spent, stumble into the village's center. Their carpet reaches its tail. They drop to the ground, gasping and proud. The WELCOMING GROUP *arrives with* PATRICIA *and* JOE, *and the whole village turns out and goes nuts. Some of them carry ducks.*

Then from the biggest hut emerges the CHIEF. *Instantly everything stops, and all the natives are lying facedown on the ground, utterly silent. Only* JOE *and* PATRICIA *are left standing to face the* CHIEF. *The* CHIEF *is a big, impressive man with gray hair and in totally traditional native costume. Most of the other natives have some element of Western dress about their person. The* CHIEF *has a sad, rich voice, full of memory and knowledge. He holds a tiki teddy bear. It has atrophied little arms and legs; its hair is standing on end.*

JOE: What is that? A teddy bear?

CHIEF: No. It is my soul.

JOE: I hope you don't lose it.

CHIEF: So do I. I am tobi. Chief.

JOE: This is Patricia Graynamore. I'm Joe Banks. You speak English.

CHIEF: I have learned. You have come to stop the anger of the Woo?

(The CHIEF *points upward.* JOE *looks where he points.*
Joe's point of view: volcano (Big Woo). Smoke steadily issues from the mouth of the Big Woo.
JOE *looks away from the volcano. He looks into the eyes of the* CHIEF.*)*

JOE: Yes.

CHIEF: There was worry that you would not come. You were to come before this.

JOE: Well. I'm here now.

(*The* CHIEF *nods sadly.*)

CHIEF (looking at PATRICIA): You're with him?

PATRICIA: Yes.

(*The* CHIEF *nods sadly.*)

CHIEF: Tonight we will have a big feast. And, then, at the end of the feast, we will climb to the top of the Big Woo, and you will jump in. Okay?

JOE: Okay.

CHIEF: The women will take this woman and make her clean for the feast. (*Shouts to the native women:*) Pelica! Pelica!

(*The native women rise quickly to their feet, giggling and excited, and make off with* PATRICIA.)

PATRICIA (calling out as she is taken): Joe!

JOE: Patricia! (*To the* CHIEF:) Is she gonna be all right?

(*The* CHIEF *nods wearily.*)

CHIEF: And the men will take you and make you right for the feast. (*Shouts to the native men:*) Oliva'! Oliva'!

(*The native men leap up with a shout, seize* JOE, *and carry him off. Other native men follow, carrying the trunks. The* CHIEF, *weary, heads back inside his hut.*)

EXTERIOR: CLEARING. DAY.

The clearing has been set up to clean JOE. *What can only be described as a giant bassinet made out of beautiful, soft greenery has been set up in the clearing, along with many coconut bowls. Into this a violently protesting* JOE, *stark naked, is being pressed by the laughing native men. They dump many bowls of water over him while he desperately tries to hide his genitals, first with his hands and then by turning facedown in the bassinet. Then the men take mounds of fresh fruit that has been cut up and rub them into Joe's flesh.*

    Then six of the native men produce big, shining fish. They hold these fish by the tails. Other men hold JOE *still. Then the men rhythmically beat* JOE *with the fish. They hum to keep time. They are giving him a massage. At first he reacts by screaming, but then he starts to groan, as one does from an important massage.*

EXTERIOR: CLEARING. DAY. A FEW MINUTES LATER.

One of the natives holds forward a tray covered with a thin blue material. JOE *looks at it with interest. The native gently, physically closes Joe's eyes, then blows the contents of the tray—a thin, bright blue powder—directly into Joe's face.* JOE *opens his eyes, a wiser man. They lick the powder off his face.*

EXTERIOR: CLEARING. DAY. A WHILE LATER.

The men are dousing JOE *with water again, only he's sitting up now, eating a piece of fruit.* EMO, *the lookout, offers him a Jump, but* JOE *shakes his head.* EMO *looks amazed and comments to the others in a low voice, in another language. Their reply to Emo's comment is a low "whoa!"; they are incredulous. Then they go back to dousing* JOE. *He*

*likes this treatment by now. Then a look of concern passes over his face,
and he looks down.*

*Joe's point of view: Joe's bare feet. Two natives are chewing the
toenails on his feet.*

JOE: Hey, stop that!

(*The two natives look at him blankly and go back to what they're doing.*
JOE *accepts it. Another native is massaging his scalp, adding a little oil
to Joe's hair. The native combs the hair with his fingers.* JOE *is starting
to look like his old self. Something on the edge of the clearing catches
his eye.*

*Joe's point of view: four steamer trunks, a little stained with salt
but otherwise none the worse for wear.*

JOE, *looking at the trunks, gets an idea.*)

EXTERIOR: ANOTHER CLEARING. DAY.

PATRICIA *is near the end of a makeover by the native women. They are
adorning her freshly washed hair with beautiful flowers and wrap-
ping her sparkling body in a pretty sarong.*

EXTERIOR: THE ISLAND. SUNSET.

The sun sets behind the Big Woo.

EXTERIOR: BONFIRE. NIGHT.

The fire is going full blast in the village. Music.

EXTERIOR: VILLAGE. NIGHT.

*Fire plays on Patricia's face as she's escorted by four village women
into the village feast.*

Patricia's point of view (handheld): as she walks through the village.
    On PATRICIA *(intercut) as she's led through the village.*

PATRICIA: Where's my friend?

(Patricia's point of view [handheld]:)

PATRICIA (continuing): Where's Joe Banks?

(Men dance on dusty drums.
    Natives jump crisscross over the fire, with the band in the background.
    A pig roasts on a spit over a fire.
    On PATRICIA [intercut] as she's led through the village.)

PATRICIA: Is my friend here?

(Patricia's point of view [handheld]: Fire-eaters are on either side of a small volcano.
    The music changes to a new cue: the drum vamp.
    The Fire God emerges from the small volcano.
    PATRICIA *reacts and looks at:)*

EXTERIOR: VILLAGE. NIGHT.

BAW *comes into the playing area, a half-moon circle of natives. He clicks the sticks of his fingers. He looks sternly from side to side, with his hands on his hips.*

BAW (crying out): Oliva'!

(This is the cue for the storytelling music to begin. BAW *does a little Waponi dance in a tight circle as he recites:)*

BAW: A whila way Waponi Woo
I sangda wangda offda blue
I sangda wangda and I aw saw
The whorl in all a-raw dindour!
Meckalecka?
Yapa
Yapa*ya*
Yapa
Yapa*ya*
Yapa
Yapa*ya*
Sup up vulca.

(*The women scream.*)

BAW: Terra not firma.
To take to tobi, put the pants!

(*The men cheer, and* BAW *picks up the tiki doll to hand it to the Fire God, who then goes back into the volcano.*)

INTERIOR: VILLAGE. NIGHT.

PATRICIA *is standing. Everyone else is below frame. There is dead silence.*
Patricia's point of view: the CHIEF. *He's decked out, and he sits in his chair. His teddy bear/soul doll is in another, and there are empty chairs on each side.*
PATRICIA *is gestured to sit in the chair on the Chief's left.*

CHIEF: You look good, now.

PATRICIA: Thank you.

CHIEF: Joe Banks said your name is Graynamore.

PATRICIA: Yes, it is.

CHIEF: I've had talks with Samuel Harvey Graynamore.

PATRICIA: He's my father.

(*The* CHIEF *nods sadly.*)

CHIEF: Your father is like the Big Woo. He must be fed, or he will destroy the world.

PATRICIA: Do you know where my friend, Joe Banks, is?

CHIEF: Maybe he ran away? Maybe he don't want to jump in the Big Woo.

CHIEF (calling to the natives): Oliva'! Oliva'! Bum bum bum.

EXTERIOR: VILLAGE. NIGHT.

Two natives swing on grass ropes, from the top of the frame. They pass each other on their way to the gongs that hang at either end of the frame. They slam into the gongs and then fall into two little broken piles.
     The CHIEF *reacts.*

EXTERIOR: VILLAGE. NIGHT.

Back to the gong scene as others bearing stretchers quickly carry the men away and as big drums are upended and rolled away in the wake of the stretchers, off to the right.

EXTERIOR: VILLAGE. NIGHT.

The natives all rise and face the Big Woo and sing.

NATIVES: WO-O-O-O-O.

EXTERIOR: VOLCANO. NIGHT.

The volcano erupts. The CHIEF *reacts to the eruption.*

CHIEF: The Woo wants his flesh!

EXTERIOR: VILLAGE. NIGHT.

Natives react and scream, and their screams turn to cheers as we cut to: JOE.
    He appears at the top of a grand staircase. He descends as the music resumes.
    The people face him and cheer as they turn with him as he walks across to the CHIEF, *and stands before him.*

CHIEF: So. You didn't run away.

JOE: No. I made a deal and I'll stick by it.

(*The* CHIEF *nods sadly.* JOE *sits down in the third chair.*)

JOE: How do you like my tux?

PATRICIA: Pretty great.

JOE: I thought I might as well go out in style.

PATRICIA: You're really going to do it?

JOE: Yeah.

(JOE *and* PATRICIA *have been talking across the* CHIEF, *who sits between them. Now a groaning native, holding his jaw, comes forward and, after prostrating himself, speaks excitedly to the* CHIEF, *addressing him as tobi, and continuing in another language. The* CHIEF *listens and then waves him away. The groaning native departs.*)

PATRICIA: What's wrong with that man?

CHIEF: His teeth have holes in them from drinking orange soda. Jump.

(*The* CHIEF *hates Jump.*)

JOE: What did he want you to do about it?

CHIEF: There are those who want a man who will fix the holes.

PATRICIA: A dentist.

CHIEF: Yes.

(*The* CHIEF *hates this idea. The volcano thunders again. This time it shakes the ground a little. They look.*

The CHIEF *and company's point of view: Big Woo. This time the volcano lets out two tongues of flame and a shower of sparks.*

The CHIEF *and company look at the volcano. The* CHIEF *then looks at* JOE.)

CHIEF: Joe Banks. We are the children of children, and we live as we are shown. Now a change has come. The Waponis like this soda, and no one among my people will jump into the Big Woo. They trade with this man, (*to* PATRICIA) your father, for a hero. We have no hero of our own. So we give this man the right to dig holes in the ground under us like the Jump digs holes in our teeth, and in some short time we will be nothing but holes. I am the tobi. I cannot be the hero. It is my place to hope for my people. But the Woo calls, and no one from among my people says, "I will go to my end for the rest of you." Joe Banks. We are not your people. Let us die. Take a boat and your woman and go. (*Jerks his thumb:*) Don't jump in the Big Woo.

JOE: I have no people of my own, Chief. I'm my only hope for a hero.

(*The Big Woo thunders again. They all look.
    The feast grows quiet and somber.*)

CHIEF: Once more I'll call among the Waponis for a hero.

(*The* CHIEF *stands. The Waponis abase themselves.*)

CHIEF (solemnly): Who knew woe sue-weigh? Who knew woe? (*He waits; as no one moves, he calls out once more.*) Drama said, said sue-weigh? (*He waits; when no one moves, he is disgusted with them; he speaks with finality and dismissal.*) I na box, bum, pelica. Box.

(*The Waponis slowly get up, shamefaced. The* CHIEF *sits.*)

CHIEF (to JOE and PATRICIA): They are all afraid to die. There is no hero among them. They deserve to die.

(JOE *stands.*)

JOE: Take me to the volcano.

(*Natives cheer. They form an aisle again, leading off in the direction of the Big Woo. Flaming torches dot the aisle. The natives start the same call and response they had going when Joe's raft was first sighted.* EMO *calls and the natives respond. This call and response continues through all the following.* JOE *walks off, down the aisle. The* CHIEF *follows him. Before* PATRICIA *can follow the* CHIEF, *the crowd closes in, following* JOE *up the mountain.* PATRICIA *tries to reach* JOE.)

EXTERIOR: VILLAGE. NIGHT.

PATRICIA: Joe! Joe!

(*But her voice can't be heard above the din of the call and response. She's restrained by the women in the village.*)

EXTERIOR: FOOT OF TRAIL. NIGHT.

A head torchbearer leads the way up the mountain path. He carries a heavy, lit torch that he swings from side to side with a ritual motion. With each swing he lights another permanent tiki sconce along the path's upward progress. He is followed by JOE, *dapper and alone.* JOE *in turn is followed by the* CHIEF, *who walks with a ritual movement, not unlike the bent-kneed gait of a sumo wrestler, leaning first on one leg, then on the other. He is assisted in this gyration by two lackeys, one to his left, one to his right, who catch him as he leans to his most extreme angle and who gently shove him back the other way. Behind the* CHIEF, *comes the general native population, all of whom carry torches.*

Patricia's point of view: The whole village is going up the trail, with JOE *and the* CHIEF *at the head of the column. Some of the natives carry ducks.*

EXTERIOR: SIDE OF THE BIG WOO. TRAIL. NIGHT.

Flaming torches now delineate the trail up the mountain. The line they describe looks very like a German expressionist version of a lightning bolt. The Big Woo is rumbling more and more. The whole sky over the mountain is suffused with red.

EXTERIOR: WITHIN COLUMN. NIGHT.

PATRICIA *struggles. She's slowly struggling up the length of the column.*

PATRICIA (starting to get hysterical): Joe! Joe! Don't do it! Don't do it!

EXTERIOR: HEAD OF COLUMN. NIGHT.

JOE *and the* CHIEF *are silent and solemn and focused. They arrive at a spot just below the rim of the volcano. There is a little well-worn trail leading from where they stand to the rim.*

JOE: Is there any ceremony or anything?

CHIEF: No. You just jump in.

(JOE *nods.* PATRICIA *breaks through the crowd and throws herself at Joe's feet. She's sobbing.*)

PATRICIA: Don't do it! Please don't do it, Joe! I love you! I've fallen in love with you! I've never loved anybody! I don't know how it happened! And I've never even slept with you or anything, and now you're going to kill yourself!

(JOE *pulls her to her feet. The* CHIEF *takes a step away, to give them privacy.*)

JOE: You love me?

PATRICIA: Yes, I love you! I can feel my heart! I feel like I'm going crazy! You can't die and leave me here on this stinking earth without you!

JOE: I've got to do it.

PATRICIA: Why? The Chief doesn't even want you to do it.

JOE: 'Cause I've wasted my whole life. And now I'm going to die. I've got a chance to die like a man, and I'm going to take it! I've got to take it!

PATRICIA: I love you!

JOE: I love you, too. I've never loved anybody, either. It's great. I'm glad. But the timing stinks.

(JOE *kisses* PATRICIA, *waves to the* CHIEF, *and starts to walk up the little path. The natives are silent, staring. The* CHIEF *is sad.* PATRICIA *is rooted, staring after him, stricken. When* JOE *has just about reached the sum-*

mit, PATRICIA *wakes from her trance and bolts up the little path after him.*

EXTERIOR: UNDERSIDE OF PLATFORM. NIGHT.

Throughout the following, occasionally we cut to a carved wooden figure of an alarmed but committed little man, who is under the platform holding it up. Of course, he's actually an inanimate strut, but as his little knees quake ever more violently under the platform's oppressive weight, we fear for the moment when he, and therefore the platform on which JOE *and* PATRICIA *stand, will give way and fall into the volcano.*

EXTERIOR: LITTLE SHELF ON MOUTH OF THE BIG WOO. NIGHT.

Behind PATRICIA *and* JOE *are flames and sparks and smoke.*

PATRICIA: Joe!

JOE: Get out of here! Go back down!

PATRICIA: No.

JOE: Please let me do what I've got to do!

PATRICIA: Marry me!

JOE: What!

PATRICIA: Marry me! (*Shouting down the hill.*) Chief! Chief! Could you come up here, please?

JOE: What the hell are you doing?

PATRICIA: I want him to marry us.

JOE: I'm jumping into a volcano!

PATRICIA: So marry me, and then jump into the volcano.

(*The* CHIEF *arrives*)

CHIEF: What?

PATRICIA: Could you marry us?

CHIEF: Okay.

JOE: I don't want to get married!

PATRICIA: What's the problem? You afraid of the commitment? You'll have to love me and honor me for about thirty seconds! You can't handle that?

JOE: (to the CHIEF) All right. Marry us.

PATRICIA: Thank you!

JOE: You're welcome!

CHIEF: Do you want to marry her?

JOE: Yes!

CHIEF: Do you want to marry him?

PATRICIA: Yes!

CHIEF: You're married.

PATRICIA: Thank you, Chief.

CHIEF: I'm going now.

(*The* CHIEF *leaves. The volcano has been roaring louder and louder.* JOE *stares into it.*)

PATRICIA: Don't jump in.

JOE: I want you to listen to me, Patricia, because these are my last words. I gotta be brave. I gotta jump in. Good-bye.

EXTERIOR: TONGUE OF VOLCANO PLATFORM. NIGHT.

JOE *is already out on the diving board.* PATRICIA *joins him.*

JOE: Patricia. Don't come out here.

PATRICIA: You're not the only one with last words. I have last words, too.

JOE: All right, talk. Say your say.

PATRICIA: I can't think of anything. Listen, I'm jumping in with you.

JOE: Oh no you're not!

PATRICIA: Whither thou goest, I go.

JOE: I'll knock you out, I'll throw you down.

PATRICIA: And take away my freedom of choice?

(*An eruption shakes them. They clutch each other.*)

PATRICIA (continuing with a new, quiet sincerity): Joe, nobody knows anything. We'll take this leap, and we'll see. We'll jump and we'll see. That's life.

JOE: I saw the moon when we were out there on the ocean. Shining down on everything. I'd been miserable for so long. Years of my life wasted, afraid. I've been a long time coming here to meet you. A long time on a crooked road. Did I ever tell you that the first time I saw you, I felt like I had seen you before?

PATRICIA: You're not going anywhere without me.

(*They kiss. Another quake from below. They look down at the magma and then at each other. They are shining with a light sweat.*)

JOE: So what are we hoping for here?

PATRICIA: A miracle.

JOE: Okay. I love you.

PATRICIA: You do?

JOE: Yeah. This is it.

PATRICIA: Okay.

JOE: This is it.

PATRICIA: Okay.

JOE: Give me your hand.

(*Close-up of them clasping hands.*)

JOE: This is it.

PATRICIA: I'm with you, baby.

JOE: Okay.

(*New angle: They jump in and are ejected from the volcano.*)

EXTERIOR: OCEAN. NIGHT.

JOE *and* PATRICIA *plunge into the water and resurface.*

JOE: Patricia?

PATRICIA: Joe?

JOE: Why aren't you dead?

PATRICIA: Why aren't you dead?

JOE: The volcano. . . it blew us out. We jumped in and it blew us out.

(JOE *starts to laugh as it dawns on him.* PATRICIA *smiles, pleased.*)

PATRICIA: It's a miracle, isn't it?

JOE: Sure it's a miracle. I would say it's at least a miracle. There goes Waponi Woo.

EXTERIOR: ISLAND. NIGHT.

The island is exploding and sinking.

EXTERIOR: OCEAN. NIGHT.

PATRICIA: We sure lucked out.

JOE: Yeah! Well, yeah, but . . .

PATRICIA: But what?

JOE: I hate to bring it up but, we're a thousand miles from no place. We're gonna drown.

PATRICIA: Well, I think we're gonna be all right.

JOE: I don't see how.

(*Angle on water: The four trunks pop up.*)

PATRICIA: See?

(*They swim out of frame in the direction of the trunks.*)

EXTERIOR: RAFT CONSTRUCTED. NIGHT.

JOE *and* PATRICIA *are on the raft.*

PATRICIA: Isn't this romantic? Who gets a honeymoon like this?

JOE: Yeah. But there's this . . .

PATRICIA: What's the matter?

JOE: I still have this . . . I still have a problem.

PATRICIA: What?

JOE: I have a brain cloud.

PATRICIA: We jumped into the volcano, but that worked out. We fell in the ocean, but now we have a raft. So you have a brain cloud. It's always going to be something, Joe.

(*New angle: They kiss in silhouette on the raft.*)

PATRICIA: What is a brain cloud anyway?

JOE: Well, it's a . . . maybe I should get a second opinion.

PATRICIA: You didn't get a second opinion about something called a brain cloud?

(PATRICIA *chuckles.*)

JOE: All right, all right. I guess I just felt . . .

PATRICIA: What are you, a hypochondriac?

JOE: A bit. I *was*. No more.

PATRICIA: I don't think there's anything wrong with you.

JOE: But Dr. Ellison told me . . .

PATRICIA: So, some quack told you . . . Dr. Ellison?

JOE: Yeah?

PATRICIA: That's my father's doctor.

JOE: It is?

PATRICIA: Yeah. Dr. Ellison doesn't have any other patients. My father owns Dr. Ellison.

JOE: But why? . . .

PATRICIA: He set you up.

JOE: Who?

PATRICIA: My father.

JOE: You mean he? . . .

PATRICIA: Yeah.

JOE: Set me up?

PATRICIA: Yeah.

JOE: No.

PATRICIA: Yeah.

JOE: No.

(JOE *starts hitting his head with the palm of his hand.*)

PATRICIA: Hey, Joe, Joe.

JOE: My whole life I've been a fall guy. I don't have a brain cloud.

PATRICIA: A brain cloud? You think they could've thought up something better than a brain cloud.

JOE: My whole life . . .

PATRICIA: Joe?

JOE: What?

PATRICIA: Your whole life is ahead of you.

JOE: Oh, yeah, I guess that's true. And you know what else?

PATRICIA: What?

JOE: I still have my luggage.

PATRICIA: Where do you think we're going to end up?

JOE: Away from the things of man, my dear, away from the things of man.

(*"And They Lived Happily Ever After" appears on screen as a music box begins to play.*)

FADE OUT

THE END

Five Corners

The cast of *Five Corners* includes:

Linda	Jodie Foster
Harry	Tim Robbins
James	Todd Graff
Heinz Sabantino	John Turturro
Melanie	Elizabeth Berridge
Mrs. Sabantino	Rose Gregorio
Mazola	Gregory Rozakis
Sullivan	John Seitz

Music	James Newton Howard
Costume Designer	Peggy Farrell
Production Designer	Adrianne Lobel
Editor	Andy Blumenthal
Director of Photography	Fred Murphy
Executive Producers	George Harrison and Denis O'Brien
Producers	Forrest Murray and Tony Bill
Writer	John Patrick Shanley
Director	Tony Bill

EXTERIOR: FIVE CORNERS. NIGHT. A GREAT BIG MOON IN THE SKY.

Music: The likes of Joe Cocker and Gracie Slick, burned out, funky, and full of romance, sing "Santa Lucia" as a duet as the credits roll.

> *Now under the nickel moon,*
> *Streetlights are glowing.*
> *O'er the blue windows,*
> *New winds are blowing.*
> *Here hearts are beating fast,*
> *Pure joy invites us,*
> *And though it cannot last,*
> *All things delight us.*
> *Look how the night flies by,*
> *Wild before it dies,*
> *Santa Lucia,*
> *Santa Lucia.*

EXTERIOR: TRUGLIO'S FIRE ESCAPE. NIGHT.

The moon turns into a scarily carved jack o'lantern with a candle burning within. The song concludes as the credits roll.

> *Home of street poetry,*
> *Realm of rough harmony,*
> *Santa Lucia,*
> *Santa Lucia.*

The camera pulls back slowly to reveal Lucky Truglio's fire escape. LUCKY *plays a beat-up violin. The tune is "Santa Lucia." Beside him sits the jack o'lantern. He is lit by the soft golden light of his living room window.* LUCKY *plays with a fervor inspired by the sight he sees across the way.*

EXTERIOR: JAMES'S ROOF. NIGHT.

Lucky Truglio's point of view: on the roof across the way the silhouette of a guy and girl kissing passionately, high above them the moon.

EXTERIOR: JAMES'S ROOF. NIGHT.

The kissing couple: At the moment that they break apart for air, JAMES, *a slender, intense, handsome, somewhat gawky guy of twenty-one, his eyes brilliant from kissing, gasps for breath.* LINDA, *twenty-two, pretty and tough and strong, ignoring the stars in her own eyes, puts a cigarette in her mouth.* JAMES *plucks it out and tosses it. He goes to kiss her again. She wants to kiss him but instead, she puts another cigarette in her mouth. He plucks the cigarette and tosses it this time as well. Now he pulls her lips slowly to his.*

LINDA (blurting out): Listen, Jimmy, I don't wanna see you anymore.

(JAMES *is surprised and utterly devastated.*)
    Linda's point of view: HEINZ *on the rooftop.*)

EXTERIOR. TRUGLIO'S FIRE ESCAPE. NIGHT.

LUCKY *is still playing on his fire escape. The window behind him flies open, and his wife,* MRS. TRUGLIO, *sticks her big head out.*

MRS. TRUGLIO (yelling): Lucky, would you shut up with that and get in the house!

(LUCKY *hits a very sour note, breaks off playing, and makes to go in. He looks across the way one more time.*)

EXTERIOR: JAMES'S ROOF. NIGHT.

Now there is only the silouhette of JAMES *alone, his head hanging.*

EXTERIOR: TRUGLIO'S FIRE ESCAPE. NIGHT.

LUCKY *goes in his window.*
      The camera lingers and then comes in close on the jack o'lantern again.

EXTERIOR: SHOPMERIT. NIGHT.

The jack o'lantern turns into Castro's grinning face. CASTRO *is wearing a hat just like Fidel Castro, and stuck in his grinning mouth is the smoking stub of a lit cigar. He's seventeen, cute as hell, and full of mischief, the original imp. The camera pulls back slightly, revealing that his face is next to a big red plastic O. He sticks a cherry bomb behind the O and lights it with his cigar.*

CASTRO (yelling): Drop me!

(CASTRO *drops out of sight as the letter blows to bits.*
      CASTRO *lands on the sidewalk next to* WILLIE, *who's brushing off his shoulders.* WILLIE *is very plump, seventeen, and already looks like someone's uncle. He is also a German immigrant.*)

WILLIE: Vow!

CASTRO: Am I not wonderful?

WILLIE: You are zumting, I swear!

CASTRO: Okay, gimme another lift.

(WILLIE *hunkers down, so* CASTRO *can climb on his shoulders.*
      We see WILLIE, CASTRO, *and the sign that once reads* SHOPMERIT *but is now missing the* O.)

INTERIOR: RED IMPALA PARKED OUTSIDE A BAR. NIGHT.

SAL INZIO, *a chubby Italian guy, twenty, black leather jacket, greased hair, sits unhappily behind the wheel. In the backseat are two girls,* MELANIE *and* BRITA. MELANIE *is Italian, twenty, heavily made-up, lots of teased hair.* BRITA *is Nordic, twenty-two, also heavily made-up.* MELANIE *is stoned; she is often stoned.* BRITA *is stoned, she is always stoned.* BRITA *is holding open a brown paper bag while* MELANIE *squeezes tubes of airplane glue into it.*

SAL: What are you doin' now?

MELANIE: Glue.

SAL: You just took the pills.

BRITA: Those downs were garbage.

(*"Garbage" is Brita's favorite word, and she lingers over it lovingly.*)

SAL: Melanie, why don't you sit up here with me?

MELANIE: Don't mess up my thoughts, Sal. This is hard. (*She finishes squeezing the tubes.*) Okay. That's it.

(BRITA *rolls back the top of the bag and puts it over her nose and mouth. She breathes in heavily a few times and offers the bag to* MELANIE, *who takes it and does the same.* MELANIE *takes the bag away from her face. She's really ripped.*)

MELANIE: I'm flyin', man! I'm flyin' from my friggin' feet! Brita! Can you see me?

BRITA: Go, cousin! Fly your friggin' wings!

SAL: What a pair a freakin' debutantes! Melanie, you got glue on your beak! All right, I can goddamn fly, too!

(SAL *throws the car in gear and peels out.*)

EXTERIOR: SHOPMERIT. NIGHT.

A close-up of CASTRO, *his face next to a big red plastic R. He sticks a cherry bomb behind the letter and lights it with his cigar.*

CASTRO: (yelling): Drop me!

(CASTRO *drops out of sight as the letter blows to bits.*
      Now CASTRO, WILLIE, *the sign, and the street behind them can be seen.* CASTRO *and* WILLIE *have their backs to us as they look up at the sign. It now reads* SH   IT.)

INTERIOR: SAL'S IMPALA. STREET. NIGHT

SAL *is hunched over the wheel of his red Impala, very pissed off, driving very fast.*

EXTERIOR: SHOPMERIT. NIGHT.

CASTRO *and* WILLIE, *their backs still to us, regard the sign overhead. We hear their voices.*

WILLIE: It is not as it should be.

CASTRO: It's beautiful!

WILLIE: There's too much space between the letters. My eye cannot see it together as one word.

(*Sal's red Impala screeches to a halt in the street behind* WILLIE *and* CASTRO. *They turn around.* SAL *rolls down the window on the passenger side.*)

SAL (calling out to WILLIE and CASTRO): Hey, you wanna couple a broads?

(CASTRO *and* WILLIE *approach the car.*)

CASTRO: *Qué pasa,* my friend?

SAL: I wanna know if you're willin' to take a couple a broads off my hands?

(CASTRO *looks in the car.*)

CASTRO: What's wrong with 'em?

INTERIOR: SAL'S IMPALA. NIGHT.

Castro's point of view: the backseat. MELANIE *and* BRITA *stare stupidly at* CASTRO.

EXTERIOR. SHOPMERIT. NIGHT.

SAL *leans out the window.*

SAL (speaking to WILLIE and CASTRO confidentially): They're totally ripped outta their gourds, all right? I'm tired a lookin' at 'em in my rear-view mirror, and I want 'em outta the car, *capisce?* You want 'em or not?

(WILLIE, *very excited and puzzled, taps* CASTRO.)

WILLIE (speaking confidentially to CASTRO): Vhat is he saying?

CASTRO: He wants us to take the girls.

WILLIE: Really? That's marvelous. Isn't it?

(CASTRO *doesn't answer.*)

CASTRO (turning back to SAL): Five dollars.

SAL: Five dollars what?

CASTRO: Five dollars we'll take the broads.

(SAL *looks at the girls. They're totally vacated.* SAL *decides.*)

SAL (handing CASTRO five dollars): They're all yours.

(CASTRO *and* WILLIE *help the girls out of the car. The car screeches away, leaving lots of rubber. The girls look after the car absently.*)

WILLIE (to BRITA): Boy, are vee gonna have a lotta fun!

(BRITA *doesn't respond. She's unaware of Willie's existence.* MELANIE *becomes gradually aware of* CASTRO.)

MELANIE: Who are you?

CASTRO: I'm Castro.

MELANIE: Where's your beard?

CASTRO: I left it in my other suit.

(CASTRO *puts his hat on her and kisses* MELANIE *on both cheeks, like a Frenchman. She's hazily puzzled.*

A lot of rubber can be heard returning. Sal's car has returned, having quickly rounded the block. It halts by CASTRO *and* WILLIE. SAL *sticks his head out the window.*)

SAL: Hey. I forgot their luggage.

(SAL *sticks his hands out the window. In each is a used glue bag. He drops them in the street and peels out again. He's gone.*)

MELANIE: What's goin' on?

CASTRO: Happy Halloween.

(MELANIE *looks at him, tilting her head like a curious bird.*)

EXTERIOR: TRUGLIO'S FIRE ESCAPE. MORNING. EARLY SUNLIGHT.

*The place where*LUCKY *played his violin the night before is empty except for some flowerpots and a mop.*

EXTERIOR: JAMES'S ROOF. DAY.

The sun-reddened roof where JAMES *and* LINDA *kissed the night before.*

EXTERIOR: SHOPMERIT. DAY.

The letters are missing from the sign. MURRAY *and* GEORGE, *the store-owners, are unlocking the metal accordion gates. They are white-haired, old-world Jews.* GEORGE *picks up a piece of red plastic from the sidewalk and thinks to look up. He points to the vandalized sign.* MURRAY *looks up, sees the sign, tears off his hat, and throws it on the ground.*

A STREETCLEANER *sweeps past* MURRAY *and* GEORGE *with his heavily bristled broom.*

EXTERIOR: FIVE CORNERS. DAY.

The wind blows empty and hollow through Five Corners.

*Three street signs fan out from a pole. The signs say*ARCHER STREET, TAYLOR AVENUE, *and* FTETLEY AVENUE.

The STREETCLEANER *sweeps his way down the block. The wind stirs up the confettilike remains of thousands and thousands of autumn leaves.*

EXTERIOR: MR. GLASCOW'S APARTMENT. DAY.

Establishing shot.

INTERIOR: A SMALL, NEAT, DRAB APARTMENT FULL OF BOOKS. DAY.

Music: some rather tight-assed Bach is playing on a not very good radio. The camera pans over a few of the book titles: The Teaching of Algebra, Understanding Algebra, Introduction to Algebra.

Now we see MR. GLASCOW, *in his cheap summer suit, correcting papers at a little table. He's a very bald, judgmental, anal, evil guy. A cruel little smile plays on his thin lips as he red-pencils student tests with a touch of savagery.*

The tests are in two piles, corrected and uncorrected. Mr. Glascow's hand writes in red, "58% YOU HAVE FAILED!" *and tosses the paper on the corrected pile. The pencil quickly goes through the next test, checking correct answers, and* x*ing the others. This test has a lot of* X*'s. He writes* "16%" *on the top of the page, followed by* "YOU HAVE NO HOPE OF PASSING THIS COURSE."

We see the whole of the mean little apartment. MR. GLASCOW *puts the tests in his briefcase, snaps down the lid efficiently, and makes for the door.*

EXTERIOR: MR. GLASCOW'S APARTMENT. DAY.

Point of view from the apartment, which is part of a green-lawned housing complex made of dark red brick. The housing complex is called Parkchester and is located in the East Bronx. MR. GLASCOW *comes out the entranceway.*

EXTERIOR: PARKCHESTER. OVAL. DAY.

A public fountain in Parkchester. MR. GLASCOW *scatters some pigeons that an old lady is trying to teach a young girl to feed.*

EXTERIOR: STREETCLEANER SWEEPING ALONG THE CURB. DAY.

He spots a dollar bill before his broom. His eyes light up. He reaches for it. A foot snaps down on it. He looks up. It's MR. GLASCOW. *He smiles in triumph, reaches down, and snatches up the bill.*

MR. GLASCOW: Herman, isn't it? Herman Hillman?

STREETCLEANER (puzzled): Yeah?

MR. GLASCOW: I was your algebra teacher, Herman. I see you ended up just about where I thought you would.

(MR. GLASCOW *stuffs the bill into his pocket and brushes by the* STREET-CLEANER.)

EXTERIOR: VACANT LOT. DAY.

The lot, replete with trees, bushes, and garbage, rises up from the side-walk. MR. GLASCOW *walks toward an elevated train station that is about a half a block away. He walks toward us. We hear a small, dull thud. An almost imperceptible shock goes through his body. He looks puzzled. He turns around to see if someone is behind him, but there's nobody there. When he turns, we see that a big arrow with red feathers is sticking out of his back. Seeing that there's nobody behind him, he starts walking again. But then he stops. Now he suspects that there's something in his back. He reaches to touch it. But he never makes it. He falls face first, dead on the ground, the big arrow sticking out of his cheap suit like the ultimate red pencil.*

EXTERIOR: MILLARD FILLMORE HIGH SCHOOL. DAY.

A second-rate public high school in the Bronx. We're at the main entrance, where one late student runs up the front steps and enters.

INTERIOR: SCHOOL RESTROOM. DAY.

CASTRO *smokes a cigar.* WILLIE *stands next to him, reading Sgt. Rock comic book; he shakes his head in disbelief.*

WILLIE: All zey do in this book is kill German guys.

CASTRO: You shouldn't read Sgt. Rock, Willie. It always upsets you.

(*An electric school bell rings loudly.*)

CASTRO: Here we go.

INTERIOR: CLASSROOM. DAY.

It's full of students, but there is no teacher. Lots of noise and movement. CASTRO *sits placidly, his hat on his desk, no cigar.* WILLIE *continues to read and be shocked by the antics of Sgt. Rock. A middle-aged* MATRON *enters, a member of the faculty.*

MATRON: All right. All right. Quiet, please! Please take your seats. Thank you. It seems Mr. Glascow's a few minutes late this morning, so I'll moderate till he arrives. My name is Mrs. Paddock. Stop brushing your hair, dear, you're only making it worse. Sit, please? Thank you. Now where did you leave off yesterday?

GOOD GIRL: We had the midterm.

MATRON: Oh. So then today you would have picked up with . . .

(*But right then another member of the faculty, a* FAT GUY *in short sleeves, obviously upset, enters, goes to the* MATRON, *and whispers emphatically in her ear. She's shocked.*)

MATRON (unintentionally raising her voice): He was what?

FAT GUY (still trying to speak confidentially): He was murdered.

MATRON (forgetting herself): Murdered!

(*The* GOOD GIRL, *who, like all good girls, is sitting at the front of the room, hears the conversation between the two faculty members first. Her reaction is immediate and hysterical. She jumps out of her seat.*)

GOOD GIRL (yelling to the class): Oh, my God, Mr. Glascow's been murdered!

(*The class's reaction is stunned silence for a moment. Then* CASTRO *starts to applaud. Others follow suit. Soon the whole class is applauding. A* STUPID GIRL *leans over to a* GUY *in the next row.*)

STUPID GIRL (asking seriously): Does this mean we all pass?

(*The* GUY *shrugs, not knowing.*)

EXTERIOR: A LONG STRETCH OF SIDEWALK. DAY.

Along the sidewalk bops HEINZ, *in a strap T-shirt, carrying an old gym bag.* HEINZ *is a very bad, peculiar guy. His skin is waxy and white; his eyes are black, bright, and insane. He's very muscular. His hair is black, cut very short, almost a crew cut. Around the crown of his head is a large circular scar where no hair grows. Needless to say, this is a strange, dangerous fellow.*

INTERIOR: SHOPMERIT, AN OLD-FASHIONED DELI. DAY.

MURRAY *and* GEORGE *are behind the counter.* GEORGE *is contentedly decorating a tray of potato salad with carrot sticks and parsley.* MURRAY *is fuming.*

MURRAY: Why did I ever leave Russia!

GEORGE: Because they burned down your house.

MURRAY: So here they blow up my store. What's the difference?

GEORGE: They blew up some letters, Murray.

MURRAY: So far!

GEORGE: So far. So while you're waiting for the next attack, why not decorate the macaroni salad? Do that thing with the tomato that I can't do. Uh-oh.

(*George's point of view: the entrance.*
HEINZ *is walking in. He smiles. This is not a good thing when* HEINZ *does it. He looks around like somebody who hasn't been in a store in a long time.*

MURRAY *and* GEORGE *wait behind the counter as* HEINZ *walks in. They're holding their collective breath, waiting for* HEINZ *to strike.*)

GEORGE: Hi, Heinz. Long time, no see.

HEINZ: I was in prison.

MURRAY: We know.

GEORGE: But, you're out now.

HEINZ: Yeah. Just. (*Notices the pie on the counter.*) How much for the pie?

MURRAY: Two dollars.

(HEINZ *spits on the pie.*)

HEINZ: How much is it now?

MURRAY: Now? Now, it's nothing.

(HEINZ *nods, walks away with the pie, leaving* MURRAY *and* GEORGE *looking after him.*)

GEORGE: So they let him out.

MURRAY: That boy is a real Cossack.

EXTERIOR: SHOPMERIT. DAY.

HEINZ *walks to the curb with his pie, sits down, and starts to eat it with his hands. A mailman comes walking down the block. He sees* HEINZ *and quickly crosses the street.*

EXTERIOR: SAL'S HOUSE. DAY.

Establishing shot.

INTERIOR: SAL'S BEDROOM. DAY.

SAL *is sleeping.* MRS. INZIO *enters. She's dressed for the day. She's Sal's mother. She pulls open the big track curtains, and sunlight floods the room.* SAL *is not asleep. He's lying on his bed, staring at the ceiling.*

MRS. INZIO: Good mornin'!

SAL: Good mornin'.

MRS. INZIO: Why you sleepin' so late?

SAL: I wasn't sleepin'. I ain't slept all night.

MRS. INZIO: Then what are you still doin' in the bed?

SAL: I'm depressed, Ma. I'm feelin' real depressed.

MRS. INZIO: Whatsamatter, baby?

SAL: You know Melanie?

MRS. INZIO: What d'you mean, do I know Melanie? A course I know Melanie!

SAL: Well, we hadda fight last night.

MRS. INZIO: So what? So make it up.

SAL: I don't know.

MRS. INZIO: I know. Make it up with her. She'll make up with you, Sally. She loves you.

SAL: I don't know, Ma. I gave her to some guy.

MRS. INZIO: You gave her?

SAL: I got mad, and I paid some guy five dollars to just take her away.

MRS. INZIO: You shouldn't a done that, Sal. That was hard.

SAL: I know. I feel bad.

MRS. INZIO: All right. First thing. Don't tell your father. His eyes are all popped out as it is.

SAL: Okay.

MRS. INZIO: Second thing. Find Melanie.

SAL: Okay. I miss her already.

MRS. INZIO: Now what do you want for breakfast?

INTERIOR: PET STORE. DAY.

A small tropical fish is being chased by a net.
   The net slowly, gracefully follows the fish and catches it. It's obviously being guided by a practiced hand.
   LINDA *lifts the fish from its tank. She places it in a water-filled plastic bag as* TIM, *a serious kid, watches. A bell jingles as the street door opens.* LINDA *looks to the door.* TIM, *who's quite short, tries to get a better look at the fish in the bag.* JAMES *walks in. Through the big window behind him can be seen an entrance to the Bronx Zoo; there's a prominent*

sign. Linda's attitude toward JAMES *is apprehensive but firm. The kid,* TIM, *whom* LINDA *has forgotten, is peering upward into the bag she's holding.*

LINDA (to JAMES): What are you doing here? (*To* TIM:) What are you staring at?

TIM: That's the wrong fish.

(TIM *is caught between* JAMES *and* LINDA.)

JAMES: Forgive me, but I just caught a flash why you kissed me off!

LINDA: Who asked ya?

TIM (pointing to another fish in the tank): That's the one I want.

JAMES: What d'you think? You think I don't think? I know what you're doin'. I know exactly what you're doin'!

LINDA: You don't know nothin'.

JAMES: Heinz is back. I just saw him.

LINDA (not surprised): He is?

JAMES: You're tryin' to protect me!

LINDA: I am not!

JAMES: But when it's me that should be protectin' you!

LINDA: Like the last time? No thanks!

(JAMES *falls silent. She has hurt him.* TIM *takes this opportune lull in the argument to make his point.*)

TIM (pointing to the fish LINDA is holding): See, this fish is a female fish. And it's pregnant. If I take this fish, she'll have all these baby fish. Then she'll eat the baby fish, which will make me sick. So I don't want that one. (*Pointing at a fish in the tank:*) I want this one.

LINDA (turning on TIM, thrusting the bag at him): Take this freakin' fish and get off my back! Pay my father, the guy at the register.

(TIM *takes the bag, resigned.*)

TIM (addressing the fish as he walks to the register): But I know you're gonna make me sick.

LINDA (yelling to her father at the register): I'm takin' lunch, Dad. Hold down the fort.

(*Her father, a classy but dissolute old guy, nods to her vaguely.* LINDA *heads out the door.* JAMES *follows her.*)

EXTERIOR: PET SHOP. DAY.

LINDA: Look. I'm sorry. Listen, James. Maybe I ain't goin' about this the ideal way, but I'm scared and you'll haveta excuse me. Heinz tried to rape me and you tried to stop him and *now you limp!*

EXTERIOR: FIVE CORNERS. DAY.

JAMES *struggles to keep up with her.*

JAMES: Oh, so what?

LINDA: So now Heinz is back, and I gotta get protection.

JAMES: I'll protect you!

LINDA: You know you can't.

JAMES: What, you're gonna go to the cops? They ain't gonna help you. He ain't done nothin'.

LINDA: No, not the cops. I'm gonna go to Harry.

JAMES: Harry!

LINDA: That's who stopped him the last time.

JAMES: Yeah, but that was then. Don't you know what Harry's been doin'? He ain't gonna help you with this.

LINDA: We'll see about that.

(LINDA *marches away from him.*)

JAMES (calling after her): Ain't you heard? Harry's nonviolent now!

(LINDA *is gone.* JAMES *looks after her, undecided about what to do. A Goldwater campaign truck drives by.*)

EXTERIOR: HARRY'S HOUSE. DAY.

The campaign truck drives past Harry's house, a modest, middle-class, two-family brick house.

INTERIOR: HARRY'S ROOM. DAY.

Music: Peter, Paul and Mary are singing "Blowin' in the Wind." Harry's voice can be heard singing along in his low-key way.
    There's a diploma hanging on the wall. It's from Fordham University, dated June 6, 1964, and made out to HAROLD PATRICK FITZGERALD; *it's a bachelor of arts.*
    There's a little table. On the table is a copy of On the Road, Thoreau's Civil Disobedience, *and a framed picture of Gandhi. Next to these items is a small glass of milk and a dish with two chocolate-chip*

cookies on it. Some of the milk has been drunk, and there's a bite out of one of the cookies.

There's a grouping of four pictures on the wall.

All are of the Reverend Martin Luther King, Jr. One of the pictures is of King speaking at the march on Washington, D.C., in 1963. In the other three, he is being taken to jail or is in jail.

There's a half-packed suitcase. The contents are Spartan, orderly, and spare. A couple of white dress shirts in laundry bands, two skinny ties, a coiled belt, jockey shorts, a pair of conservative trousers, two pairs of black socks.

HARRY *pulls tight a small knot in a skinny tie while he looks in the mirror. He has short, carefully combed hair and wears glasses. He's wearing a short-sleeved white shirt. In brief, he's dressed like one of the white civil rights workers in the early 1960s. But there's something incongruous about him. He's a big tough guy, a mug, a bouncer type, who dreams of being Gandhi. In his movements and speech, he struggles constantly to act like a gentle guy. He's singing along with "Blowin' in the Wind." We hear Mrs. Fitzgerald's voice through the door.*

MRS. FITZGERALD'S VOICE (yelling from downstairs): Harry!

HARRY: Yeah, Ma?

INTERIOR: HARRY'S STAIRS AND LIVING ROOM. DAY.

MRS. FITZGERALD *at the foot of the stairs. She's a handsome, intelligent woman in her midforties. She continues to yell up the stairs. Next to her is a piano.*

MRS. FITZGERALD: You promised you'd walk the Buddha!

(MRS. FITZGERALD *looks over her shoulder to where the Buddha is sulking. He's under a table. He's a big, big Saint Bernard.*)

MRS. FITZGERALD (trying to reason with the dog): Come on, baby. Come on out. (*The dog crouches further under the table. She calls up to* HARRY:) He won't cooperate with me.

INTERIOR: HARRY'S ROOM AND HALL. DAY

HARRY *comes out the door to his room, still fixing his tie.*

HARRY (calling down the stairs): I don't really have that much time, Ma, Mother. I'm supposed to meet the guys, the gentlemen from the SNCC this after—

INTERIOR: HARRY'S STAIRS AND LIVING ROOM. DAY.

MRS. FITZGERALD *is still at the foot of the stairs.*

MRS. FITZGERALD (interrupting): Excuse me, excuse me, Harry, but who belongs to this dog?

HARRY: It's my dog.

MRS. FITZGERALD: That's right. The Buddha belongs to you. I cannot walk the Buddha. I cannot do anything with the Buddha that the Buddha does not want me to do.

HARRY (coming down the stairs): Okay, I'll walk him. C'mere, Buddha Boy.

(*The dog immediately comes, holding his leash.* HARRY *grabs his leash and starts to hook it to his collar.*)

MRS. FITZGERALD (still not pleased): What is this SNCC?

HARRY: The Student Non-Violent Coordinating Committee.

MRS. FITZGERALD: I don't like it that it has "Violent" in the title.

HARRY: Non-Violent.

MRS. FITZGERALD: This is the Negroes, right?

HARRY: That's right.

MRS. FITZGERALD: Where you meeting these guys?

HARRY: Harlem.

MRS. FITZGERALD: Harlem. You're a pip. Listen, Harry. You cannot go to Mississippi.

HARRY: Why not?

MRS. FITZGERALD: Becausa the dog. Who's gonna take care of this monster dog?

HARRY: My best girl.

MRS. FITZGERALD: No, I will not. That's your dog. That ain't my dog. I never woulda gotten a dog like that.

HARRY: I gotta get movin', Ma, Mother. You wouldn't want me to blow an interview. C'mon, Buddha!

(*The dog starts to pull him away.*)

EXTERIOR: HARRY'S HOUSE. DAY.

The front door opens, and out comes the Buddha pulling HARRY.

EXTERIOR: CASTRO'S BUILDING. DAY.

HARRY *walks by, and the camera tilts up to a window, which belongs to Castro's apartment.*

INTERIOR: CASTRO'S APARTMENT. DAY.

The camera leaves the window and inspects the apartment. There are two single beds in an otherwise bare room. A front page from the Daily News is taped up by way of decoration. A girl sleeps in each of the beds.

The girls are MELANIE *and* BRITA. MELANIE *wakes up. She looks around. She is completely bewildered. She has no idea where she is.*

MELANIE: Brita. Brita. Brita. (BRITA *stirs and wakes.*) Where are we?

BRITA: I gotta headache.

MELANIE: Where are we?

BRITA: I don't know. This ain't my house.

MELANIE: This ain't my house, either.

BRITA: Whose house is this?

MELANIE: What did we do last night?

BRITA: We were with Sal.

MELANIE: This ain't Sal's house. Wait a minute. There were some guys.

BRITA: Yeah?

MELANIE: Yeah.

BRITA (looking under her sheet): I ain't wearin' no clothes.

MELANIE (looking under her sheet): I ain't wearin' no clothes, neither. (*Calls out:*) Is there anybody here?

BRITA (leaning over and finding her clothes under her bed): Here's my clothes.

MELANIE: I don't think there's anybody here. (*Looks under her bed.*) Yeah, here's my clothes.

BRITA: So who were these guys last night?

MELANIE: I don't know. I ain't awake yet.

BRITA: Me neither.

(*They both fall back to sleep.*)

INTERIOR: SHOPMERIT. DAY.

MURRAY *and* GEORGE *are behind their counter.* SAL *walks in. He's a little embarrassed by what he's doing.*

SAL: Ah, excuse me.

GEORGE: Yes, can I help you?

SAL: I'm looking for somebody.

MURRAY: There's only the two of us here.

SAL: I know that. I'm looking for some girls.

GEORGE: Girls?

MURRAY: This is a delicatessen.

EXTERIOR: HARRY'S HOUSE. DAY.

LINDA *walks up to the front door and knocks.* MRS. FITZGERALD *opens the door. They talk. She invites* LINDA *in. The door closes.*

EXTERIOR: THE PUBLIC FOUNTAIN IN PARKCHESTER. DAY.

HEINZ *is sitting on a bench, smoking a cigarette.* HARRY *approaches, walking the Buddha.* HARRY *sees* HEINZ *and stops.* HEINZ *sees* HARRY *and slowly stands.*

HARRY: Hi, Heinz.

HEINZ: Fuck you.

HARRY: So they let you out.

HEINZ: I don't let no hair grow over to hide this scar you gave me, Harry.

HARRY: You should. You look like shit.

HEINZ: I don't wanna forget!

HARRY: What? That some goon hit you with a beer pitcher? That don't seem like no golden memory to me. Why don't you forget it? I'm gonna try to forget it. I'm not proud of it.

HEINZ: I hadda lotta time to think when I was in that fuckin' hole.

HARRY: It's a shame you didn't use it.

(HEINZ *takes a step toward* HARRY. *The Buddha growls.* HEINZ *steps back, respectful of the dog.*)

HEINZ: Yeah, well, why don't you go walk your dog. Leave me to smoke my cigarette.

HARRY: Look, Heinz. I wanna say somethin' to you. (*Hesitates.*) I love you. (HEINZ *doesn't react.*) I did a lotta soul-searchin' while you were gone. I've had some bad shit in my life. And I've hadda change of heart. I don't wanna do the caveman shit anymore. I wanna help people.

HEINZ: You *love* me?

HARRY: Yeah.

(HARRY *turns and walks away with the Buddha.* HEINZ *looks after, stunned.*)

INTERIOR: HARRY'S LIVING ROOM AND KITCHEN. DAY.

LINDA *is sitting on the edge of an upholstered chair in the living room.* MRS. FITZGERALD *can be seen moving around in the kitchen.*

MRS. FITZGERALD: Do you use milk in your coffee?

LINDA: Yeah, I'll take some.

MRS. FITZGERALD: It's funny how things are, you know? How things are set up. You're the first girl ever to knock on that door and ask for Harry. You know him from Fordham?

LINDA: No, from the neighborhood.

MRS. FITZGERALD: It's funny. I figured he'd meet a girl at school and get married. (*She comes into the living room with two cups of coffee.*) And here he graduated in June, and he's still as single as he ever was. Right?

LINDA: Right. I mean, I guess so.

MRS. FITZGERALD: He got so serious after his father died. His father was a hero cop. (*Picks up a picture of a smiling man and shows it to* LINDA.) You get to be a hero cop by being killed. (*Puts the picture down.*)

LINDA: I know. About that.

MRS. FITZGERALD: Are you with the student not-violent Negro thing?

LINDA: No.

MRS. FITZGERALD: Harry's got it in his head to be a hero, too. Harry's gonna go down to Mississippi, him and a buncha other heroes, and they're gonna register Negroes for the vote. And these hillbilly cops down there, with their third-grade educations and their shotguns and their love of the Negro people, they're gonna welcome Harry the hero, my son, and make him feel ta home.

LINDA: Maybe I should go.

MRS. FITZGERALD: No. I'm sorry. He's packin' his bag. It's just on my mind. So why do you wanna see Harry?

(*The doorbell rings, then rings again. Then there is impatient knocking on the door.* MRS. FITZGERALD *gets up, puzzled.*)

MRS. FITZGERALD: Who's that?

(MRS. FITZGERALD *opens the front door. It's* JAMES.)

JAMES (in a state): Excuse me, excuse me, Mrs. Fitzgerald, but Linda's here, right?

LINDA: What are you doin' here?

(JAMES *is so excited he brushes right on by* MRS. FITZGERALD *to talk to* LINDA.)

JAMES: I just figured it out! You gotta thing for this guy! This whole number about protection is just smoke! You're throwin' me over, so's you can make a play for Harry Fitzgerald! (*To* MRS. FITZGERALD, *who has followed him in:*) Your son! Excuse me, Mrs. Fitzgerald, but I love this girl, and she's doin' a number on me! (*To* LINDA:) I figured it out, Linda. Tell me I'm wrong!

LINDA: You're wrong!

JAMES: Bullhockey! (*To* MRS. FITZGERALD:) Maybe you don't understand, so lemme explain what's goin' on here.

MRS. FITZGERALD: I wish you would.

JAMES: This one here is my girl, and last night she breaks up with me. I feel bad. You can understand that?

MRS. FITZGERALD: Sure.

JAMES: And she doesn't tell me *why!* So today I'm eatin' my heart out when I see Heinz.

MRS. FITZGERALD: Heinz.

JAMES: Bad boy from way back. Been in the big house a couple a years. Busted my hip, tried to rape Linda, etcetera. Your son Harry saved the situation. Iced Heinz completely with a pitcher of beer. But now, today, this one, she tells me she left me 'causa Heinz bein' back . . .

LINDA: *You* said that!

JAMES: You didn't contradict me . . . and that she's goin' ta Harry for protection! Meanwhile, the whole world knows that Harry's gone out to lunch with the Gandhi thing!

MRS. FITZGERALD: You want some coffee?

JAMES: No thanks. I think a cup of coffee right now would give me a heart attack. So when I had a moment to think about it, I'm thinking it definitely don't add up like she's tellin' me. And then I understand! It must be that she got a thing for Harry, and that she's just usin' Heinz for smoke to blow on me!

LINDA: Oh, James, please.

JAMES: Well, what else would it be?

MRS. FITZGERALD: Would you like to sit down?

JAMES: I can't sit down, Mrs. Fitzgerald, I'm a man on the move!

(*The front door opens, and* HARRY *enters with the Buddha. He stops short when he sees there's company.*)

HARRY: What's this?

JAMES: This? This is your life, clown!

EXTERIOR: THE FORTY-THIRD PRECINCT. DAY.

Cops are walking in and out. A couple of the old, dark green New York City cop cars are parked outside.
        JOHN SULLIVAN, *a rough-looking Irish detective, enters the building.*

INTERIOR: THE FORTY-THIRD PRECINCT DESK. DAY.

SAL *is talking to the* DESK SERGEANT. *The* DESK SERGEANT *is not sympathetic. Painters are working in the background.*

SERGEANT: Why don't you wait a little while. They'll turn up.

SAL: But neither of their own mothers ain't heard from 'em.

SERGEANT: Then why ain't their mothers in here complainin'?

SAL: Because they gotta shitty attitude. Like you.

SERGEANT: Well, take a lesson, why don't ya? Don't worry about it.

(SULLIVAN *walks by.*)

SULLIVAN: Hi, Phil.

SERGEANT: Hi, Sullivan. What'd it look like?

SULLIVAN (keeps walking): Homicide.

(SULLIVAN *walks on into his office.*)

SAL: Look, I feel responsible for these chicks. I gotta find 'em.

SERGEANT: All right, so go find 'em. Go with God. I'm not stoppin' ya.

(SAL, *dissatisfied, stands his ground uncertainly. The sergeant's phone rings.*)

SERGEANT (answering): Forty-third Precinct. (*Puts his hand over the receiver and speaks to* SAL.) Seriously, buddy, trust me on this. Just wait it out. They'll turn up. (*Goes back to phone.*) Yeah? I can't understand you, Ma'am. You're gonna haveta stop cryin'.

(SAL *takes out his comb, combs his hair aggressively at the* SERGEANT, *and then leaves.*)

INTERIOR: THE DETECTIVES' OFFICE. DAY.

SULLIVAN *is just sitting down at his desk. At the next desk is* MAZOLA, *a greasy detective with a Band-Aid on his cheek.*

MAZOLA: So was it really an arrow?

SULLIVAN: Right in the back.

MAZOLA: Whaddaya make a that?

SULLIVAN: Indians. (*He takes forms out of a drawer and starts filling them out. He stops a minute, noticing the Band-Aid.*) What happened here, somebody tag you?

MAZOLA: Nah, it's a pimple. You know there useta be Indians around here.

SULLIVAN (not interested): Is that right?

MAZOLA: Sure. This whole area here was Indians. It was called Keskeeskek.

SULLIVAN: Is that right?

MAZOLA: Sure.

SULLIVAN: What happened?

MAZOLA: Whaddaya mean?

SULLIVAN: Why ain't they here now?

MAZOLA: The neighborhood changed. (*Smiles.*) So who killed this . . . What was he?

SULLIVAN: Algebra teacher. I don't know.

MAZOLA: Heinz Sabantino's back on the street, you know.

SULLIVAN: I know.

MAZOLA: Think it mighta been him?

SULLIVAN: Maybe. Only where would he a learned the art of the bow and arrow?

MAZOLA: Coulda picked it up in the pen.

SULLIVAN: Who from?

MAZOLA: An Indian, a camp counselor. I don't know.

SULLIVAN: So we moved in, and the Indians moved out.

MAZOLA: Pretty much. The Indians moved out, and this Dutch family moved in.

SULLIVAN: Who were they?

MAZOLA: They were the Broncs. Something like John and Katrina Bronc. People used to say, "Let's go over to the Broncs tonight." That's why it's called the Bronx, see? It was their place.

SULLIVAN: So we changed it from Keskeeskek to the Bronx.

MAZOLA: That was the drill.

SULLIVAN: Then after us probably there's probably somebody next in line.

MAZOLA: Probably.

SULLIVAN: Jeez, are they gonna be some sorry shitheads.

INTERIOR: CASTRO'S BUILDING STAIRWELL. DAY.

MELANIE *and* BRITA *are leaving, walking down the stairs.*

MELANIE: Let's get outta here.

BRITA: Should we leave 'em a note?

MELANIE: We don't even know who they are.

BRITA: Boy, this is weird. This is like the weirdest thing that ever has happened to me.

(*On a landing they meet* CASTRO *and* WILLIE, *who are standing there holding cans of Schaeffer beer. They both smile brightly.*)

MELANIE: It's them!

BRITA: Who? The dudes from last night?

WILLIE: Hi, Brita. Did you get zum good sleep?

BRITA: He knows my name. And he's Dutch or something.

WILLIE: German.

BRITA: German.

MELANIE: Is that your apartment?

WILLIE: No, not exactly.

CASTRO: This is an apartment over which we have use.

WILLIE: Until ze zuperintendent finds out.

INTERIOR: SABANTINO TENEMENT HALLWAY. DAY.

Within, relentlessly cheerful Muzak can be heard. HEINZ *hesitates, sighs, steels himself, and punches the door. Mrs. Sabantino's voice comes from inside.* MRS. SABANTINO *is relentlessly pleasant and cheerful.*

MRS. SABANTINO'S VOICE: Is someone there?

HEINZ: It's me.

(MRS. SABANTINO *opens the door. Cheerful Muzak floods the hallway. She's a little woman, but her height has been augmented by high heels and Corinthian curls, a hairdo based on a Greek column. Her hair is dyed bright red. She is dressed in bright, happy clothes. And she's crazy. She lives in a delusion where everything is nice.*)

MRS. SABANTINO: Heinz? Is that you?

(HEINZ *remains surly and alienated in his mother's presence. But she doesn't notice. Her cheerfulness drives him slowly insane.*)

HEINZ: Yeah.

MRS. SABANTINO: I can't believe it's you!

INTERIOR: SABANTINO APARTMENT. DAY.

HEINZ *pushes past* MRS. SABANTINO, *into the apartment. The Muzak is roaring. There are framed happy sayings on all the walls, along with big, Kodak-style pictures of children playing with dogs and the like. There are bright yellows and oranges everywhere.* HEINZ *goes to the radio and turns off the Muzak.*

HEINZ (murmuring to himself): God damn.

MRS. SABANTINO: I do play it a little loud, but it's so beautiful! It makes me feel so good. I got your letters all the time you were gone.

HEINZ: I didn't write.

MRS. SABANTINO: Oh I know you did. Maybe I didn't get 'em all the time, but I know you wrote your mother. How's the asthma?

HEINZ: I ain't had asthma since I was twelve.

MRS. SABANTINO: Yeah, you've been gone a long time. What a weird haircut. I'm sure it's the style now. This, what I have, they call Corinthian curls. Ya like it?

HEINZ: I wanna change my clothes. My clothes still here?

MRS. SABANTINO: Yeah.

HEINZ: I wanna change my clothes. Use the bathroom.

MRS. SABANTINO: Okay.

INTERIOR: SABANTINO BATHROOM. DAY.

HEINZ *is washing his hands. The walls and ceiling are covered with big flowers with smiling faces. On the curtain rod is a pair of drying nylons. He looks at them and touches one thoughtfully. He rubs his cheek with it. Then he turns to go. Almost as an afterthought, he steps back, snatches one of the nylons, and stuffs it in his pocket.*

EXTERIOR: HARRY'S HOUSE. DAY.

Establishing shot.

INTERIOR: HARRY'S LIVING ROOM. DAY.

HARRY *and* LINDA *are sitting, drinking coffee.* MRS. FITZGERALD *has repaired some distance away, to the piano, where she stands and drinks her coffee.* JAMES *is lying on the floor, staring at the ceiling, singing "We Shall Overcome".*

LINDA (to HARRY): That's about all I can think of to say.

HARRY: There's not really that much I can do anyway, but . . .

LINDA: James, why don't you get off the floor? James? (*No reply. The song goes on. She addresses* HARRY *again:*) I don't know who else I can ask.

HARRY: You should go to the police.

LINDA: He ain't done nothin' yet.

HARRY: Well, I can't help you. I've got stuff of my own to do. You don't even know that he's gonna bother you. When I talked to him today . . .

(JAMES *stops singing and sits up.*)

JAMES: You talked to Heinz?

HARRY: Yeah. And I told him that I loved him.

(JAMES *stands up*.)

JAMES: You told Heinz Sabantino that you loved him?

HARRY: Yeah, I did.

JAMES: And this is who you come to for protection? Excuse me, Linda, but I gotta have a chuckle over this one. This guy's further out than Sputnik. Listen, I'm late for work. This has been great, but I gotta go. When you're ready to ask for my help, you know where I am. Mrs. Fitzgerald? Nice to meet you.

MRS. FITZGERALD: Nice to meet you, James.

JAMES: Sorry for my intensity. All good things to you in Mississippi, Harry. It ain't worth it to be jealous with you. You're crazy. You're leaving town. It's not worth it. (*To* LINDA, *indicating* HARRY.) This is not a rival. This is a phenomenon. Don't rush. Finish your conversation. I gotta fly.

(JAMES *goes to the door and leaves. The Goldwater truck rolls by*.)

LINDA: You gotta excuse James. He acts that way 'cause he's nervous about himself.

HARRY: That's okay.

LINDA: You saved him, too, you know. I guess that makes him feel weird. He limps around, and I don't think he feels, you know, like enough of a man.

MRS. FITZGERALD: Who does?

EXTERIOR: THE PARKCHESTER CAFÉ. DAY.

*The Goldwater truck rolls by the Parkchester Café, which is a little
neighborhood bar next to a wide street called White Plains Road. Over
White Plains Road wheels a flock of pigeons from a local coop.* JAMES
appears on the street and enters the bar.

INTERIOR: THE PARKCHESTER CAFÉ. DAY.

A big, gray-haired Irishman, ED, *is the day bartender.* JAMES *walks in;
he has come to relieve* ED. JAMES *is the night bartender. A very* OLD GUY
*sits at one end of the bar, reading his newspaper through thick glasses.
His mouth is always open. This is how he breathes. When* ED *sees* JAMES,
he takes off his apron and prepares to go.

JAMES: Quiet?

ED: So far.

JAMES (indicating the OLD GUY): How's he?

ED: One more, and he gets a knock.

OLD GUY: That's right.

(JAMES *is now in his apron, and* ED *prepares to go.*)

ED: So long.

JAMES: 'Bye.

(*As* ED *walks out,* SAL *walks in.*)

SAL: Ah, excuse me, chief. I'm lookin' for somebody. Maybe you seen
'em.

(JAMES *shakes his head in answer to Sal's question.* SAL *gets in the Impala and starts it up.*)

EXTERIOR: HARRY'S HOUSE. DAY.

SAL *drives by in the Impala.*
 The front door opens. LINDA *comes out, followed by* HARRY. *They walk down the stairs together.*

LINDA: I understand. You got your own things to do. I'm just scared is all. But that's my problem.

HARRY: You probably won't even hear from the guy. All that junk was a long time ago.

LINDA: But what if I do hear from him?

HARRY: All right, if you hear from him, call me.

LINDA: Thanks.

(*They've reached the sidewalk.*)

HARRY: Yeah. Well, I'm probably gonna be around only a couple more days, and then you're strictly on your own. He probably won't bother you. Okay, take it easy.

(HARRY *walks out down the sidewalk.* LINDA *looks after him a moment, then walks away in the other direction.*)

EXTERIOR: ASPHALT PATH LEADING TO BUILDING. DAY.

It's well lit by streetlights. The building is part of the Parkchester housing complex. CASTRO, MELANIE, BRITA *and* WILLIE *are walking up the path to the building.* CASTRO *and* MELANIE *walk in front;* BRITA *and* WILLIE *trail behind.*

MELANIE: I thought we were going for a ride.

CASTRO: We are.

(*Meanwhile,* BRITA *is in the middle of telling a long story to* WILLIE.)

BRITA: . . . So I took two of 'em. It was like eleven o'clock, and nothin' happened. And then, like ten minutes later or somethin', my mother walks in, and she tries to hand me this vacuum. And I go to take it, but it's like I have no arms. I can't feel my arms at all! They're like these two salamis hangin' down!

WILLIE: Vow!

BRITA: These downs, these downs were the most serious kind of deep garbage I ever had. I should call my mother. Ah, screw her. What's your name again?

WILLIE: Willie.

BRITA: And you're German?

WILLIE: That's right.

BRITA: You're German, what are you doin' here?

WILLIE: My father came here to work for his company for some years. Then he will go back to Germany.

BRITA: What about you?

WILLIE: Yes, then I will go back to Germany, too. Maybe.

(*The four of them walk into the building.*)

INTERIOR: BUILDING ELEVATOR. DAY.

The elevator opens on the third floor, and they get off. WILLIE *holds the door open.*

CASTRO: Okay.

MELANIE: Okay, what?

BRITA (to WILLIE): She left the bag open for like two hours. The glue was like a friggin' rock.

WILLIE: Vhat a shame!

CASTRO: You got the whatnot, Willie?

WILLIE: Yeah.

(WILLIE *takes a can opener out of his pocket and hands it to* CASTRO. BRITA *pays no attention, but* MELANIE *is a little alarmed. The can opener is heavily wrapped with black insulation tape on one end.*)

CASTRO: This is a whatnot.

MELANIE: What's it for?

CASTRO: It's a key. We're on the third floor, right? (*He steps into the elevator, and presses the second floor button.*) So I press the second floor (*steps back out of the elevator*), and I take this and I stick it in here. (*He sticks the metal end of his gizmo into a hole near the top of the elevator doorframe.*) Like so.

(*As* MELANIE, BRITA, *and* WILLIE *watch and as* CASTRO *continues to apply his gizmo, the inner door slides closed.* WILLIE *holds the outer door and presses the button for the other elevator. The elevator* CASTRO *is working on descends out of view; it has gone to the second floor. The black elevator shaft appears in the doorway.* CASTRO *removes the can opener and hands it to* WILLIE, *whose elevator has just arrived.* WILLIE *sets about the operation that* CASTRO *has just completed. The top of the elevator, which in Castro's case is now at floor level, has a girder across it that functions like a bench. Out of the center of the girder come four cables that continue up, out of sight.* CASTRO *takes Melanie's arm gently.*)

CASTRO: C'mon. This is the ride I promised you.

MELANIE (a little horrified): On there?

CASTRO: C'mon. It's a goof.

BRITA: Wow.

WILLIE: And here's ours.

(*The other elevator has now been brought to the same position.* MELANIE *and* CASTRO *step through the door into one shaft as* BRITA *and* WILLIE *step through the other door into the other shaft.*)

INTERIOR: HARLEM COFFEE SHOP. DAY.

Everybody in this coffee shop is black. HARRY *walks in. The* COUNTER SERVER, *a big black woman in a serving uniform that looks like armor plating, eyes him suspiciously.*

SERVER: What you want, dear?

(*An* OLD BLACK GUY, *wearing a strap T-shirt with holes in it, cackles with delight.*)

OLD BLACK GUY: He don't want nothin', Nancy. He's just crazy, right?

HARRY: I'm meeting some friends.

(HARRY *squeezes past a big, mean-looking black man.*)

OLD BLACK GUY: You ain't got no friends here, sonny. Gimme a dollar, and I may get you outta here alive.

SERVER: Stop talkin' so bad, old man. May be somebody here don't know you, take you seriously.

HARRY (seeing someone): There they are.

(HARRY *walks away. The* SERVER *and the* OLD BLACK GUY *look after.*
    Two young black men, ARTHUR *and* SAMUEL, *are sitting at a booth.*
ARTHUR *is a stoical, intellectual pacifist.* SAMUEL *is not stoical and doesn't
like white people very much. They are both organizers for the movement.
They are sitting on the same side of the booth, and a cup of coffee is in
front of each guy. Black coffee.* HARRY *approaches. He's awkward and
eager. He sticks out his hand to* ARTHUR, *who shakes it briefly.*)

HARRY: Hello, Arthur!

ARTHUR: Hello, Brother Harold. Sit down.

(HARRY *sits. He smiles at* SAMUEL, *who doesn't smile back.*)

HARRY: We haven't met, have we?

SAMUEL: You're not sure?

HARRY (sticking out his hand): I'm Harry Fitzgerald.

(SAMUEL *doesn't shake his hand. Instead he picks up his coffee and sips.*)

ARTHUR: This is Brother Samuel Kemp. He's been down in Mississippi
for us for some time now. He's been working with Brother Stokely
Carmichael.

(*The* SERVER *walks up to the booth.*)

SERVER (addressing HARRY): Can I get you somethin'?

HARRY: I'll have coffee, too. Black.

(*The* SERVER *leaves.*)

SAMUEL: The purpose of the Mississippi Project is to get some rich white kids down there, working beside those of us Negroes who've been beaten up enough to satisfy a lifetime in the cause of the movement without the population up north getting upset about it. Now we figure if some rich white kids get beat up in the cause of the movement, that'll get the TV cameras rolling real good.

ARTHUR: Brother Samuel doesn't like the Mississippi Project very much.

(*The* SERVER *returns and serves Harry's coffee.*)

SERVER: There you go.

HARRY: Thank you.

(*The* SERVER *leaves.* HARRY *sips his coffee and puts it down.*)

HARRY: I want you to like me, Mr. Kemp.

SAMUEL: I don't like you. I don't like the idea of you.

HARRY: What I mean is, I want you to approve me for this project. I want to be on that bus the day after tomorrow.

SAMUEL: Why should I approve you? Why should Brother Arthur approve you? You look to me like you're made out of sweet butter, and when that Mississippi sun lands on you, you're going to shimmer down into some grease. They got state troopers down there waiting for you Harvard types with a knife and fork. Why don't you go home?

HARRY: I can understand if you don't like me, Mr. Kemp. I can. I may not like you. I don't know yet. But lemme straighten you out on a couple a things. I'm not rich. I didn't go to Harvard. I went to Fordham, which ain't Harvard. And I come from a place in the Bronx called Five Corners. The movement has not been to this place. If a Negro, if you, for instance, were to walk through Five Corners, before you'd gone one block, people would come outta their houses and stomp your ass into the ground. 'Causa the color of your skin. Two years ago I woulda been one of those people. But then somethin' happened, and I had a change of heart. My father was a cop, and he got shot by a kid, some screwed-up kid. And when I was sittin' home with my mother, watchin' the news about it on TV, the next thing they showed after that was Dr. Martin Luther King speaking. He was talking about the power of love in the face of senseless cruelty and violence. And I heard him, Mr. Kemp. I guess something had knocked the wax outta my ears. 'Cause I heard him loud and clear. That's why I'm sitting here now.

SAMUEL: Was this kid who killed your father black?

HARRY: I don't remember.

(SAMUEL *is a little irritated by this answer, and* ARTHUR *is a little amused.* HARRY *sips his coffee.*)

INTERIOR: THE ELEVATOR SHAFT. DAY.

MELANIE *and* CASTRO *are sitting on top of the elevator. It's pretty dark and kind of romantic.* WILLIE *and* BRITA *are sitting on top of the other elevator.* MELANIE *looks up. The little square windows on each floor above her make a dotted line of little lights.* MELANIE *drops her head and looks at* CASTRO.

MELANIE: It's dark in here.

CASTRO (smiles): Yeah.

(*The spirit of the moment is like a pajama party where everybody whispers.*)

MELANIE (calling across to BRITA): Brita!

(BRITA *and* WILLIE *are getting along quite well.*)

BRITA: Hey, Melanie, dig this! It's like outer space!

(MELANIE *looks at* CASTRO *with the first pangs of romantic affection.*)

MELANIE: So is like Castro your real name?

(*We see* CASTRO, *with* BRITA *and* WILLIE *on the other elevator behind him.*)

CASTRO: It's what I go by.

(BRITA *and* WILLIE *sink out of sight.* MELANIE, *only a little surprised and a little sorry, notices them disappear.*)

MELANIE: Oh, they're gone.

(CASTRO *doesn't bother to look behind him.*)

CASTRO: They'll be back.

(CASTRO *leans forward until his face is in front of the cables.* MELANIE *leans forward, and they kiss. Each of them is holding the cables with one hand and touching the other's face with the other hand.*
  We watch them kiss, and now we see the other shaft behind them. Then the other elevator rises into view. WILLIE *and* BRITA *are kissing in just the same way. Their elevator continues to rise, leaving* MELANIE *and* CASTRO *still kissing, oblivious that their friends have just floated by and away.*)

INTERIOR: PET SHOP. DAY.

LINDA *closes up the shop. She puts a newly cleaned catch tray back in the bottom of a macaw's cage and then turns off the lights in the fish tanks. She locks the front door and goes to the back of the shop. All the while she sings "Swing Low, Sweet Chariot" to herself.*

EXTERIOR: PET SHOP. DAY.

HEINZ *appears at the front door and peers in the window. He can't see* LINDA. *Then he rings the bell for the upstairs apartment. No answer. He walks away.*

INTERIOR: ELEVATOR SHAFT. DAY.

The elevators are now on the same level. MELANIE *and* BRITA, *on their respective elevators, are now standing, facing each other, singing the end of the "Star-Spangled Banner." Their hands, naturally, are on their hearts.*

MELANIE and BRITA: O say does that star-spangled banner yet wave
O'er the land of the free
And the home of the brave.

CASTRO: Very moving.

WILLIE: *I* feel patriotic! Hey, you two, come on over here! We'll all be on one!

CASTRO: All right.

(CASTRO *crosses from one elevator to the other.*)

CASTRO: Come on, Melanie.

MELANIE: I ain't walkin' around in here.

BRITA: Don't be a chickenass, Melanie. It's like the sidewalk.

CASTRO: No, that's okay. I'll come back.

MELANIE: No, stay there. I'm comin'.

(MELANIE *stands up and starts to cross to the other elevator. But when she steps off her elevator and onto the girder, the elevator with* CASTRO *and company suddenly goes down.* MELANIE *looks down, frightened. The elevator with her friends is receding quickly, sinking down several floors.* MELANIE *is watching this chasm open at her feet.*)

MELANIE: Oh, shit. Oh, shit.

CASTRO (calling up): Get back on the other elevator.

(MELANIE *peers back cautiously, preparing to take Castro's suggestion, but at that moment, the other elevator goes down, leaving* MELANIE *stranded on the narrow girder. She's petrified with fear.*)

MELANIE: Oh, no.

(*Melanie's point of view:* CASTRO *and company. They're all looking up.*)

CASTRO (calls up soothingly): It's okay, Melanie. It's gonna be okay.

(*We see* MELANIE *now, utterly alone, standing on this small thing in this weird twilight world.*)

MELANIE (her small voice peeping out): Oh, shit.

CASTRO'S VOICE (from somewhere down below, out of view, he's trying to sound calm, like a hypnotist): Be cool. Be cool. This is just, like, a temporary situation.

BRITA'S VOICE (awed): Oh, my God, Melanie. You're gonna die!

CASTRO'S VOICE (still the hypnotist): Shut up, Brita. Melanie's gonna be fine. (*To* MELANIE:) In a minute, this elevator is gonna come up, and you'll just step on. That's all.

BRITA'S VOICE: I'll never forget you, cousin. We've been through some serious, deep garbage together.

WILLIE'S VOICE: What a disaster!

CASTRO'S VOICE: Shut up, Willie.

MELANIE: I think I'm gonna throw up.

CASTRO'S, WILLIE'S and BRITA'S VOICES: Don't throw up!

(*The hum of the elevator motor starting up can be heard.*)

CASTRO'S VOICE: We're comin' up! We're comin' up!

BRITA'S VOICE: We're comin', cousin.

WILLIE'S VOICE: Here we come!

(CASTRO *and company's elevator stops a floor beneath* MELANIE.)

CASTRO: Damn it!

MELANIE: Oh, man.

(MELANIE *closes her eyes and leans against the wall.*)

CASTRO: Melanie? Melanie?

(*Slowly* MELANIE *turns and looks down at* CASTRO. *He's trying to look ingratiating. The distance is about twelve feet.*)

CASTRO: Jump.

MELANIE (uncertain): I ain't jumpin' nowhere.

CASTRO: It's not far.

MELANIE: Yeah, well, it's far enough.

BRITA: Hey, Melanie. Jump, man! Fuck it!

MELANIE: Why don't you jump off somethin' if you're so freakin' hot to jump!

(CASTRO *digs into his pocket and comes out with a five dollar bill.*)

CASTRO: Melanie? Melanie, I'll give you five dollars if you jump.

MELANIE (just about forgetting about her danger): I know where you got that five dollars. Don't think I forget shit just 'cause I was high.

CASTRO: So? I'm offerin' to give it to you. You can take it and shove it up the guy's nose.

(*The elevator that* CASTRO *and company are on starts to rise.* CASTRO *continues to hold out the bill. They rise to Melanie's level.* MELANIE *smiles. She's touched. She takes the bill.*)

MELANIE: Thanks.

CASTRO (genially): You know, if you take one step back, you're gonna die.

(MELANIE *suddenly remembers the gaping shaft just inches behind her and jumps forward into Castro's arms.*)

BRITA: She's saved! You're saved!

WILLIE: It's wonderful!

MELANIE (to CASTRO): Get me offa this thing.

INTERIOR: LINDA'S APARTMENT. DAY.

The beautiful arias of Madama Butterfly *can be heard.* LINDA, *holding a little blue plate with a freshly made sandwich on it, comes out of the kitchen and into the living room. It's a small room with comfortable, old, lumpy furniture and many plants. Her dad lies sleeping on the couch, his mouth open. On the coffee table is an ashtray full of dead butts and a half-empty bottle of rye.*

Taking all this in, LINDA *nestles down into a chair and opens her book,* All about Guppies, *which sports a nice picture of a fan-tailed guppy. She starts to eat and read.*

EXTERIOR: FIVE CORNERS. VARIOUS SHOTS. SUNSET.

The neighborhood closes up for the night and the sun goes down.

INTERIOR: LINDA'S APARTMENT. NIGHT.

Close-up of the little blue plate, which now holds nothing but the crumbs of the consumed sandwich. The camera pulls back, and we see LINDA *asleep, the book on her lap. There is a moment of quiet informed by the gently skipping record. Then the calm is broken by the ring of the telephone.* LINDA *starts and wakes. The phone rings twice more, and she picks it up.*

LINDA: Hello?

HEINZ'S VOICE (heard on the telephone): Hello, Linda. It's me. Heinz.

LINDA: Hi, Heinz.

EXTERIOR: A TELEPHONE BOOTH. PARKCHESTER. NIGHT.

HEINZ *is inside.*

INTERIOR: A TELEPHONE BOOTH. PARKCHESTER. NIGHT.

HEINZ *is on the phone. He's very excited. He can hardly keep from being carried away by uncontrollable giggles.*

HEINZ: Did you know I was back? Oh, you did, huh? (*Giggles.*) Listen, listen! I got you a present! A present! Guess what it is. (*She won't guess. He gets angry.*) I SAID GUESS! (*He listens, giggles, very excited.*) No! Wrong! Listen, listen! I want you to meet me at the Oval and fountain in Parkchester at twelve o'clock. No, tonight!

LINDA (on the phone): You can forget that. I don't meet nobody at twelve o'clock nowhere.

HEINZ'S VOICE: You'll meet me.

LINDA: Or what?

HEINZ (on the phone): Or I'll go look up your gimp boyfriend, James. I know the bar he works at. Maybe he'll be glad to see me.

LINDA (on the phone): I'm not even seein' him anymore. We broke up.

HEINZ'S VOICE: Then you won't care if I pay him a visit.

(LINDA *pauses.* HEINZ *has called her bluff.*)

LINDA: All right. I'll meet ya at twelve. I'll be there.

(LINDA *hangs up the phone. She's scared.*)

INTERIOR: HARRY'S LIVING ROOM. NIGHT.

MRS. FITZGERALD *is sitting at the upright piano. She's singing Stephen Foster's "The Erie Canal." She knows the words and sings them in a serious, even a grim way. She's worried about* HARRY *being in Harlem, and this is how she deals with it. There's a drink next to her on one side of the keyboard and a cigarette burning in a little ashtray on the other side. She stops playing to take a sip of her drink. When she reaches for her drink, her focus goes beyond, to the picture of her husband on a nearby table. She looks at the picture, sips her drink, puts it down, and starts to play again.*

The phone rings. Her reaction is immediate. She stops playing abruptly and stands. She quickly takes another sip of her drink and picks up the phone.

MRS. FITZGERALD: Hello, Harry?

INTERIOR: LINDA'S KITCHEN. NIGHT.

LINDA *is on the phone. She's nervous and very disappointed that* HARRY *is not there.*

LINDA: Oh. Then he's not there!

MRS. FITZGERALD'S VOICE: Who is this?

(MRS. FITZGERALD *is on phone, listening with a frown. We can't hear.*)

MRS. FITZGERALD: Well, I thought he told you he wasn't gonna get mixed up with Heinz? Uh-huh. He did. Well, that's like him. (*Listens.*) I don't know when he'll be back.

(LINDA *is on the phone.*)

LINDA: Just tell 'em I gotta meet Heinz at the Oval in Parkchester at twelve tonight. And that if Harry was there, too, I'd feel a heck of a lot safer. Will you tell him that?

(MRS. FITZGERALD *is on phone. She considers a moment.*)

MRS. FITZGERALD: All right. I'll tell him.

(LINDA *is on the phone. She is a little relieved. She hangs up the phone.*)

INTERIOR: HARRY'S LIVING ROOM. NIGHT.

MRS. FITZGERALD *is back at the piano. She has had a couple of drinks now and a few cigarettes. She's singing "When You Were Sweet Sixteen";*

it's a short song, and she sings it all. She's very loose and sentimental now, and sings the song with the whole of her heart. In the middle of her big finish, the door slams behind her. She pauses but doesn't look around. She knows it's HARRY. *Instead she decides to finish the song. Then she turns around.* HARRY *is at the door.*

HARRY: Looks like you're havin' a big night.

MRS. FITZGERALD: Yeah, well, I didn't feel like watchin' TV.

(MRS. FITZGERALD *casually crooks her head and glances at a clock on the wall.* HARRY *doesn't notice. The time is a quarter to twelve.* MRS. FITZGERALD *seems casual and genial.*)

MRS. FITZGERALD: Want a drink?

(HARRY *starts to say no but changes his mind.*)

HARRY: All right.

MRS. FITZGERALD: I guess it didn't go well.

(MRS. FITZGERALD *gets up from the piano and heads toward the kitchen.* HARRY *walks in and sits down. It's obvious he's tired.*)

HARRY: Why you say that?

MRS. FITZGERALD: 'Cause you haven't said yes to a drink in about a century.

HARRY: You're right. It didn't go great. It went okay. Where's the Buddha?

(MRS. FITZGERALD *opens the door to the kitchen. The Buddha runs out.*)

MRS. FITZGERALD: I keep him in there when I sing. He howls.

(*The Buddha runs to* HARRY. HARRY *receives the dog affectionately, but his mind is elsewhere.*)

EXTERIOR: THE PET STORE. NIGHT.

LINDA *comes out the front door and locks it behind her. She walks off.*

INTERIOR: PARKCHESTER CAFÉ. NIGHT.

JAMES *is trying to reason with the very* OLD GUY *with thick glasses, who is totally smashed. It should be pointed out, though, that the* OLD GUY *appears virtually the same drunk or sober.*

JAMES: Come on now, call it a night.

OLD GUY: No. I ain't finished readin' the paper.

JAMES: You can't even see that paper. Look, I'll call you a cab. I'm gonna call you a cab.

OLD GUY: Okay, Jimmy.

(JAMES *picks up the phone behind the bar.*)

EXTERIOR: A STREET. NIGHT.

LINDA *is passing a pay phone. She stops, decides, and quickly dials. But she gets a loud busy signal. She hangs up the phone and walks on.*

INTERIOR: PARKCHESTER CAFÉ. NIGHT.

JAMES *is on the phone. He is just finishing his conversation with the cab service.*

JAMES: Okay, thanks. (*He hangs up and addresses the* OLD GUY:) He'll be here, ten or fifteen minutes.

INTERIOR: HARRY'S LIVING ROOM. NIGHT.

HARRY *and* MRS. FITZGERALD *are having drinks.*

MRS. FITZGERALD: So, what happened? They think you're too white?

(MRS. FITZGERALD *steals another look at the clock. The time is five to twelve.*)

HARRY: No, it's the other way 'round. I might not be white enough. All the people they got goin' down there are from Harvard and Yale and like that. The white cream, you know? They figure if those Mississippi cops touch a Harvard man . . . well, you know, that that'd be a big deal.

MRS. FITZGERALD (incredulous): You're not white enough?

HARRY: Yeah. You know. I'm a Bronx boy. I'm just a Bronx boy.

(MRS. FITZGERALD *doesn't like what she's hearing.*)

INTERIOR: POOL HALL. NIGHT.

CASTRO, MELANIE, WILLIE, *and* BRITA *are shooting pool. They're laughing.*

WILLIE: So I asked Castro, "Should we leave her sleeping on her stomach like this? Vhat if she suffocates on her pillow?" You were snoring like a motorcycle.

BRITA: I was not!

WILLIE: Yes! Like a motorcycle going over a cliff! So we thought it better, and I held your shoulders and Castro took your ankles, and we counted three and flipped you over like you flip over the egg in the pan!

(MELANIE *and* BRITA *are loving Willie's story.*)

MELANIE: Was she wearing clothes when you did this number?

WILLIE: Not a stitch!

BRITA: Shut up!

(MELANIE *pulls* CASTRO *aside. She has been wanting to ask him a question privately. She feels awkward about asking.*)

MELANIE: Did we do anything last night?

CASTRO: Whaddaya mean?

MELANIE: I mean I woke up with no clothes on.

CASTRO: No, I didn't do anything.

(*This answer pleases* MELANIE. *From outside, squealing tires and a loud car horn are heard. Once, twice.* MELANIE *looks from* CASTRO *to the sound of the horn. Her face registers guilty surprise.* SAL *barges in.*)

SAL'S VOICE: Where the hell you been?! I've been through three friggin' neighborhoods lookin' for you! Where you been? You been all your time with these guys?

MELANIE (turning to CASTRO): Excuse me.

(MELANIE *starts yelling at* SAL *while still beside* CASTRO *and during the following, walks away from* CASTRO *and toward* SAL.)

MELANIE: Where have I been! Excuse me if I don't feel like explainin' that to you, Sal! I gotta five dollar bill here you gave these guys, bigshot!

SAL: What!

MELANIE: What what?! Don't gimme that what shit!

SAL: Your mother is like insane! She don't know where you are! She's sittin' there by the phone starin' at the phone like it was a crystal ball or some shit! But it don't ring 'cause you don't call!

(BRITA *and* WILLIE *are watching.*)

MELANIE'S VOICE: Shut up about my mother! Don't you mention my friggin' mother to me! If I was ta tell your father what you did last night, he'd strangle you with his bare hands! He'd choke you to death!

(BRITA *has seen all this before. She's almost bored.*)

BRITA: They're engaged. You'd swear ta God they was already married.

SAL'S VOICE: Where'd you sleep last night?

MELANIE'S VOICE: None of your goddamn business!

BRITA: I'm the maid of honor. I'm engaged, too.

WILLIE: Really!

SAL'S VOICE (trying to make peace now): I was just pissed off 'cause you were so stoned.

BRITA: Yeah. To her brother Ronny. He's in the navy.

(CASTRO *watches the fight and the reconciliation with a bemused expression.*)

MELANIE'S VOICE: Well, you never wanna do nothing!

(MELANIE *and* SAL *are talking low now.* SAL *puts his hand on her shoulder. She knocks it off. He puts it there again. This time, she leaves it.*)

EXTERIOR: PARKCHESTER OVAL AND FOUNTAIN. NIGHT.

The fountain is in a miniature park in the center of a traffic circle. There's no traffic though, because of the hour. The fountain, which is lit up, is surrounded by a well-manicured circle of hedges. LINDA *walks into view, outside the circle of hedges. She looks around at the deserted streets and then at the Oval. She takes a breath and walks in the direction of the fountain. When she steps within the circle of hedges, she sees* HEINZ. *He's sitting on one of the benches that ring the fountain. He's idly playing with a baseball bat. Behind the bench, not very noticeable, is a large burlap bag that's tied at the top. He looks up, sees* LINDA, *and smiles. He puts the bat down and stands up.*

INTERIOR: HARRY'S LIVING ROOM. NIGHT.

The clock reads one minute after twelve. MRS. FITZGERALD *is looking at it.*

HARRY: Why do you keep looking at the clock?

MRS. FITZGERALD (a little drunk): As you get older, Harry, you become more conscious of the time.

EXTERIOR: PARKCHESTER OVAL AND FOUNTAIN. NIGHT.

LINDA *approaches* HEINZ *at the fountain.*

LINDA: Hi, Heinz.

HEINZ: Hi.

LINDA: How you been?

HEINZ: I missed you.

LINDA: You did?

HEINZ: Yeah, outta the whole world you were the only one I missed.

LINDA: Thanks. That's nice.

HEINZ: I brought you a present.

(HEINZ *goes to the bench, reaches behind it, and lifts out the burlap sack. He brings it over to* LINDA *and sets it down on the ground by the fountain's edge.*)

HEINZ: Turn your back.

LINDA: Why?

HEINZ (sudden cracked anger): 'Cause it's a surprise!

LINDA: Okay!

(LINDA *turns toward us and away from* HEINZ. *We can only dimly see* HEINZ *untying the bag. As he works, he talks to her.*)

HEINZ: Don't turn around till I say.

LINDA: I won't.

HEINZ: I really tried to think of somethin' you would like.

LINDA: That's nice, Heinz.

HEINZ: 'Cause I want you to like me.

LINDA: I like you, Heinz.

(*There is a splash, and then another, not very loud.* HEINZ *stands up.*)

HEINZ: Okay, you can turn around now.

(LINDA *turns around.* HEINZ *is standing there, smiling his crazy smile, the bag empty at his feet. But there's nothing to be seen.*)

LINDA (puzzled): I don't see it. Where is it?

(HEINZ *is really getting off on this. He starts to giggle.*)

HEINZ: That's 'cause you're not lookin' in the right place. Look in the water!

(LINDA *is puzzled a moment more, but then she sees the present. She's amazed by what she sees and very pleased. She gasps in wonder.*
    Linda's point of view: the fountain. Standing on the ledge of the fountain, looking at LINDA *with a distinguished deadpan, is a shining wet penguin. A second penguin is swimming in the water.*)

EXTERIOR: STREET NEAR PARKCHESTER. NIGHT.

CASTRO *and* WILLIE *are still on the sidewalk looking at Sal's car, which is out of view.* WILLIE *looks glum.* CASTRO *is expressionless. A car door slamming can be heard.*
    It's the red Impala, which is starting up. SAL *is driving, and* MELANIE *and* BRITA *are in the back. They are both looking at* CASTRO *and* WILLIE *wistfully.* MELANIE *rolls down her window and waves. The car pulls away.* CASTRO *and* WILLIE *are left alone.* WILLIE *is depressed;* CASTRO *is philosophical. He pulls out a cigar and lights it. They both still look after the departed car.*

WILLIE: Gee, Castro, this makes me feel kinda down.

CASTRO: Yeah.

(*They start to walk.*)

WILLIE: I liked zat Brita. She hadda sense of humor.

CASTRO: Yeah.

WILLIE: You like that Melanie, too, huh?

(*They walk around a corner. They are further away, and we see them at a distance. They are approaching the fountain at the Oval.*)

CASTRO'S VOICE: Yeah, I guess so. Listen, Willie. Let's face it, you an' me, 'causa the kinda guys we are, I think we're always gonna be on the outside lookin' in. I think we're always gonna be goin' in and outta other people's stuff.

WILLIE: Maybe we should become cowboys and go out West and live outside the law.

CASTRO: Maybe we already have.

(*They are crossing the street, in the general direction of the fountain.* WILLIE *stops, seeing something.* CASTRO *stops, too.*)

WILLIE (pointing toward the fountain): What's that?

CASTRO: What?

WILLIE: I think I see something, I don't know vhat.

(CASTRO *and* WILLIE *immediately and stealthily run up to the bushes surrounding the fountain. They part a hedge and peer through.*)

EXTERIOR: PARKCHESTER OVAL AND FOUNTAIN. NIGHT.

Castro and Willie's point of view: HEINZ, LINDA *and one penguin can be seen.* LINDA *is saying something, but nothing can be heard.*

WILLIE (whispering): It's that crazy Heinz! They let him out!

(CASTRO *continues to look through the hedge intently.*)

CASTRO: So I see.

WILLIE: Vhat is that?

CASTRO: It's a penguin.

EXTERIOR: PARKCHESTER OVAL AND FOUNTAIN. NIGHT.

Now we leave the point of view of CASTRO *and* WILLIE, *and return to* HEINZ *and* LINDA. LINDA *is enraptured by the sight of the penguins.*

LINDA: They're so cute!

(HEINZ *watches* LINDA *watch the penguins.*)

HEINZ: I wanted to get you a present. I tried to think a somethin' that you'd like.

LINDA: Yeah, sure. They're unbelievable. Where'd you get them?

HEINZ: From the zoo.

LINDA: You stole 'em outta the Bronx Zoo?

HEINZ: Yeah. I climbed over the fence with a bag. It's easy. They keep 'em outside.

LINDA: You gotta take 'em back, you know.

HEINZ: What?

LINDA: Otherwise they'll die. They need special stuff.

HEINZ: They're a present!

LINDA: I know, Heinz, but serious now, you gotta take 'em back.

HEINZ: I thought you'd like 'em 'cause you like animals!

LINDA: I do like 'em, that ain't the point.

HEINZ: Then you take 'em then!

LINDA: I can't take 'em, Heinz! It wouldn't be right! They're like wild things, they're not like dogs or some shit! They belong in the zoo!

(HEINZ *picks up the baseball bat. He stares at* LINDA.)

HEINZ: You don't want my present?

(LINDA *stares back defiantly. She has decided to face him down.*)

LINDA: No.

(HEINZ *looks away from her.*
Heinz's point of view: the penguin takes a step.
LINDA, *horrified, realizes what* HEINZ *is about to do. She opens her mouth to protest.*
HEINZ, *snapping back the bat, swings viciously.*
LINDA, *out of view, screams.*)

LINDA'S VOICE: No!

(LINDA *ineffectually reaches out to stop* HEINZ.
We hear the terrible dull thud, and the odd cry of the stricken penguin. LINDA *covers her eyes.*
HEINZ *repeatedly clubs the bird, but this we cannot see. But we can see the red blood glistening on the bat. We hear* LINDA *sobbing.* HEINZ, *satisfied and fired up, drops the bat abruptly and turns to* LINDA. LINDA *is sobbing and half bent over.* HEINZ *approaches her. He is gentle, even solicitous. He strokes her hair.*)

HEINZ *(speaking to her softly)*: It's all right. It's all right. It's just that when somebody gives you a present, you should take it, that's all. It's all right. There's another one in the fountain. I'll give you that one, and this time you'll take it, right?

(LINDA *looks up at him. Her eyes are swollen with tears. She nods.* HEINZ *smiles and leaves her side. She looks after him. His splashing as he enters the fountain can be heard.* LINDA *reaches into a pocket, pulls out a pack of cigarettes, takes one out, and, her hands shaking crazily, tries to light it, and fails.* HEINZ *returns. His pants are soaked, and he has got the burlap bag with something struggling in it. He ties the top with a piece of cord. Then he takes* LINDA *by the shoulders and straightens her up. She is completely cooperative; she has gone to jelly with fear.* HEINZ *speaks to her gently.*)

HEINZ: Now, here's your present, Linda.

LINDA: Uh-huh.

HEINZ: What do you say?

LINDA: Thank you?

HEINZ: You're welcome. Are you gonna give me somethin'?

LINDA: Whaddaya want?

HEINZ: A thank-you kiss.

(LINDA *takes the unlit cigarette out of her mouth, kisses him chastely, and puts the cigarette back in her mouth.*)

HEINZ: That's good.

(HEINZ *sticks his hand in his pocket absently. He discovers his mother's nylon. He fingers it absently. He looks at it.*)

LINDA (attempting to be casual): Ah, look, Heinz, ah, I better be gettin' home.

HEINZ: No, not yet.

LINDA: Yeah, I should. My father's not feelin' good, like I told you on the phone. And I've gotta take care of your present. Set him up with water and stuff.

HEINZ: Gimme another kiss.

(LINDA *glances down. She sees, between Heinz's pointy shoes, the discarded bloody baseball bat. The handle is facing her. She drops her cigarette.*)

LINDA: Oh.

(LINDA *goes down on one knee before* HEINZ. *He smiles, looking down on her. She looks off to her right, as if she sees something.*)

LINDA: Is that a cop?

(HEINZ *looks.* LINDA *grabs the bat and slams it up into Heinz's crotch as hard as she can.* HEINZ *is surprised and in much pain.* LINDA *slams the bat upward again! And again!* HEINZ *staggers back. He falls to his knees.* LINDA *stands, letting her savage hatred of him show on her face for the first time. He falls forward, groaning. She casts the bat aside and starts to leave. Then she returns, picks up the bag, and goes.*)

INTERIOR: HARRY'S LIVING ROOM. NIGHT.

MRS. FITZGERALD *and* HARRY *are sitting, finishing their drinks. The Buddha is at Harry's feet asleep.* MRS. FITZGERALD *is a bit in her cups;* HARRY *is just tired. He finishes his drink and puts it down. He stands up.*

HARRY: I'm gonna hit the sack.

MRS. FITZGERALD: Sure you won't have one more?

HARRY: Arthur's gonna call me tomorrow. . .

MRS. FITZGERALD (cutting in): Arthur the Negro?

HARRY: Yeah, Arthur the Negro's gonna call me tomorrow and gimme the verdict whether I go or not. Not that it didn't seem pretty clear, like I said.

(HARRY *has reached the foot of the stairs.* MRS. FITZGERALD *glances at the clock. The time is twenty to one.* MRS. FITZGERALD *turns.*)

MRS. FITZGERALD (calling casually): Oh! Speaking of calls, you got a call.

(HARRY *stops on the stairs. He senses something too casual about what she said.*)

HARRY: I did? Who?

MRS. FITZGERALD: That girl, what was her name, she was here today.

(HARRY *takes a step back.*)

HARRY (concerned): Linda called? What did she say?

MRS. FITZGERALD: Oh, you know, it was something like this afternoon. You already said no . . .

HARRY: Be more specific, please.

MRS. FITZGERALD (suddenly angry and emotional): Don't play the cop with me, sonny boy!

HARRY: What did she say?

MRS. FITZGERALD: She hadda meet Heinz somewhere, and she was scared.

HARRY: Where?

MRS. FITZGERALD: At the fountain, the Oval in Parkchester. At midnight.

HARRY: Why didn't you tell me?

MRS. FITZGERALD: You already said no . . .

HARRY: WHY DIDN'T YOU TELL ME?

MRS. FITZGERALD: FIGURE IT OUT! You're so determined to kill yourself, one way or the other! If they won't let you go to Mississippi, then you'll go out and lock horns with some nutcase here! You're just like your goddamn father, Lord have mercy on his dumbass hero soul. (*Tired.*) I'm goin' to bed.

(HARRY *goes to the front door.*)

HARRY: I'm going out.

MRS. FITZGERALD: Take the Buddha.

HARRY: What?

MRS. FITZGERALD: Take the Buddha. He needs the walk.

(*The Buddha catches on, rouses himself, and barks.* HARRY *grabs the leash, which is by the door.*)

HARRY: Okay. C'mon, Buddha.

(*The Buddha runs to him.* HARRY *quickly attaches the leash and opens the door.*)

HARRY (not looking at his mother): 'Bye.

(*And* HARRY *is gone. The door shuts behind him and the Buddha.* MRS. FITZGERALD *is alone, staring after him.*)

MRS. FITZGERALD: 'Bye.

EXTERIOR: HARRY'S HOUSE. NIGHT.

HARRY *runs down the steps with the Buddha, hits the sidewalk, and heads off.*

EXTERIOR: THE PARKCHESTER CAFÉ. NIGHT.

It's very quiet. One by one, the lights go off inside. The entrance door opens, and JAMES *steps out. He starts to lock up.*

LINDA'S VOICE (in an urgent whisper): James! James!

(JAMES *looks around, puzzled. Then he sees* LINDA, *and his face registers concern and pleasure.*)

JAMES: Linda!

(LINDA *is standing hard against the building, in a shadow. She has got the burlap bag. She's out of breath, and she's scared.*)

LINDA: Can we go inside?

JAMES: Sure.

(JAMES *fumbles briefly with his keys and opens the door. He holds it open.* LINDA *walks quickly past him and inside. He looks after her. He's in love with her.*)

EXTERIOR: PARKCHESTER OVAL AND FOUNTAIN. NIGHT.

HARRY *approaches the Oval with the Buddha. He enters through the hedges to the fountain proper. He looks around but sees nothing. The Buddha starts sniffing the ground and pulls him.* HARRY *sees something on the ground. It frightens him and makes him angry. We see the temper rising that* HARRY *tries hard to disguise. He is looking at a section of the fountain ledge that is covered with blood.* HARRY *bends over, touching it with his finger. He looks at the blood on his finger.*

HARRY: Linda? (*A cold realization.*) Heinz!

EXTERIOR: THE PARKCHESTER CAFÉ. NIGHT.

Establishing shot.

INTERIOR: THE PARKCHESTER CAFÉ. NIGHT.

All of the stools are up on the bar except for two that have been taken down. LINDA *and* JAMES *sit on these two stools. Between them, in the space on the bar created by the absence of the two stools, stands the penguin.* LINDA *is used to the penguin.* JAMES *has trouble taking his eyes off it.*

LINDA: James?

JAMES: Yeah?

LINDA: I want you to do something for me.

JAMES: Yeah? What?

LINDA: I wanna leave the penguin here.

JAMES: What?

LINDA: I want you to hold on to the penguin for me.

JAMES: Oh, no. Why don't you put it in your store? You've got the cages and everything.

LINDA: I can't go back there. Heinz might be waitin'.

JAMES: Listen, I don't know, why don't you call the cops?

LINDA: That ain't gonna get it. 'Cause he murdered a penguin? How much time is he gonna get for that?

JAMES: I don't know.

LINDA: And who's ta say they won't take his side against me? He didn't lay a glove on me, and I nailed him with a bat in the jewels. Listen, just lemme do this my way. I'm tired, I'm nervous, I need some sleep. I can stay with my Aunt Pam, she don't give a shit I show up late. Then we can figure this out tomorrow. But that means you gotta keep the penguin tonight, okay?

JAMES: Okay.

EXTERIOR: THE FORTY-THIRD PRECINCT. NIGHT.

It's all lit up. HARRY *and the Buddha appear at a run and go inside.*

INTERIOR: THE FORTY-THIRD PRECINCT. NIGHT.

The DESK SERGEANT *is on the phone, with a serious expression.*

SERGEANT: No, Millie, I am not gonna hit the kid. I don't care what he did. I don't like hitting my own son. If I wanna hit somebody, I get plenty a candidates at the job.

(HARRY *strides past the* SERGEANT *without looking or stopping.*)

SERGEANT (seeing HARRY): Hey! (*To himself:*) Oh well, he looked like he knew where he was going. (*To phone:*) You're preventin' me from doin' my job properly here.

INTERIOR: DETECTIVES' OFFICE. NIGHT.

As HARRY *opens the door.* SULLIVAN *is sleeping with his face in his fedora.* MAZOLA *is eating a sandwich.*

MAZOLA: Can I help you?

HARRY: I need help!

(SULLIVAN *slowly wakes up, lifting his head.*)

MAZOLA (to HARRY): Did you explain your problem to the sergeant at the desk?

SULLIVAN (looking at HARRY, recognizing him): You look just like Ed Fitzgerald, may he rest in peace.

HARRY: I'm his son.

SULLIVAN: Did anybody ever tell you that he saved my life?

HARRY: Are you Bigfoot Sullivan?

(SULLIVAN *smiles, lifts one of his feet, and slams it down on the desk. It's enormous.*)

SULLIVAN: The very same!

HARRY: Listen! I need help now. Fast!

EXTERIOR: SQUAD CAR. NIGHT.

Through the windshield we can see HARRY *and* SULLIVAN *are in the backseat.* MAZOLA *is driving and trying to eat his sandwich. The Buddha occupies the seat next to him.* MAZOLA *says something to* SULLIVAN *and gestures with his sandwich hand. The Buddha sees the sandwich and snaps it up.* MAZOLA *is incredulous and then depressed.*

INTERIOR: THE PARKCHESTER CAFÉ. NIGHT.

JAMES *is wheeling a number of cases of beer out of a storage room with a hand truck.* LINDA *grabs one off the top and lays it on top of several others.* LINDA *and* JAMES *are in the process of building something to hold the penguin. It's a rectangular enclosure made out of cases of beer, and it's just about finished. In it stands the penguin in a pan of water.* JAMES *puts the last two cases of beer on the structure and mops his forehead.*

JAMES: That should hold him.

LINDA: Do you have any fish?

JAMES: Fish?

LINDA: I just thought he might be hungry.

JAMES: No, I don't have any fish. We'll just have to hope he likes beer.

(*Impulsively,* LINDA *kisses* JAMES. *A fairly long kiss. She lets him go. He's pleasantly stunned.*)

LINDA: Thanks, James.

JAMES: What kind of fish does he like? Maybe I can find some fish.

EXTERIOR: THE PARKCHESTER CAFÉ. NIGHT.

JAMES *and* LINDA *stand at the entrance door. He locks up.*

LINDA: I don't wanna walk back into the neighborhood. My Aunt Pam's only two stops on the train.

JAMES: Okay. So we'll take the train.

LINDA: We?

JAMES: Absolutely. Don't get me mixed up with Dr. Harry Martin Luther Gandhi Fitzgerald, all right? I mean, I'm protectin' you now.

(JAMES *says this last only half in fun. They kiss again. They start walking away from the bar.*)

EXTERIOR: ALLEY NEXT TO PARKCHESTER CAFÉ. NIGHT.

Heinz's head leans out of the shadows. He was standing just out of view, around the corner. He nods.
    LINDA *and* JAMES *are walking along. They are a little awkward together because they are in love. They don't look at each other. Their eyes are shining.*

JAMES (stopping): Wait a minute!

(JAMES *looks at her.*)

LINDA: What?

JAMES: Nothing.

LINDA: Okay.

(*They start walking again.*)

JAMES (stopping again): No, wait a minute!

LINDA: What is it?

JAMES: Linda. You gotta kiss me right now about six times.

LINDA: Come on, we're in a hurry.

JAMES: There's gotta be time for this.

LINDA: What if I don't want to.

JAMES: You have to. It's like your duty. This is like a medical emergency.

(LINDA *relents and kisses* JAMES *quickly and fondly, but not on the lips.*)

LINDA: One. Two. Three. Four. Five.

JAMES: Six!

(JAMES *kisses* LINDA *long and hard on the mouth, and she responds.*)

EXTERIOR: PARKCHESTER OVAL AND FOUNTAIN. NIGHT.

SULLIVAN, HARRY, *and the Buddha stand by the fountain, looking at the blood. In the background the squad car can be seen at curbside, its lit gum ball turning silently.* MAZOLA *is looking in the hedges.* SULLIVAN *bends down to touch the blood. The Buddha pulls the leash out of Harry's hand and runs off in the direction of* MAZOLA, *with a single woof!* SULLIVAN, *suspecting the worst, looks at* HARRY.

SULLIVAN: She was supposed to meet Heinz here at midnight?

HARRY: Yeah.

(*The Buddha barks once, twice, three times.*)

MAZOLA: I think he found somethin'!

(*The Buddha is very excited. He has found something in the ground ivy by the hedge.* MAZOLA *reaches into the undergrowth.* SULLIVAN *and* HARRY *join the Buddha. The three look to see what* MAZOLA *is revealing.* MAZOLA *grins.*)

MAZOLA: It's a bird! It's a big, dead bird! I thought it was a bloody foot or some shit, but it's just a big dead . . . penguin?

(SULLIVAN *and* HARRY *are both very relieved.*)

SULLIVAN: So some nutcase killed a bird. That's bird blood over there. It's just bird blood.

MAZOLA's voice: I think it's a penguin.

HARRY (relieved but still uncertain): Where's Linda then?

SULLIVAN: She's probably where we should be. Home in bed.

EXTERIOR: THE SUBWAY ENTRANCE. NIGHT.

We see the subway entrance from across the two-way street in front of it. There's a goodly amount of traffic going both ways on this street. LINDA *and* JAMES *go down a small staircase entrance to the subway. This is the side opposite the main subway entrance.*

JAMES: You got any tokens?

LINDA: Yeah, I got two.

JAMES: Can I bum one?

LINDA: No. Sure.

INTERIOR: THE SUBWAY STATION. NIGHT.

It's deserted and brightly lit. A wall of steel bars that run floor to ceiling stretch away to the right as far as can be seen. To the left the bars end in a wall. The couple approach an automatic turnstile. In the space that one enters by passing through the turnstile are some steel columns and a couple of big trash bins. JAMES *is about to put his token in the slot when he remembers to be gallant. He steps aside and bows to* LINDA.

JAMES: After you, my lady.

LINDA: Why thank you!

(LINDA *puts her token in and goes through. Immediately a guy wearing a stocking over his face, obviously* HEINZ, *leaps out of hiding from behind a garbage bin and grabs* LINDA. *She screams.* HEINZ *giggles.*

JAMES *is momentarily stunned by the violent turn things have taken. Then he snaps out of it. We see the token in James's hand. The hand is shaking and in a terrible hurry to put the token in the slot; it fumbles. The token misses and falls to the floor. The token rolls.* JAMES *scrambles after it, but the token rolls through the bars.* LINDA *screams and* JAMES *looks up.*

James's point of view: LINDA *and* HEINZ *fighting.* HEINZ *slaps her. She punches him. She's tough but no match for* HEINZ. *He rips her blouse.* JAMES, *stricken by what he sees, looks through the bars in horror. He throws himself to the floor and jams his arms through the bars, trying to reach the token. But it's out of reach. He jumps to his feet and looks around wildly for a way in.* LINDA *is desperately defending herself from the masked attacker.*)

LINDA (calling out): For the love a God, hurry! Hurry!

(JAMES *takes a running start and tries to slam through the automatic turnstile. Once, twice. But it doesn't budge. He looks to the right. The wall of bars stretches away, out of view.* JAMES, *torn, considers. He looks from* LINDA *and* HEINZ *to the corridor on his right, and back. He decides. He starts to run away from the scene of the attack, along the wall of bars. He, of course, runs with a limp. He has only gone about twenty feet when Linda's scream stops him.*)

LINDA: James! Don't leave me!

(JAMES *starts to run back. We see the struggle indistinctly, from James's point of view. Linda's blouse is torn off, and her breasts are visible.* JAMES *is totally conflicted. He knows it's senseless to run back again, but emotionally it feels wrong to run away from the woman he wants to save.*

He pulls himself together, turns around, and runs away along the bars. He runs as fast as he can. His hip starts to act up, and his limp gets worse. We hear his labored breathing and, in the distance, Linda's cries. The cries gradually fade away. Finally, up ahead, he sees the token booth.)

INTERIOR: SUBWAY TOKEN BOOTH. NIGHT.

A TRAINMAN *and a* COP *are standing at the token booth, chatting idly with the* TOKEN TELLER. *They look up when they hear the disturbance at the door. They see* JAMES. *He's wild. He takes no notice of them. He runs past, jumps the turnstile, and keeps going. The* TRAINMAN *looks at the* COP. *They look after* JAMES *blankly; then they look at each other again. The* TOKEN TELLER *snaps them out of it.*

TELLER: Hey! Do something!

(The TRAINMAN *and the* COP *take off in pursuit of* JAMES.*)*

INTERIOR: SUBWAY STAIRS. NIGHT.

JAMES *is within the cage formed by the wall of bars. He is panting, wild-eyed, and in great pain from his hip. He runs along the bars. In the distance behind him can dimly be seen the pursuing* TRAINMAN *and* COP. JAMES *sees the big trash bins ahead. He approaches the spot where the struggle took place. No one is there. He reaches the spot. Behind him, we see the* TRAINMAN *and the* COP *approaching at a run.* JAMES *picks up Linda's shredded blouse from the ground. It's dirty, and there's a little blood on it.* JAMES *starts to cry. The* TRAINMAN *and the* COP *arrive.* JAMES *is unaware of them. The* TRAINMAN *is angry; the* COP, *compassionate.*

TRAINMAN: What the hell you think you doin'? You gotta case of somethin' you think . . .

(The COP *puts a hand on the* TRAINMAN, *gently stopping him. The* COP *talks to* JAMES, *who is quietly crying.)*

COP: What's the matter, fella?

(JAMES *looks at the* COP, *seeing him for the first time.*)

JAMES: I was supposed to protect her. But I couldn't get to her. I just couldn't get to her.

EXTERIOR: PARKCHESTER OVAL AND FOUNTAIN. NIGHT.

MAZOLA *pulls a neat white handkerchief out of his pocket, bends down, and respectfully covers the body of the dead penguin. He stands. He and* SULLIVAN *regard the little covered body. In the background, a distance away,* HARRY *can be seen entering a phone booth, which lights up. He has got the Buddha with him.*

MAZOLA (indicating HARRY): Who's he callin'?

SULLIVAN (continues to look at the little corpse): He's callin' her house ta see if she's there. A penguin.

MAZOLA: Yeah.

SULLIVAN: Who'd kill a penguin?

MAZOLA: An Eskimo might. For food.

SULLIVAN: An Eskimo, huh? No Eskimos around here.

MAZOLA: Nope. But an Eskimo is a kind of Indian.

SULLIVAN: You tryin' to pin this one on the Indians, too?

MAZOLA: Nah. This was Heinz. There's no Eskimos in the Bronx. Yet.

(HARRY *comes out of the phone booth. He's worried.*)

HARRY: She's not there. She never got home.

SULLIVAN (to MAZOLA): Call in, okay? See if anything's been reported.

(MAZOLA *heads for the squad car.* HARRY *takes his place by* SULLIVAN. *He has got the Buddha with him. The dog sniffs around the penguin like mad.*)

SULLIVAN: That's some dog. Saint Bernard, right?

HARRY: Yeah.

SULLIVAN: Acts like a friggin' bloodhound.

HARRY: Well, they're rescue dogs, you know. They use 'em for findin' people that get lost in the Alps.

(HARRY *and* SULLIVAN *get the same idea at the same moment. They both wonder if it would work.*)

MAZOLA'S VOICE (breaking their link): Hey!

(MAZOLA *is at the squad car. He has been talking on the radio through the driver's window.*)

MAZOLA (still on the line but talking to SULLIVAN and HARRY): They just brought in a guy we should see.

INTERIOR: DETECTIVES' OFFICE. NIGHT.

JAMES *is sitting surrounded by* HARRY, MAZOLA, *and* SULLIVAN. *He's still crying a little.*

JAMES: I don't know.

MAZOLA: Did you see where he went?

JAMES: No, they were gone. That was all I found. (*Indicates item on table:*) It's her blouse.

SULLIVAN (to MAZOLA): Somebody check on Heinz's mother?

MAZOLA: We sent a patrolman over there, but he says she ain't seen him.

SULLIVAN: Did the patrolman stay?

MAZOLA: No.

SULLIVAN: Send a plainclothes over there. Have him stake the place out. And don't bother to let the old lady know.

MAZOLA: Right.

(MAZOLA *leaves the office.*)

SULLIVAN (calling after him as he goes): Then meet me out front! (*He grabs the torn blouse off the desk and looks at* HARRY.) I think we both had the same stupid idea. (*To* JAMES:) I need your help to find this girl. Are you okay enough ta help?

JAMES: Try to keep me out of it, and you'll have a fight on your hands.

SULLIVAN: Good! Let's go!

EXTERIOR: THE FORTY-THIRD PRECINCT. NIGHT.

In the backseat of the squad car are SULLIVAN *and* HARRY. *In the front seat is* MAZOLA *at the wheel, next to him is the Buddha, and next to the Buddha is* JAMES. *The car peels out.*

INTERIOR: THE FORTY-THIRD PRECINCT. NIGHT.

The DESK SERGEANT. *A* PATROLMAN *comes in off the street. He has got a cup of coffee.*

PATROLMAN: Hey, I seen Sullivan just goin'. He travels with a dog now, huh?

SERGEANT: Yeah, he's a regular Sergeant Preston.

(*The Sergeant's phone rings .*)

SERGEANT (answering): Forty-third Precinct. No, he just went.

EXTERIOR: A TELEPHONE BOOTH ACROSS FROM SHOPMERIT. NIGHT.

The phone booth is in a block of tenements. In the phone booth is the PLAINCLOTHESMAN.

PLAINCLOTHESMAN: Well, I'm just checkin' to say that I'm here. (*He looks up at a nearby tenement, at one dark window in particular.*) The windows are dark, and nothin's goin' on.

INTERIOR: THE FORTY-THIRD PRECINCT. NIGHT.

The SERGEANT *is on the phone.*

SERGEANT: All right. Call in on the hour. And don't fall asleep.

(*The* SERGEANT *hangs up.*)

EXTERIOR: THE SUBWAY ENTRANCE. NIGHT.

The squad car pulls up to the subway entrance. Everybody piles out, SULLIVAN *leading the way.* HARRY *has the Buddha on his leash. They go through the swinging doors.*

INTERIOR: THE SUBWAY STATION PLATFORM. NIGHT.

The barred and bleak underground no-man's-land where HEINZ *and* LINDA *struggled.* SULLIVAN, MAZOLA, JAMES, HARRY, *and the Buddha stand on the spot.* SULLIVAN *has the torn blouse in his hand.*

SULLIVAN (addressing JAMES): This is where you last saw 'em?

JAMES: Yeah.

SULLIVAN: All right. (*Embarrassed.*) Listen, what's the dog's name?

HARRY: The Buddha.

SULLIVAN: The Buddha. All right. Ah, give the Buddha this blouse to smell.

(HARRY *takes the blouse.*)

JAMES (looking at HARRY): I'm gonna be the one that saves her.

HARRY: That's fine with me. I don't know if this is gonna work. This ain't exactly the Alps.

JAMES (to SULLIVAN): I don't see why you drafted this nutcase to do your job, Mr. Dragnet!

SULLIVAN (getting angry): Look, you! I gotta all points out for Heinz right now! I got his apartment staked out. And that's about all that I can do that makes any real sense! But that's not enough for me, all right? So I'm down here in the friggin' subway with a Saint Bernard doin' somethin' that like as not, back at the precinct, is gonna get me nominated for Hoople of the Year! Now I can live with that, but, please, don't make me think about it too much. This guy is here because he owns the dog. I'm not gonna start askin' why you're here unless you start bustin' my hump. (*To* HARRY:) So give the dog the stupid blouse to smell, an let's see what happens.

(HARRY *holds the blouse to the Buddha's nose. The Buddha smells it.*)

MAZOLA: He's smellin' it.

(*The Buddha starts smelling so hard that* HARRY *puts the blouse down. The Buddha buries his face in the blouse.*)

SULLIVAN: I think he's eatin' the friggin' thing.

(*The Buddha raises his head and howls. Then he takes off. He waits for them at a revolving exit.*)

HARRY: You know I think he's doin' it! I think he's on the trail!

SULLIVAN: Okay. I guess we follow the dog.

(*They start after the Buddha, who awaits them eagerly.* HARRY *attaches his leash, and they go through the revolving exit. The others follow.*)

EXTERIOR: A SMALL SUBWAY STREET EXIT. NIGHT.

The Buddha emerges first, straining on his leash, followed by HARRY, *then* MAZOLA, SULLIVAN, *and* JAMES.

JAMES (speaking confidentially to SULLIVAN as they follow the rest): Look, I didn't mean to give you a lotta shit. I appreciate what you're doin'.

SULLIVAN: She your girlfriend?

JAMES: No. Yeah. It's on and off.

SULLIVAN: Don't worry about nothin'. Guys like this Heinz, they get wound up real good, then they bust like a two-dollar watch.

JAMES: Do you know Heinz?

SULLIVAN: I've seen him. I know his rap sheet.

JAMES: But you don't know him?

SULLIVAN: I ain't had dinner with him.

JAMES: He's very crazy, and he's gotta thing about Linda. The last time he came for her, she was on a date with me. Found us in this bar. Started talkin' to her, yellin' at her. Just like I wasn't there, like I was a piece a cheesecloth nothin' between him and her. And then he started to, like, *rape* her, in a bar, in this the middle of this bar, with me standin' there next to his face. So I made ta save her, and ta make him see me, take me into account. He threw me down on the floor, which broke a couple a my ribs, and then he stomped me on my hip, three, four times, I don't know. My hip made a sound like somebody bit into a real big ice cube, and it broke. I don't remember nothin' after that. They tell me Harry there broke a beer pitcher on Heinz's head, and that stopped him. But the last thing I remember was lyin' on the floor, my bones broken up like breadsticks, knowin' that Heinz has crippled me without ever looking at me. Without ever even seeing me.

SULLIVAN: We'll get him.

JAMES: I guess what I'm sayin' is he won't really notice you till you kill him.

(SULLIVAN *is disturbed by this idea. He looks at* JAMES. *They have both been walking very fast all the while.*
     Meanwhile, the Buddha, who's been pulling HARRY *along, stops.*
     The Buddha looks confused, uncertain. He whines a little. The others catch up.)

MAZOLA: What's a matter?

HARRY: I don't know.

SULLIVAN: Did he lose the scent?

HARRY: I don't know if he ever had it.

SULLIVAN: Well, it was an idea.

(*Suddenly the dog howls mightily and takes off again.* HARRY *is caught off guard and loses the leash. The Buddha takes off down a long street.*)

JAMES: He's got it!

SULLIVAN: Follow that dog! Don't lose that dog!

(*They take off in pursuit of the Buddha, who's already a good distance away. The dog howls again, heroic and far off. The humans trail some distance behind, already breathing hard.*)

EXTERIOR: A LONG LONELY STREET. NIGHT.

This is a street of run-down factories and garages. Walking down the sidewalk toward a couple of parked cars comes HEINZ. *He has a scratch on his face and nail scratches on his arm. In his arms is* LINDA, *unconscious. Her face is somewhat bruised, but otherwise she seems unharmed. She is naked from the waist up, and her breathing is apparent. There is a peculiar tranquility about the two of them.* HEINZ *walks, looking at her. He loves her. He loves her like King Kong loved Fay Wray. He reaches the parked car. He lays her tenderly down on the hood. He tries the door. It's locked. With one expert kick, he destroys a side window. He reaches in and opens the back door. He leaves it open, goes, picks up* LINDA, *takes her, and lays her gently in the backseat. He arranges her hair. He kisses, chastely, a spot between her breasts. Then he gets out, closes the back door, opens the front door, and slides in. He leans under the steering column and, with a practiced touch, pulls out the ignition wires. He uses his teeth to strip them. He stops, puzzled by something. He hears a low panting. He looks at* LINDA. *No, she's not doing it. Then he looks out the driver's window. The Buddha has his big face pressed against the glass, and he's panting.*

MAZOLA'S VOICE (coming in from the passenger window): All right, my friend. Don't move, please.

(HEINZ *looks cautiously over his shoulder. He sees through the window that* SULLIVAN, JAMES, *and* HARRY *are still running to catch up. Then he sees* MAZOLA *pointing his revolver in the broken passenger window.* HEINZ *is lying on the front seat. He snaps his foot up, catching Mazola's gun hand at the wrist, grinding it into the broken glass of the window.* MAZOLA *screams and fires, hitting* HEINZ *in the shoulder. The gun falls in the car.* MAZOLA *staggers back a foot, holding his hand.* HEINZ *sees* SULLIVAN *pulling his revolver and aiming. He ducks under the wheel as* SULLIVAN *fires and a bullet shatters the windshield.* HEINZ *grabs the ignition wires.* JAMES *grabs Sullivan's gun arm.*)

JAMES: Linda's in there!

(*The car starts up. The Buddha is standing in front of it. In the car* HEINZ *grabs the gun off the floor as* MAZOLA *tries to reach in and grab it.* HEINZ *shoots* MAZOLA, *who pitches backward into the dark.* HEINZ *throws the car in gear and slams on the gas. The car screeches forward. The Buddha is in front of it.* HARRY *realizes what's happening at the last moment, but he's too far away to save the dog.*)

HARRY: Buddha!

(JAMES *dives in front of the oncoming car, knocking the dog clear by a hair. Meanwhile* HARRY *has bolted for the driver's side. As the car speeds away, it strikes him a glancing blow, which throws him to the ground.* SULLIVAN *is running toward* MAZOLA, *who's lying in a lump on the sidewalk. He reaches him.*)

SULLIVAN: Mazola?

MAZOLA: Yeah?

SULLIVAN: Are you dead?

MAZOLA: No. Is Heinz dead?

SULLIVAN: No.

MAZOLA: Then the night's over for me, but not for you.

(SULLIVAN *pulls off his tie and makes a tourniquet for* MAZOLA.)

SULLIVAN: I'll have you in Jacobi emergency in ten minutes.

(*Meanwhile* HARRY *slowly gets up and brushes himself off.* JAMES *starts to get up, but it's hard for him.* HARRY *tries to help him.*)

JAMES: Get your hands off me!

HARRY: Thanks.

JAMES: For what?

HARRY: Saving the dog.

JAMES: Did I save that damn dog? I can't imagine what I was thinking about.

(JAMES *gets up. He looks after the car. So does* HARRY.)

HARRY: We'll get him.

JAMES: Why does everybody keep saying we'll get him? I don't want him. I want her.

(SULLIVAN *approaches them, wiping his hands.*)

SULLIVAN: That's it for you guys. From here on in it's strictly OK Corral.

EXTERIOR: BRITA'S HOUSE. NIGHT.

The red Impala pulls up. BRITA *gets out the curb door. We hear her murmuring good night to* SAL *and* MELANIE. *She goes up the steps to the house. In the car* SAL *is behind the wheel.* MELANIE *is in the backseat. The car is running, but* SAL *doesn't put it in gear. They both sit there a minute without speaking.*

SAL: Why don't you sit up here with me?

(MELANIE *doesn't answer. She's sullen. After a second, she gets out of the backseat wordlessly and gets in the front.*)

MELANIE: Okay?

SAL: I don't like it you're always sittin' in the backseat with Brita.

MELANIE: I like to.

SAL: And you're all the time gettin' high. Tonight's the first time I seen you an' Brita straight at one an' the same time in like forever.

MELANIE: Sal, take me home. I am very tired.

INTERIOR: SAL'S IMPALA OUTSIDE BRITA'S HOUSE. NIGHT.

SAL *throws the car in gear and pulls away from the curb. He drives silently.*

SAL: All right.

MELANIE: All right what?

SAL: All right. I'm sorry. I apologize.

MELANIE: I do not accept.

(SAL *continues to look ahead and drive. But softly, quietly, he breaks. His eyes fill with tears.*)

SAL (his voice a husky whisper): C'mon! What do you want me to say? I'm sorry, I said. Don't do this to me, Melanie. I've been sick about doin' what I did, but you've been fucked up all the time! I figure we're gonna have kids. I don't want their mother in the backseat poppin' pills with Brita.

(MELANIE *looks at* SAL. *She's finding out what she wanted to know, that he loves her. She starts to put out a hand to touch his face. A screech is heard. She looks out, startled, through the windshield. Oncoming headlights are shining in her face.*)

SAL'S VOICE: Oh shit!

EXTERIOR: LONELY STREET. NIGHT.

Sal's face is lit by headlights. He cuts the steering wheel furiously. Tires screech. It's HEINZ, *driving madly. His face is brilliantly lit for a minute by Sal's headlights. Sal's car goes into a spin on the dark street. When the spin stops,* HEINZ *is gone.* SAL *and* MELANIE *are stunned. A moment passes.* SAL *has just seen his life pass before his eyes.*

MELANIE: You all right?

SAL: Yeah. You?

MELANIE: Yeah. What was that?

SAL: Some friggin' total maniac.

MELANIE: Wow. I thought we were dead.

SAL: Listen. Listen, you wanna do me a favor? Why don't you drive the car?

MELANIE: You're gonna let me drive your car?

SAL: I've hadda bad couple a days here. My nerves are shot. Okay?

MELANIE: Okay.

EXTERIOR: LONELY STREET. NIGHT.

MELANIE *and* SAL *get out from their respective doors. They walk to the front of the car. As they pass each other,* MELANIE *casually touches Sal's cheek, hesitates, gives him a peck, and continues to the driver's side. As she opens her door,* SAL *opens the passenger door. They both get in and slam their doors behind them.* MELANIE *starts the car and smiles to herself.*

EXTERIOR: THE TELEPHONE BOOTH OUTSIDE HEINZ'S HOUSE. NIGHT.

The PLAINCLOTHESMAN *is standing in the booth, leaning against the wall. He looks up at Heinz's window; it's still dark. He's relaxed and bored. He lights a cigarette, exhales, and starts to sing to himself.*

PLAINCLOTHESMAN: In Dublin's fair city,
   Where the girls are so pretty,
   I first set my eyes on sweet Molly Malone,
   She wheeled her wheelbarrow
   Through streets broad and narrow,
   Crying, "Cockles and mussels, alive, alive, oh!"

   She died of a fever,
   And none could relieve her,
   And that was the end of sweet Molly Malone,
   But her ghost wheels her barrow
   Through streets broad and narrow
   Crying, "Cockles and mussels, alive, alive, oh!"

(*During the latter part of the song, a tire screeches distantly and then a headlight gleams behind the* PLAINCLOTHESMAN, *but he doesn't notice. He has gotten wrapped up in the song. He turns around as he ends the song. His astonished face is illuminated by the oncoming headlights. The cigarette falls from his mouth, which is dropping open in mute horror. It's Heinz's car, up on the sidewalk, going very fast. It runs into and over the booth. It comes to rest with the booth beneath it, totally destroyed.*)

INTERIOR: TRUGLIO'S BEDROOM. NIGHT

At the moment of the crash, MRS. TRUGLIO *sits up suddenly, alarmed by the noise. She goes to the window and looks out.*

MRS. TRUGLIO (calling to her husband): Lucky! Lucky! Come look. Somebody ran over the phone booth!

(LUCKY *is still half asleep and has no intention of getting up if he can avoid it.*)

LUCKY: Was there anybody in the phone booth?

MRS. TRUGLIO: I don't know. I can't tell.

LUCKY: What time is it?

MRS. TRUGLIO: Quarter past three.

LUCKY: Nobody makes a pay call at quarter past three. Come back to bed.

(MRS. TRUGLIO *reluctantly complies.*)

EXTERIOR: THE TELEPHONE BOOTH OUTSIDE HEINZ'S HOUSE. NIGHT.

The back door of the car is now open, and HEINZ *is reaching in. He emerges, carrying* LINDA *in his arms. She still seems to be unconscious, but she is groaning quietly now and crying a little.* HEINZ *looks up at his apartment window. He is bleeding from the shoulder. He heads for the building.*

INTERIOR: SABANTINO TENEMENT HALLWAY. NIGHT.

HEINZ *rings the bell and waits. A light goes on under the door.*

MRS. SABANTINO'S VOICE (sleepy but cheerful, heard from within): Who is it?

HEINZ: It's me.

MRS. SABANTINO'S VOICE: Maybe you should come back in the morning, and we can have a nice breakfast.

HEINZ: Open the fuckin' door!

(MRS. SABANTINO *opens the door. She's dressed in a happy robe covered with leaping sheep.*)

MRS. SABANTINO: Oh. You've brought home a friend!

HEINZ (brushing past her): Yeah. I've brought home a girlfriend.

INTERIOR: SABANTINO APARTMENT. NIGHT.

MRS. SABANTINO *is still able, through a violent effort of will, not to notice that the so-called girlfriend is naked to the waist and unconscious.*

MRS. SABANTINO: A girlfriend. That's nice. You'll probably be getting married soon and leave the nest. Should I put on some music?

(HEINZ *is laying* LINDA *on the couch.* MRS. SABANTINO *has followed him into the living room.*)

HEINZ: No music.

MRS. SABANTINO: Would your friend like something to eat? A sandwich?

HEINZ: No.

MRS. SABANTINO: No, she's tired, ain't she? Let her sleep. I'll put a blankie on her.

HEINZ: No!

MRS. SABANTINO: Okay. I was havin' the most beautiful dream when you rang the bell. Your dad was alive again, and we were eatin' fish.

HEINZ: You're dreamin' right now.

MRS. SABANTINO: Me? No, no. I'm awake now, Heinz. Can't I play some nice music?

HEINZ: No! You're sleepin'!

MRS. SABANTINO: No, I'm not.

HEINZ: Wake up! Wake up!

MRS. SABANTINO: I'm not sleepin'.

HEINZ (grabbing her): Look at me! Look at me! What do you see?

MRS. SABANTINO: My boy, my little boy!

HEINZ: Wake up, I'm tellin' you! Have the cops been here?

MRS. SABANTINO: A policeman came and asked about you before, but I told him you wasn't lost, you were just out.

HEINZ: Listen! I'm gonna die tonight, Ma!

MRS. SABANTINO: No, no. Let me play some music.

HEINZ (holding her in an iron grip): I'm gonna die tonight. And just once, just once before I die, I'd like you ta see me.

MRS. SABANTINO: I see you.

(*But* HEINZ *can see she doesn't.*)

EXTERIOR: HEINZ'S STREET. NIGHT.

JAMES, HARRY, *and the Buddha are walking home. They notice the lighted window.*

HARRY: Isn't that Heinz's building?

(JAMES *looks at* HARRY.)

INTERIOR: SABANTINO APARTMENT. NIGHT.

HEINZ *is still holding* MRS. SABANTINO *in a fierce grip.*

MRS. SABANTINO: Let me go, Heinz.

HEINZ: I'm goin' to let you go.

MRS. SABANTINO: You're hurtin' me.

HEINZ: Who am I?

MRS. SABANTINO: You're my little Heinz.

HEINZ: Where have I been?

MRS. SABANTINO: I don't know.

HEINZ: I've been in jail, Ma.

MRS. SABANTINO: No.

HEINZ: I've been in jail an' now I'm out an' the cops are comin' for me again.

MRS. SABANTINO: No.

HEINZ: And they're gonna kill me.

MRS. SABANTINO: No. Lemme go.

HEINZ: I'm gonna let you go. What's my name?

MRS. SABANTINO (starts to cry): Heinz, Heinz.

HEINZ: And who am I to you?

MRS. SABANTINO: You're my boy.

HEINZ: And what's your boy gonna do tonight? Tell me! TELL ME!

MRS. SABANTINO: He's goin' ta die!

HEINZ: Thank you! Thank you! (*He kisses her. A tear falls down his face. He hugs her fiercely.*) Thank you, Ma.

(*Now* HEINZ *grabs her, and with tremendous force, he throws her right through the window, sash and all going out with her.*)

EXTERIOR: SABANTINO APARTMENT. NIGHT.

JAMES *and* HARRY *see* MRS. SABANTINO *smashing out through the window, screaming.*

JAMES: Holy shit!

HARRY: Oh, my God!

(MRS. SABANTINO *screams all the way to the ground. The Buddha yelps pitifully.*)

INTERIOR: TRUGLIO'S BEDROOM. NIGHT.

The final scream rings through the apartment. MRS. TRUGLIO *leaps up in bed.*

MRS. TRUGLIO: What's goin' on!

(MRS. TRUGLIO *runs to the window.*)

LUCKY (sitting up): What is it?

EXTERIOR: MRS. TRUGLIO'S POINT OF VIEW: HEINZ'S STREET. NIGHT.

MRS. TRUGLIO (looking out the window): Oh my God! Lucky! Call the police! There's a woman on the sidewalk! I think!

(LUCKY *reaches for the phone.*)

INTERIOR: THE FORTY-THIRD PRECINCT. NIGHT.

The DESK SERGEANT *is on the phone.*

SERGEANT: We'll be right there!

(*The* SERGEANT *hangs up.*)

INTERIOR: THE DETECTIVES' OFFICE. NIGHT.

SULLIVAN *is on the phone.*

SULLIVAN: I don't know. I really don't know.

(*The door flies open. It's the* SERGEANT.)

SERGEANT: Sullivan! I think we just found Heinz!

SULLIVAN (into phone): I call you later! (*Hangs up.*) Where?

EXTERIOR: HEINZ'S STREET. NIGHT.

Heinz's car is on top of the crushed phone booth. Mrs. Sabantino's body lies in the street. Neighborhood people, mostly in housecoats and bathrobes, are starting to appear in the street. HARRY *and* JAMES *run up to Heinz's building with the Buddha. A* GOOFY GUY *in a bathrobe tries to stop them.*

GOOFY GUY: Hey, what the hell's goin' on here?

HARRY (handing the Buddha's leash to the GOOFY GUY): Watch this dog!

(HARRY *and* JAMES *run into the building.*)

INTERIOR: HEINZ'S HALLWAY. NIGHT.

HARRY *and* JAMES *stand outside Heinz's door. They try the knob. It's locked.*

JAMES (yelling): Linda, are you in there?

INTERIOR: SABANTINO APARTMENT. NIGHT.

HEINZ *is sobbing.*
    LINDA *is on the couch. She hears* JAMES *calling and wakes up.*

LINDA: James? James?

(HEINZ *stops crying and pulls out the gun.* LINDA *sees the gun.*)

LINDA: No!

INTERIOR: HEINZ'S HALLWAY. NIGHT.

HARRY *and* JAMES *are outside the door.*

JAMES: I heard her!

(*A bullet rips through the door. It narrowly misses them.*)

HARRY: Watch out!

(*They fall back. A second bullet rips through the door.*)

INTERIOR: SABANTINO APARTMENT. NIGHT.

LINDA (looking at the door): Watch out. He'll kill you!

(HEINZ *turns on her, and as she rises from the couch, he neatly clips her on the jaw, knocking her out. He picks her up. He looks around. He sees what he's looking for.*)

INTERIOR: HEINZ'S HALLWAY. NIGHT.

JAMES *and* HARRY *are plastered against the walls. They whisper to each other.*

JAMES: I heard her!

HARRY: Me too! But he's got a gun.

JAMES: We've got to get in there!

HARRY: Yeah, but he's got a gun!

JAMES: I don't care!

HARRY: Of course you care! If he shoots you, then you'll be dead and *you can't save Linda!*

JAMES: You think too much!

(JAMES *runs back, and then runs into the door. It almost opens but doesn't. He tries again: same thing.*)

JAMES: You know, forget the gun, Harry! I could just kill myself runnin' inta this door over and over!

(HARRY *joins him. Together they knock down the door. They burst into the apartment.*)

INTERIOR: SABANTINO APARTMENT. NIGHT.

JAMES *and* HARRY *look around, but* HEINZ *and* LINDA *aren't to be seen. They see an open window in the kitchen. Outside is a fire escape.* JAMES *and* HARRY *climb out the window.*

EXTERIOR: SABANTINO FIRE ESCAPE. NIGHT.

HEINZ, *with* LINDA *in his arms, jumps from the fire escape to the other roof.* HARRY *and* JAMES *emerge onto fire escape.*

JAMES: He's on the roof.

EXTERIOR: THE STREET BELOW. NIGHT.

A goodly crowd has gathered. Four cop cars, sirens wailing and gum balls flashing, arrive and park willy-nilly. Cops are getting out. SULLIVAN *gets out. He looks around. A* PATROLMAN *runs up to him.*

SULLIVAN: Where the hell's the stakeout?

PATROLMAN (pointing to the car on top of the crushed phone booth): Under that mess. I guess he was callin' in.

SULLIVAN: Oh, shit!

PATROLMAN: The woman on the sidewalk's dead. Neighbors say it's Heinz's mother.

SULLIVAN (seeing something that strikes him): Hey you!

(*It's the* GOOFY GUY *with the Buddha in tow. He looks at* SULLIVAN *quizzically, pointing to himself.*)

SULLIVAN: Yeah, you. Where'd you get that dog?

GOOFY GUY: I'm watchin' him for a couple a guys.

SULLIVAN: Where are these guys now?

GOOFY GUY (pointing): They ran in that building about ten minutes ago.

(*It's Heinz's building.* SULLIVAN *slowly looks up the face of the building.*)

SULLIVAN: Oh, great. Great. (*Starts firing orders to the cops around him.*) There's a girl with Heinz, so no John Wayne shit. There's two other innocent goons in there, too. Two guys. All right. Take two of ya and cover the fire escape. Gimme a guy on the front door. C'mon, c'mon, get me a guy on the horn, an' clear this street! There may be fireworks. (*Speaking to another detective, confidentially:*) Tom?

TOM: Yeah?

SULLIVAN: Call in to the station. Tell 'em ta get a couple a sharpshooters over here. When they get here, put 'em up on the roof across the way. I hate this. I don't know where this clown is, but he's gotta gun, and he's surrounded with innocent people.

COP (on a megaphone): Please stand back. Please stand back. Nobody on this side of the street, please.

EXTERIOR: HEINZ'S FIRE ESCAPE AND ROOF. NIGHT.

Meanwhile, HARRY *and* JAMES *reach the top of the fire escape.*
The sky is lightening; it's predawn. They cautiously step on the roof.
They look around. The megaphone can be heard. Then, they plainly
see the silhouette of HEINZ *with* LINDA, *unconscious in his arms.* HARRY *and*
JAMES *are cautious, waiting to see what* HEINZ *is going to do.* HARRY *puts*
his finger to his lips. HEINZ *approaches the ledge of the building that faces*
the crowd and cops below. He lays her limp form gently down on the
ledge. He is streaked with blood. In his right hand is the revolver. JAMES
starts forward, but HARRY *holds him back.*

JAMES (speaking to HARRY in a fierce whisper): He's going to throw her
off!

HARRY: No.

EXTERIOR: HEINZ'S STREET. NIGHT.

In the street below, a second PATROLMAN *looks up and sees* HEINZ.

PATROLMAN (pointing): There's somebody up on the roof!

SULLIVAN (looking up): Get me some light up there.

(*The cops turn on one mini-searchlight on a squad car and a couple of*
multiple-cell flashlights. SULLIVAN *watches* HEINZ *lay* LINDA *down.*)

SULLIVAN (murmuring under his breath): C'mon, Heinz. Be a good go-
rilla. Don't kill the girl.

EXTERIOR: HEINZ'S ROOF. NIGHT.

HEINZ *is lit by lights from below. He seems almost mesmerized, emotion-*
less, but tears stream down Linda's face. He touches Linda's face gently,
kisses her, and, for the first time on the roof, lets go of her.

JAMES (punching Harry's arm and whispering): Let's rush 'em, knock 'em right off!

(JAMES *and* HARRY *jump from fire escape to roof.*)

HARRY: No. No violence.

JAMES: No violence? What are you, crazy? Save that shit for Mississippi!

(HARRY *ignores* JAMES.)

HARRY (in a strong, calm voice, calling out to HEINZ): Heinz.

(HARRY *comes forward a few steps from* JAMES. *He's standing in full view.* HEINZ *turns around and sees him.*)

HEINZ: So. It's you.

HARRY: Let her go, Heinz.

HEINZ: Do you still love me?

HARRY: Yeah.

HEINZ (smiles): C'mere. Come here ta me.

(HARRY *takes a step toward* HEINZ.)

JAMES (calling out): Don't do it! He'll kill you!

(HARRY *starts to slowly walk toward* HEINZ *again.*)

HARRY: You think too much.

EXTERIOR: HEINZ'S STREET. NIGHT.

Meanwhile, SULLIVAN, *in the street below, is on a walkie-talkie.*

SULLIVAN: Are you in place?

EXTERIOR: A ROOF OPPOSITE HEINZ'S ROOF. NIGHT.

A COP *with his hat on backward is looking through the scope of a rifle. A* SECOND COP *with a scoped rifle is on a walkie-talkie.*

SECOND COP: Yeah. But there's two other guys up there. And one of 'em is walkin' up to Heinz.

EXTERIOR: HEINZ'S STREET. NIGHT.

SULLIVAN *is on the walkie-talkie.*

SULLIVAN: Look, if you get a clear shot, take him down, he's a cop killer. But for the love a God, make sure it's a clear shot!

EXTERIOR: HEINZ'S ROOF. NIGHT.

HARRY *is walking toward* HEINZ.

HARRY: I won't raise a hand ta you, Heinz. Those days are gone with me. You can do what you want with me. But lemme take the girl off the ledge before she falls.

(JAMES *runs forward till he's the apex of a triangle between* HEINZ *and* HARRY.)

JAMES: Don't!

(HARRY *takes another step toward* HEINZ.)

HARRY: Stay outta this, James.

(HEINZ *starts to lift his gun.*)

JAMES (bolting forward): Watch out!

EXTERIOR: ROOF OPPOSITE HEINZ'S ROOF. NIGHT.

The sharpshooters are on the opposite roof.

COP (looking through the scope): He's gettin' the gun up.

SECOND COP: Take him out!

EXTERIOR: HEINZ'S ROOF. NIGHT.

HEINZ *shoots just as* JAMES *hits his arm.*
     The gun fires, winging HARRY *instead of killing him.* HARRY *is thrown back.*

EXTERIOR: ROOF OPPOSITE HEINZ'S ROOF. NIGHT.

The COP *with his hat on backward shoots.*

EXTERIOR: HEINZ'S ROOF. NIGHT.

JAMES *has lost his balance, and* HEINZ *is about to shoot him. At that moment the sharpshooter's bullet rips through Heinz's forearm, and he screams. The gun falls.* JAMES *reaches for the gun.* HEINZ *kicks* JAMES *in the stomach as he bends over.* JAMES *crumples to the ground.* HEINZ *tries to pick up the gun but has difficulty because his hand isn't really working. Through painful effort he retrieves the gun. Both* HARRY *and* JAMES *are inert.* LINDA *chooses this moment to revive, but she doesn't know where she is. She starts to roll over, but she goes the wrong way. She starts to fall off the roof. She screams, seeing the fall below her. At the moment that she truly goes over the edge, the bloody arms of* HEINZ *snatch her from death. The pain of grabbing her forces him to drop the gun.*
     HEINZ *struggles desperately to pull* LINDA *back on the ledge. He is panting and wild-eyed.* HARRY *sits up, holding his shoulder. He shakes*

his head, trying to clear it. Then he sees HEINZ *saving* LINDA. HEINZ *succeeds in getting* LINDA *on the ledge. He's panting horribly and bleeding a lot.*

EXTERIOR: ROOF OPPOSITE HEINZ'S ROOF. NIGHT.

The sharpshooters are on the opposite roof. The SECOND COP *is on the walkie-talkie.*

SECOND COP: I'm not chancing a second shot. One nudge and that girl's dead.

EXTERIOR: HEINZ'S ROOF. NIGHT.

HEINZ *is at the ledge. Suddenly* JAMES *is on Heinz's back.* HEINZ *staggers back a step and then shakes him off.*

JAMES: My name is James Carrol. You crippled me. Now look at me.

(LINDA, *on the ledge, is conscious now. She looks around. She sees* HARRY. HARRY *is slowly getting up, unseen by* HEINZ. *He mouths the word "run" to* LINDA *and points toward the fire escape.* LINDA *looks where he's pointing.* JAMES *is ineffectually pounding* HEINZ. HEINZ *throws* JAMES *into* LINDA. *They both crash into the pigeon coop, releasing the pigeons.)*

LINDA: Oh God, oh God

JAMES: I got you. I got you.

(HARRY *has grabbed* HEINZ *and is holding him over the edge of the building. After a moment of indecision,* HARRY *decides on nonviolence and lets* HEINZ *off the hook.* HEINZ *reverses the situation and now holds* HARRY *over the edge.* HEINZ *grabs* HARRY *by his hair and the seat of his pants. Harry's life is in his hands.)*

HEINZ: I've always been bad and you've always been good, ain't that right, Harry? You love me. You ain't got the right, you good boy. If I let you go, would you kill me now? If I gave you the shot? Would you throw my ass off this roof?

HARRY: No.

HEINZ: Then good boy, tell me this. What good are you to me?

(HEINZ *makes to pitch* HARRY *to his death.*)

LINDA (realizing what's happening): Heinz, don't do it!

(HEINZ *glances at her briefly. He is most certainly about to do it. There's the sound of a small, sharp thud.* HEINZ *seems to have an unexpected thought. He abruptly lets go of* HARRY.)

HEINZ: Oh! Oh-kay.

(HEINZ *slowly pivots. As he turns, we see there's a large arrow sticking out of his back, with red feathers.*)

INTERIOR: CASTRO'S APARTMENT. NIGHT.

Interior of a darkened tenement across the way from the Sabatino apartment. CASTRO *and* WILLIE *are drawing back from an open window.* CASTRO *is holding a large hunting bow, and* WILLIE *is holding an arrow. The arrow has red feathers.*

EXTERIOR: SABANTINO APARTMENT. NIGHT.

HEINZ *falls over the ledge and then bounces off a second building ledge, and continues downward.*

EXTERIOR: HEINZ'S STREET. NIGHT.

Heinz's body lies on the sidewalk, small and broken, facedown. A COP *runs up to the body, looks at it, and then runs away, around a corner.*

COP (turning and yelling to SULLIVAN): It's Heinz! He's over here! He's dead!

EXTERIOR: HEINZ'S ROOF. DAWN.

At the top of the fire escape, the sun is rising. HARRY *is recovering himself. He stands up. He groans a little and turns around.* LINDA *is with* JAMES, *her head in his lap; she's crying.* JAMES *covers her with his shirt.*

HARRY: She's all right?

(JAMES *nods.* HARRY *nods in return, absently.*)

HARRY: I'm goin' down.

(HARRY *starts walking down the fire escape.* LINDA *stops crying. She looks up at* JAMES.)

JAMES: It's over. It's over.

(*They kiss. They are pretty much in the same spot on the same roof that they were at the opening of this story. The light of dawn fills the sky.*)

EXTERIOR: TRUGLIO'S FIRE ESCAPE. DAWN.

MRS. TRUGLIO *is on the fire escape, looking down at the tragedy below. Her husband,* LUCKY, *is looking straight ahead.*

MRS. TRUGLIO: Unbelievable! What a tragedy!

EXTERIOR: HEINZ'S ROOF. DAWN.

Lucky's point of view: JAMES *and* LINDA *are kissing.* LUCKY *is beaming and* MRS. TRUGLIO *is scowling, looking* down.

EXTERIOR: TRUGLIO'S FIRE ESCAPE. DAWN.

LUCKY: Beautiful!

MRS. TRUGLIO: What d'you mean, beautiful? It's a tragedy!

(LUCKY *steps out onto the fire escape. He has his bow and his violin.*)

EXTERIOR: HEINZ'S STREET. DAWN.

The cops are trying to keep back the crowd. HEINZ *lies facedown in the center of a circle of people, the arrow sticking out of his back. One cop takes a picture.* SULLIVAN *stands by the body, regarding it.* HARRY *comes down the fire escape and joins* SULLIVAN. SULLIVAN *takes in Harry's shoulder wound.*

SULLIVAN: You better have somebody look at that.

(HARRY *nods vacantly.*)

HARRY: In a minute.

(*The other detective,* TOM, *runs up to* SULLIVAN, *and starts talking fast. Sullivan's mind is elsewhere.*)

TOM: I got three men checking the buildings for whoever . . . Hey, whoever did this killed that schoolteacher, too!

SULLIVAN: Maybe there are Indians around this friggin' neighborhood. Maybe we are headed back to the old days.

HARRY: What, you think it was that arrow killed ol' Heinz?

SULLIVAN: What's your theory?

HARRY: At least he stayed true to himself.

(*The sound of a violin playing is heard from high overhead.*)

EXTERIOR: TRUGLIO'S FIRE ESCAPE. DAWN.

MRS. TRUGLIO *is scolding* LUCKY, *who's playing "Santa Lucia" on the violin.*

MRS. TRUGLIO: Lucky, cut that out! Everybody's lookin' up here!

LUCKY: So what?

MRS. TRUGLIO: So, it's inappropriate! There's people lyin' dead down there in the street.

LUCKY: So, if you look down, it's a tragedy. But if you're lookin' some-place else, maybe it is somethin' else.

EXTERIOR: HEINZ'S ROOF. DAWN.

JAMES *and* LINDA *are kissing passionately, silhouetted in the full splendor of the rising sun. "Santa Lucia" swells from a single violin to the rhap-sody of a full orchestra. The camera rises into the sun. The music swells and, at last, dies away. The sounds of street noise, daytime noise can be heard.*

EXTERIOR: SHOPMERIT. DAY.

MRS. TRUGLIO'S VOICE (loud and clear): It was completely a night of hor-rors! The first time I got up was when Heinz ran down the policeman in the phone booth. I couldn't even get Lucky up for that one.

INTERIOR: SHOPMERIT. DAY.

MRS. TRUGLIO *is enjoying herself telling her horror story to* MURRAY *and* GEORGE.

MRS. TRUGLIO: He convinced me it was nothin'. But it was me that called the cops, you know, when Mrs. Sabantino fell to her death. Fell, he threw her out the window!

MURRAY: Such a cheerful woman.

GEORGE: She hadda screw loose.

MURRAY: Still. I saw the stain on the sidewalk.

MRS. TRUGLIO: Sad. Sad. A real tragedy.

(MURRAY *sees someone come in. He's stunned.* GEORGE *looks, and he's taken aback as well. Then* MRS. TRUGLIO *sees.*)

MRS. TRUGLIO: Oh my.

(*At the door is* SAMUEL KEMP, *the young black organizer. He is smiling.*)

SAMUEL: Hello.

MURRAY: Hello.

(SAMUEL *walks up to the counter.*)

SAMUEL: Could you tell me which way is Leland Avenue?

GEORGE: Two blacks. Blocks. (*Points over his shoulder.*) That way.

SAMUEL: Thank you. Somebody who I intend to work with told me a Negro couldn't walk through this neighborhood. Whoever heard of anything so absurd? So I thought I should come up here myself and set him straight. Thanks for the directions.

(SAMUEL *walks to the door. They all look after, dumbfounded.* SAMUEL *opens the door.*)

SAMUEL: 'Bye.

(MRS. TRUGLIO *waves good-bye.*)

EXTERIOR: THE PARKCHESTER CAFÉ. DAY.

The big, gray-haired Irishman, ED, *is unlocking the entrance to the bar. He has his paper under his arm. He walks in. Nothing happens for a minute. Then* ED *reappears, slowly backing out the front door. He is followed out by a penguin.*

Music: A guitar begins to play. It's the opening of "Blowin' in the Wind," by Peter, Paul and Mary. The song plays through the following scene and the closing credits.

EXTERIOR: HARRY'S HOUSE. DAY.

SAMUEL *walks up to the house. The* MAILMAN *passes him and does a double take, but keeps going.* SAMUEL *climbs the stairs and rings the bell. The door opens. It's* MRS. FITZGERALD. *She hesitates and then invites him in. He goes in. The door closes.*

"Blowin' in the Wind" plays. The closing credits roll in front of Harry's house.

THE END